Leckie
the education publisher
for Scotland

C000226260

Higher
HISTORY

For SQA 2019 and beyond

Course Notes

Maxine Hughes, Chris Hume

ISBN 9780008383497

Published by
Leckie
An imprint of HarperCollins Publishers
Westerhill Road, Bishopbriggs, Glasgow, G64 2QT
T: 0844 576 8126   F: 0844 576 8131

HarperCollins*Publishers*
Macken House, 39/40 Mayor Street Upper,
Dublin 1, D01 C9W8, Ireland

leckiescotland@harpercollins.co.uk

www.leckiescotland.co.uk

Publisher: Sarah Mitchell
Project Managers: Janice McNeillie and Gillian Bowman

Special thanks to
Elizabeth Fletcher (proofread)
Jouve (layout)

Printed and bound in the UK using 100% Renewable Electricity at CPI Group (UK) Ltd

A CIP Catalogue record for this book is available from the British Library.

Acknowledgements

Images:

P5 Author: Kim Traynor. Licensed under the Creative Commons Attribution-Share Alike 2.0 licence; P9 Author: Colin Smith. Licensed under the Creative Commons Attribution-Share Alike 2.0 licence; P10 © Gail Johnson/ Shutterstock.com; P11a Author: Czar Brodie. Licensed under the Creative Commons Attribution-Share Alike 3.0; P11b © UniversalImagesGroup / Getty Images; P16b Author: Phillip Capper. Licensed under the Creative Commons Attribution-Share Alike 2.0 licence; P17a Kean Collection/Getty Images; P18b Author: Bubobubo2. Licensed under the Creative Commons Attribution-Share Alike 1.0, 2.0, 2.5, 3.0 licence; P23a Author: Billreid at en.wikipedia. Licensed under the Creative Commons Attribution-Share Alike 3.0 licence; P24 © Archive Photos / Stringer / Getty Images; P26 © Jeremy Sutton-Hibbert / Contributor / Getty Images; P28 © Crown copyright. Data supplied by National Records of Scotland; P29 © Hulton Archive / Stringer / Getty Images; P31 Author: Steve F-E-Cameron. Licensed under the Creative Commons Attribution-Share Alike 1.0, 2.0, 2.5, 3.0 licence; P35 Author: Kim Traynor. Licensed under Creative Commons Attribution-Share Alike 3.0 licence; P37 © Print Collector / Contributor / Getty Images; P39 Author: Finlay McWalter; Licensed under Creative Commons Attribution-Share Alike 3.0 licence; P43 © Mary Evans Picture Library / Alamy; P44a Author: Finlay McWalter. Licensed under Creative Commons Attribution-Share Alike 3.0 licence; P44b Author: Christian Bickel. Licensed under Creative Commons Attribution-Share Alike 2.0-d licence; P52 © Topical Press Agency / Stringer / Getty Images; P55b © Time Life Pictures / Contributor / Getty Images; P57 © EyeOn / Contributor / Getty Images; P65 © Science & Society Picture Library / Contributor / Getty Images; P67a Author: Ross. Licensed under Creative Commons Attribution Share-alike license 2.0; P67b Author: Ron Almog. Licensed under Creative Commons Attribution Share-alike license 2.5; P68 © Crown copyright 2012; P71 © Chris N Illingworth and licensed for reuse under this Creative Commons Licence; P78a Licensed under Creative Commons Attribution Share-alike license 3.0; P78b Author: Mombas. Licensed under Creative Commons Attribution Share-alike license 3.0; P80b Licensed under Fair use of copyrighted material in the context of Highlanders (rugby); P88 Licensed under Creative Commons Attribution Share-alike license 3.0; P89 © World History Archive / Alamy; P98 © Heritage Images/ Getty Images; P100 © Science & Society Picture Library / Contributor / Getty Images; P101 © Science & Society Picture Library / Contributor / Getty Images; P102 © Culture Club / Contributor / Getty Images; P111 © Alain BENAINOUS / Contributor / Getty Images; P116 © © thislife pictures / Alamy; P118 © Universal History Archive / Contributor / Getty Images; P119 © Heritage Images / Contributor / Getty Images; P122a © Mansell / Contributor / Getty Images; P122b © Hulton Archive / Stringer / Getty Images; P125 Licensed under Creative Commons Attribution Share-alike license 3.0; P127 © UniversalImagesGroup / Contributor / Getty Images; P129 © Hulton Archive / Stringer / Getty Images; P138 © Margaret Bourke-White / Contributor / Getty Images; P139 © Maeers / Stringer / Getty Images; P140 © Three Lions / Stringer / Getty Images; P146 Author: Thomas Wolf. Licensed under Creative Commons Attribution Share-alike license 3.0; P157 © Alinari Archives / Contributor / Getty Images; P158 © SuperStock; P173 Author: Rama. Licensed under the Creative Commons Attribution-Share Alike 2.0 France license; P174 © INTERFOTO / Alamy; P179 Bundesarchiv, Bild 102-00015 / CC-BY-SA; P180a Author: Alfred Grohs. Licensed under Creative Commons Attribution Share-alike license 3.0; P182 © UniversalImagesGroup / Contributor / Getty Images; P184 Bundesarchiv, Bild 146-1989-040-27 / CC-BY-SA; P185 © PHAS / Contributor / Getty Images; P190 Bundesarchiv, Bild 183-R96361 / CC-BY-SA; P191 © Lordprice Collection / Alamy; P192 © Topical Press Agency / Stringer / Getty Images; P203a © World History Archive / Alamy; P203b licensed under the Creative Commons Attribution 2.0 Generic license; P206 licensed under the Creative Commons Attribution-Share Alike 3.0 Unported license; P215 Sovfoto / Contributor / Getty Images; P219 Bundesarchiv, Bild 183-S01260 / CC-BY-SA; P220 Bundesarchiv, Bild 183-H28740 / CC-BY-SA; P226 © Universal History Archive / Contributor / Getty Images; P236b © Everett Collection Historical / Alamy; P240 Creative Commons Attribution-Share Alike 3.0 Unported; P242 © World History Archive / Alamy; P250 © FPG / Staff / Getty Images; P264b © Imagno / Contributor / Getty Images; P265 © Hank Walker / Contributor / Getty Images; P268b © Underwood Archives / Contributor / Getty Images; P272 © Three Lions / Stringer / Getty Images; P273 © Hulton Archive / Stringer / Getty Images; P276a Icon Communications / Contributor / Getty Images; P277 © American Stock Archive / Contributor / Getty Images; P278 © American Stock Archive / Contributor / Getty Images; P280 © Archive Photos / Stringer / Getty Images; P283 © The Protected Art Archive / Alamy; P283 © William Vandivert / Contributor / Getty Images; P285 © Scott Olson / Staff / Getty Images; P290b © Hulton Archive / Stringer / Getty Images; P293 © Lee Lockwood / Contributor / Getty Images; P296 © Universal History Archive / Contributor / Getty Images; P297 © Francis Miller / Contributor / Getty Images; P298 © Historic Florida / Alamy; P299 © Michael Ochs Archives / Stringer / Getty Images; P300 © Stringer / Getty Images; P302 © Afro Newspaper/Gado / Contributor / Getty Images. All other images © Shutterstock.com.

Text permissions can be found on P310.

CONTENTS

Introduction

About this book

This book is designed to lead you through the new Higher History course. The book has been designed to map the course specifications and contains examples, explanations and activities to help deepen your understanding of the topics and to help prepare you for assessment.

At the beginning of each topic you will find a table explaining which activities meet which of the unit outcomes (1.1, 1.2 etc.). In most cases, if you are sitting the final exam you do not need to complete the units, although your teacher may put you forward to complete both the units and the final exam. However, for those undertaking the standalone Higher units and not going forward for the final exam, completing these activities will support a portfolio approach where you compile evidence to meet the outcomes.

In Higher History there are a choice of topics. This book covers the following topics:

* Scottish: The Wars of Independence, 1249–1328; Migration and Empire, 1830–1939
* British: Britain, 1851–1951
* European and World: Germany, 1815–1939; Russia, 1881–1921; USA, 1918–68

Features

LEARNING INTENTIONS

Learning intentions are a list of the topics covered in the section. This tells you what you should understand when you have completed the section.

In this section you will learn about:

* Scottish resistance.
* The roles of William Wallace and Andrew Murray.
* Victory at Stirling and its effects on Scots and on Scotland.
* Defeat at Falkirk and continuing Scottish resistance.

HINTS

Hints give you advice and tips to support your learning.

> ### 🔍 Hint
>
> Care must be taken when using these particular sources about Wallace as the chronicles were written well after Wallace's death. Blind Harry's work was intended as a piece of entertainment written 170 years after his death – he even has Wallace written down as being seven feet tall!

MAKE THE LINK

Make the Link helps you to connect what you are learning to other areas of study within the course and to other subjects you might be studying. History is about what has happened in the past and you will find that what you learn has links to lots of other subjects like Modern Studies, Geography, English, RMPS and many more.

Make the Link

In Modern Studies you may study terrorism. Do you think Wallace employed 'terrorist' tactics in his day?

HISTORIOGRAPHY

Historiography sections will help you to analyse the importance of historical events in Sections 2 and 3. You can use the historiography in your essays/activities to help support analysis and widen the topic of debate. To ensure that you are using historiography correctly, think about what the historian is saying and how you can use their point to reinforce your point, or even if you can argue against it. Either way, you need to explain and analyse what they are saying and then clearly relate it to what you are saying. Simply dropping in a quote from a historian is not enough and will result in you not gaining marks for analysis or evaluation, and means you will have wasted valuable time. So, if you do use historiography, really use it to analyse or evaluate the issue in more depth by fully explaining how it relates to your argument and the question more broadly.

📖 **Historiography**

Martin Pugh argues that the 1867 Reform Act 'greatly accelerated the democratisation of British politics' because it paved the way for the Third Reform Act of 1884.

ACTIVITIES

Activities will get you thinking about what you have learned and help you to practise and develop the skills you will need for your assessment. There are different kinds of activities, including individual research work, paired discussion and group work. These are designed to help you broaden your knowledge of history but also to deepen your understanding and develop your analytical skills.

🔵 Activity 17

Evaluating the success of Labour in this period

You are going to debate the following issue:

The motion: The Labour government 1945–51 was successful in creating a welfare state that catered for the needs of the British people.

Your teacher will divide the class into two groups: for and against the motion. You must come up with the strongest arguments to support your side. You will be expected to argue against the other side, using facts and historiography to support your argument. Your teacher will decide whether this is a whole class debate or if you should get into opposing pairs.

EXAM STYLE QUESTIONS

Exam style questions are included throughout each section to test your knowledge and understanding of what you have learned. Many of these questions will also help you to develop and practise the skills you will need for your final exam. Some exam style questions, when answered correctly, can count towards meeting the unit outcomes.

GO! Activity 19

Exam style questions

'The Labour government met the needs of the people 'from the cradle to the grave'.'
How valid is this view?　　　　　　　　　　　　　　　　　　　　　　　　　　　(22)
(Higher British unit outcomes: 2.1, 2.2, 2.3)

LEARNING CHECKLISTS

Each topic closes with a summary of learning statements showing what you should be able to do when you complete the unit. You can use the learning checklist to check you have a good understanding of the topics covered in the topic. Traffic lights can be used for your own self-assessment.

Learning checklist

Now that you have finished **The Wars of Independence, 1249–1328**, complete a self-evaluation of your knowledge and skills to assess what you have understood. Use traffic lights to help you make up a revision plan to help you improve in the areas you identified as red or amber.

- Describe the nature of royal authority under Alexander III and Scotland's relationship with England before 1286.　◯ ◯ ◯

- Describe and analyse the succession problem following 1286.　◯ ◯ ◯

- Describe the importance of the Guardians and the Community of the Realm.　◯ ◯ ◯

ASSESSMENTS

At Higher you will sit two papers that cover all three topics. Paper 1 requires you to write one extended response on British history and one on European and World history. You will have 1 hour and 30 minutes to write the two extended responses. There are 44 marks for Paper 1.

Paper 2 requires you to answer four questions on Scottish history. Three of these will be source handling questions and one will be a knowledge question that requires you to explain the reasons for a particular issue or event occurring. There are 36 marks for Paper 2.

Higher candidates will also sit an assignment. The assignment is a piece of work in which you decide on the issue and question yourself, conduct research on it, and then write it up in class in 1 hour 30 minutes. You can take an A4 resource sheet in to help you when you write it up, meaning you don't have to remember all of your research. This piece of work will be sent off to SQA to be assessed. It is advised that you conduct a suitable amount of research and bring in alternative points of view into your assignment to show your understanding of the issue. There are 30 marks for the assignment.

Studying this topic will provide you with an understanding of the succession problem that arose in Scotland after the death of Alexander III. You will study the appeal to Edward I of England to adjudicate between the competitors for the Scottish Crown and the political change and military conflict which arose from the subsequent Wars of Independence. You will also study the key figures of the period, John Balliol, William Wallace and Robert Bruce, and explore the themes of authority, conflict and identity in the Scottish struggle for independence.

This topic is split into four sections:

❖ Alexander III and the succession problem.

❖ John Balliol and Edward I 1292–96.

❖ William Wallace and Scottish resistance.

❖ The rise and triumph of Robert Bruce.

Activities and Outcomes

		Activity								
		1	2	3	4	5	6	7	8	9
Outcome	1.1			✓		✓		✓		✓
	1.2			✓		✓		✓		✓
	1.3			✓		✓		✓		✓
	2.1			✓		✓		✓		✓
	2.2		✓	✓	✓	✓	✓	✓	✓	✓
	2.3		✓		✓		✓		✓	

Historical Study: Scottish: The Wars of Independence, 1249–1328

Background

The Scottish Wars of Independence have attracted historical interest for generations. They are intriguing because it is the story of Scotland as a sovereign nation, which went from being a prosperous nation with strong leadership to finding itself at the brink of civil war and eventual subjugation by Edward I of England, all within a matter of years. The topic continues to fascinate because of the ultimate success of Scotland, when the odds were arguably stacked against them. The topic certainly raises several questions. How did Scotland go from being a prosperous nation to one facing civil war and domination by England? Was the fight for Independence the true birth of the Scottish nation or a contest for power between kings? Did Robert the Bruce finally re-establish the independence of medieval Scotland?

With the death of Alexander III in 1286, Scotland's leadership crisis began and previous good relations with Edward I of England turned sour when he chose John Balliol to be the next King of Scotland. Scotland's Guardians had asked Edward to help choose the next King, trusting he would do so in a fair and balanced manner, not thinking that Edward would use Scotland's succession crisis as a stepping stone to increase his own power over the Scots. Balliol's reign was unsuccessful, in part due to his lack of capability as King, but also because of Edward's unalterable determination to be overlord of Scotland.

The failure of John Balliol to rule as an effective King of Scotland led to his disposal by Edward. Balliol and the other nobles of Scotland had refused to fight for Edward against France so Edward invaded Scotland and stripped Balliol of his title. Perhaps the two most famous challengers to Edward's rule were William Wallace and Robert the Bruce. Both challenged Edward's rule in Scotland and fought for its independence, although their motives were quite different. Wallace fought for the restoration of Balliol to the Crown whereas Bruce had further ambitions to be King of Scotland himself. It is also worth noting that Bruce did not always fight for Scottish independence, in fact he fought for Edward and against Balliol. The Wallace- and Murray-led battles of Stirling Bridge in 1297 and Wallace-led Falkirk in 1298 were key moments in Scottish history.

However, the Bruce-led Scottish victory at the Battle of Bannockburn in 1314 is probably the most famous Scottish victory of them all.

Figure 1: *Statue of Robert the Bruce.*

Nevertheless, the victory at Bannockburn did not secure Scottish independence and it took further campaigning by Bruce and his men in Ireland and England before Scotland was granted its independence in 1328.

GO! Activity 1

With a partner, mind map what you know about the following:

- William Wallace
- Robert the Bruce
- Battle of Stirling Bridge
- Battle of Falkirk
- Battle of Bannockburn.

Share your ideas with the rest of the class to find out your prior knowledge of the Wars of Independence.

Highlight the points that you think are TRUE in one colour and that are MYTH in another. As you find out about each person or event in turn, you can revisit your mindmap and see if you were correct. You should note any changes required!

Make the Link

If you take Modern Studies, you will learn about the campaign for Scottish independence over recent years.

1 Alexander III and the succession problem

In this section you will learn about:

- The succession problem.
- The Guardians.
- The Treaty of Birgham.
- The death of the Maid of Norway.
- The Scottish appeal to Edward I – the decision at Norham.
- Bruce versus Balliol.
- The Great Cause and Edward's decision.

Background: the nature of royal authority under Alexander III and the relationship with England before 1286

Figure 2: *Alexander III was crowned King of Scotland in 1249 aged only seven. He characterised what has become known as a Golden Age in Scotland until his death in 1286.*

> **Make the Link**
>
> In Business Management or Economics you may learn more about the roles these industries play and have played in Scotland's economy.

Alexander was crowned King of Scotland at only seven years of age. His reign, from 1249 to 1286, is often known as a Golden Age, largely because Alexander achieved peace and prosperity for Scotland. Scotland's economy improved in these years. For example, there was shipbuilding at Inverness, Glasgow exported timber to Ireland and there was an increase in exports of wool to Belgium. Since the economy was doing well, it could in turn support the Crown and Alexander was able to expand Scottish territories. He took advantage of the civil war in England to strengthen Scottish expansion to the west. From the time of the Vikings, the Western Isles had been ruled by Norway but in 1263 they were gained control of by Alexander. He took the Isle of Man in 1264 and in 1265 managed to get the nobles in the north and west, in Ross, Caithness and Skye, to submit to his rule. The Treaty of Perth was signed in 1266 which gave Alexander control of the Western Isles. This territorial expansion won Alexander many admirers and supporters and made him every bit as strong a leader as Edward I in England. Further, the Treaty of Perth heralded a time of peace between Norway and Scotland, leading eventually to Alexander's daughter marrying the King of Norway.

Prior to 1286, Scotland's relationship with England was relatively strong, perhaps made more secure with the marriage of Edward's sister Margaret to Alexander. The two leaders had a strong respect for each other and this helped to boost Anglo-Scottish relations. Any arguments between Edward and Alexander tended to be about overlordship of land, particularly in the north of England.

The regions of Cumbria and Northumberland had often been the subject of conflict between Scotland and England but after the Treaty of York in 1237 Scotland had officially given up claims to both regions. However, England remained concerned about a Scottish invasion and sceptical over Scotland's promise not to invade. England had real ambitions in France and did not want any battles with the Scots to get in the way of foreign expansion. Edward also knew that in the past other Scottish kings such as William the Lion had agreed to English overlordship of Scotland. However, Alexander was different and he refused to acknowledge Edward's overlordship of Scotland and refused to pay him homage.

Alexander believed in the divine right of kingship. He thought he was God's intended appointee on earth as the King of Scotland and is on record as saying to Edward: 'No man has the right to homage for my kingdom for I hold it of God alone.' Therefore, Edward could not, by the rule of God, be overlord of Scotland. Many historians think that it was Alexander's assertive personality along with their family ties that kept the relationship between Alexander and Edward, and indeed Scotland and England, so strong.

Although royal relations were strong, the relationship between the Scottish and English churches was not. The Archbishop of York thought he should have control over Scotland's church because there was no Scottish archbishop. However, Rome supported a religiously independent Scotland and granted her status as the 'Special Daughter' of Rome. Historians agree that the Scottish bishops supported Scottish independence in the period from 1286 onwards because they did not want to be ruled by the English church.

The succession problem

The succession problem began in 1286 with the death of Alexander. Prior to Alexander's death, his wife and two sons had died and Alexander had re-married a French noble called Yolande in the hope that the marriage would produce an heir. However, after a meeting in Edinburgh on 19 March 1286 Alexander attempted to ride home to Fife in dark and stormy weather. He made it quite close to home before

🔍 Hint

Overlordship means to have supremacy over other lords. As we shall see, Edward later claimed overlordship of Scotland, which meant that he effectively controlled the noblemen of Scotland and they had to do as Edward asked them.

🔍 Hint

Paying homage meant to acknowledge another leader as overlord and offer them loyalty especially through military service. In return, the overlord would grant land ownership. This was part of the feudal system.

🔍 Hint

The feudal system was introduced into Britain by William the Conqueror after the Norman invasion of 1066. It was introduced to Scotland at the time of David I. Under the feudal system all lands belonged to the king but could be given to nobles and knights as he saw fit. The peasants on the land would be loyal to a particular noble and pay them in kind, with barley or military service, in return for living on the land.

Figure 3: *Margaret, Maid of Norway was only an infant when she inherited the Crown of Scotland in 1286. This portrait is part of a mural in the Scottish National Portrait Gallery.*

> **Hint**
>
> A regent is someone who rules in place of a monarch if there is a reason the monarch cannot do so themselves. In the case of the Maid of Norway she was too young to rule at the time of her succession.

Figure 4: *The seal of Bishop Fraser of St Andrews.*

> **Hint**
>
> Seals were used as the 'signature' of a family or person. They were normally characterised by something related to the person, often the family coat of arms.

becoming separated from his men and, in the dark and poor weather conditions, fell off his horse and was killed. This posed a huge problem for Scotland. The marriage to Yolande had not produced an heir and Alexander's only living relative was Margaret, Maid of Norway, his granddaughter from the marriage of Alexander's daughter to the King of Norway, who was only about three years old at the time of his death.

Many Scottish nobles feared a civil war in Scotland over who should succeed Alexander as king, given that both the Bruce family and the Balliol family had strong claims to the throne. However, in an Act of Parliament in 1284, Alexander had stated that Margaret, Maid of Norway should become queen in the event of his death so the nobles agreed that this was the preferred option. Few were inclined to get Edward I involved at this stage although some had thought to ask him for help considering his good relationship with Alexander.

While it was felt that the succession problem had been resolved, the option of Margaret becoming queen raised difficult issues in the short term. Margaret was far too young to rule Scotland. She was also female and Norwegian. A regent or regents would have to be put in place to help her rule until she was old enough and she would have to be carefully guarded in case anyone with ambitions to rule Scotland should attack or kidnap her.

The Guardians

The choice of who to choose to help Margaret rule was difficult. Nobles with some knowledge and experience of authority were needed as well as some people who would offer religious guidance. Further, those who were appointed would be responsible for selecting a husband for Margaret and they needed to be wary of heightening the chances of civil war in Scotland depending on who they chose.

In the end, the following people were chosen as Guardians:

- Bishop Fraser of St Andrews
- Bishop Wishart of Glasgow
- Baron John Comyn of Badenoch
- Baron James the Steward
- Earl of Buchan – Alexander Comyn
- Earl of Fife – Duncan.

The Bruce and Balliol families were left out of the Guardianship, possibly due to the potential for trouble. The Guardians and the nobility of Scotland signed an oath of fealty to Margaret.

The Bruce family reacted badly and attacked the Comyns. However, they failed to make any major progress and the army of the Guardians quickly stamped out the rebellion. It served as a reminder of the political volatility of the succession question and other problems followed: for example, the Comyns argued with other nobles and the Earl of Fife was murdered.

Nevertheless, the Guardians, overall, were successful in ruling Scotland in the years following Alexander's death. They promoted the 'Community of the Realm' – the idea that upholding the Kingdom of Scotland itself was more important than the political ambitions of individual families. The fact that the Guardians included representatives of the church, barons and earls showed an attempt at balance in the rule of Scotland in the absence of a monarch. Further, the Guardians were determined to keep Scotland an independent country and free from the overlordship of England.

The Treaty of Birgham 1290

Soon after Margaret inherited the Scottish throne there was a proposal to marry her to Edward I's son, also called Edward. It was a proposal gladly welcomed by both Scotland and England. From England's point of view, it would secure a political relationship with Scotland and the marriage would mean that young Edward would inherit the rule of Scotland. From Scotland's point of view, it stopped the threat of civil war and preserved the prior relationship with England. However, the Guardians were not so foolish as to give away Scottish independence with the marriage so the Treaty of Birgham was drawn up to guarantee the sovereign independence of both Scotland and England.

The Treaty guaranteed the following:

- Edward I would respect the borders between England and Scotland and each country would remain separate.
- Edward agreed that no parliament governing Scotland would be held in England.
- Scottish laws, customs, rights and freedoms would be preserved.
- The Scottish church would remain free from interference from the English church.

However, fundamentally, the Treaty was a marriage contract and was entirely dependent on the marriage of young Edward and the Maid of Norway.

The death of the Maid of Norway

The decision was made to bring Margaret to Scotland to marry Edward in 1290. However, on the journey from Norway the young princess took sick and the ship she was travelling in had to land in Orkney, where she died. With her death, the Treaty of Birgham was null and void and the succession problem was again top of the political agenda in Scotland. Civil war loomed in the background as the Guardians decided how best to resolve the crisis. The ambitions of Edward I also concerned many as, earlier in 1290, he had taken control of the Isle of Man and demanded the Scottish church pay taxes to England – perhaps a warning sign of what was to come.

The Scottish appeal to Edward I – the decision at Norham

The Guardians asked Edward I for help in deciding who should rule Scotland. Robert Bruce had also asked Edward for help in the hope that Edward would favour the Bruce family. It may seem an odd choice to ask Edward for help considering his ambitions to be overlord of Scotland but, from the point of view of the Scots at the time, it probably seemed like a sensible option. Edward was an extremely skilled statesman and well trained in law and particularly understood the law of primogeniture.

Figure 5: *The Maid of Norway – stained glass window in Lerwick Town Hall.*

Hint

Primogeniture is the law by which the eldest born male inherits. Until recently, in the case of royalty, the eldest born male is heir to the throne. Edward would have to follow this rule to pick the true heir to the Scottish throne.

Further, Edward was a good choice because he was already a King by divine right, therefore his choice would have religious approval. He also had the force of arms to enforce his decision, removing the threat of any backlash by families such as the Bruces.

Edward had also been Alexander's brother-in-law so there was already a strong political relationship between Scotland and England. It may be that the Scots asked for Edward's help because they thought that involving him in the choice of the next king would prevent him from having ambitions to take Scotland himself. In total, there were 13 valid claimants to the throne. All of the claimants and the Guardians travelled to Upsettlington on the Scottish side of the border with England and waited patiently for Edward, who was stationed with a garrison over the border, to come and meet them to begin the selection process. However, Edward wanted to keep the upper hand and made the claimants come over the border to him at Norham castle. This was a clever move by Edward. It put him firmly in control and many Scots felt threatened by him and his army. They feared an invasion if they did not accept his demands. However, the Guardians stated it would be up to the next King of Scotland to accept Edward's demands so he would have to choose a king first.

Figure 6: *Norham castle in the north of England was the chosen place for the selection process for the new King of Scotland.*

Edward made each of the claimants accept his overlordship before they were able to proceed. The claimants probably thought this was only to be for a temporary period until the succession crisis was resolved. Also, they needed Edward's help to choose a new king or face the real possibility of a civil war over succession.

Bruce versus Balliol

The two families with the strongest claim were the Bruce family and the Balliol family. The Bruce family capitulated to Edward quite early on in the decision-making process, thinking that, if they accepted Edward's overlordship sooner, it would win them favour with the King of England. John Balliol held out and was the last of the candidates to accept Edward's overlordship. John Balliol is often judged to have been the weaker of the two candidates but as this instance shows, Balliol was not necessarily ready to give in to Edward's demands as soon as they were requested.

Make the Link

In Geography or Modern Studies you may learn about countries around the world that have been annexed or invaded by neighbouring countries in recent years. You will of course also see this if you study the Germany topic.

The Great Cause and Edward's decision

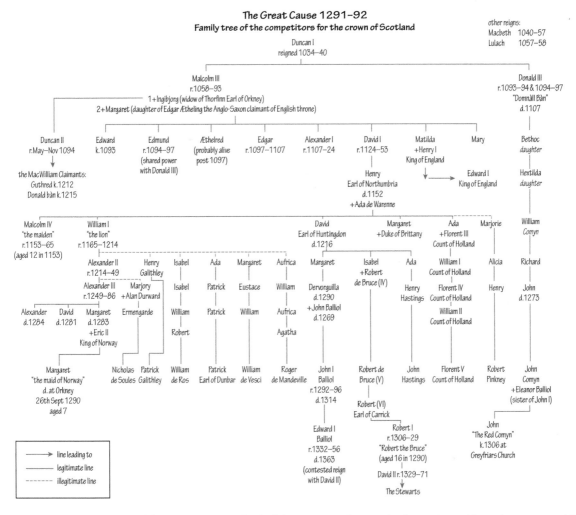

Figure 7: *This detailed royal family tree shows who had the strongest claim to the throne. It would require someone skilled in the law of primogeniture to help make the legally correct choice.*

The selection process became known as the Great Cause. After careful consideration Edward whittled the number of claimants down to three – John Balliol, Robert Bruce and John Hastings. Edward again forced the claimants to accept his overlordship – it became clear that this was not to be on a temporary basis and the Guardians were worried at the implications of this for Scotland. Edward had spent time prior to the meeting at Norham looking for justification for overlordship of Scotland and had recently gained control of Wales. Further, Edward probably wanted to control the Scots to gain their military support for his continued campaigns in France.

Edward also deliberately took a long time to make his decision, probably thinking that if he delayed then the possibility of his continuing position as overlord of Scotland would be stronger as any new Scottish king would find it difficult to assert their authority. It took over a year for Edward to state his decision – he announced that John Balliol would be the next King of Scotland on 17 November 1292. By the law of primogeniture, John Balliol was chosen as the rightful heir to the throne of Scotland.

Figure 8: *An artist's impression of John Balliol, who was chosen as the new King of Scotland in 1292.*

GO! Activity 2

1. With a partner, go through the text of this section and produce an information poster on the following:
   - Explain the reason why the Golden Age of Scotland came to an end in 1286.
   - Explain the reason why there was a succession crisis in Scotland between 1286 and 1292.
   - Explain the reasons why Edward I of England was asked to help choose the next King of Scotland.
   (Higher Scottish unit outcomes: 2.2)
2. Now, with your partner, offer your analysis of the following:
   - Analyse the difficulties the death of Alexander III caused for Scotland.
   - Analyse the difficulties the death of Margaret, Maid of Norway caused for Scotland.
   - Analyse the importance of the role of the Guardians of Scotland up to 1291.
   (Higher Scottish unit outcomes: 2.3)

GO! Activity 3

Exam style questions

Source A is an extract from the Treaty of Birgham (1290).

> We [Edward I] promise…that the kingdom of Scotland shall remain separate and divided from the kingdom of England by its rightful boundaries and borders as has been observed up to now and that it shall be free in itself and independent, reserving always the right of our lord or whoever which has belonged to him or to anyone in the borders elsewhere.

1. Evaluate the usefulness of Source A as evidence of the Guardians' desire to protect the independence of Scotland.   **(8)**

   In reaching a conclusion you should refer to:
   - the origin and possible purpose of the source;
   - the content of the source;
   - recalled knowledge.
   (Higher Scottish unit outcomes: 1.1, 2.1)

Source B is from Geoffrey W.S. Barrow, *Robert Bruce and the Community of the Realm of Scotland* (2005).

> The atmosphere in the summer of 1290 was hopeful, even joyful. Then tragic events in late September 1290 set in motion a struggle for the throne between a number of claimants, of whom two were of outstanding importance: Robert Bruce of Annandale and John Balliol, Lord of Galloway. While the nobles were gathering at Perth, Robert Bruce, in his seventieth year, had arrived unexpectedly with a strong body of armed men. It looked as though the question of the succession would be settled by open war between the two claimants and their supporters. Bishop Fraser went so far as to write to the English king in October 1290, suggesting that if John Balliol was to come to Edward, the king would be well advised to reach an understanding with him, as the likely king of Scots.

Source C is from Michael Penman, *The Scottish Civil War* (2002).

> As part of the legal process to decide between the claimants to the Scottish throne, Robert Bruce and John Balliol (who was aided by Comyn) now had to choose forty auditors each to represent their interests in legal proceedings at Berwick in front of the English King Edward I, alongside his own twenty-four jurors. But once seated there was an almost immediate adjournment for ten months. What this did was to leave Edward firmly in charge of the Scottish realm. This cannot have come as a surprise; Edward I had long since ordered his lawyers to search for documentary proof of the English monarchy's claim to Scotland. In the end, Edward I announced John Balliol as 'king of Scots' on 17 November 1292. But the outcome of what is now known as the 'Great Cause' was surely a foregone conclusion.

2. How much do sources B and C reveal differing interpretations about the role of Edward during the Great Cause? **(10)**

   Compare the sources overall and in detail.

   (Higher Scottish unit outcomes: 1.3)

Source D is from Michael Brown, *The Wars of Scotland* (2004).

> The situation was by no means hopeless (following the death of Prince Alexander in 1284)… Within days of his son's death, the king obtained a promise from his magnates that they would accept the child, Margaret, Maid of Norway, as his heir. This was only an insurance policy. In October 1285 Alexander remarried, wedding Yolanda of Dreux, from a French noble family. He hoped that this match would produce a child of his own to succeed him. It was his enthusiasm to return to his young queen that led the king to leave Edinburgh and cross the Forth on the evening of 19 March 1286. Setting out from Queensferry to the royal manor at Kinghorn, Alexander was thrown from his horse and died, his neck broken.

3. How fully does Source D demonstrate the problems caused by the death of Alexander III in 1286? **(10)**

   Use the source and recalled knowledge.

   (Higher Scottish unit outcomes: 1.2, 2.2)

4. Explain the reasons why there was a succession problem in Scotland between 1286 and 1292.

   (Higher Scottish unit outcome 2.2) **(8)**

2 John Balliol and Edward I, 1292–96

In this section you will learn about:

- Balliol's rule.
- Edward's overlordship.
- The Anglo-French war and the Franco-Scottish Treaty.
- The Scottish response.
- The subjugation of Scotland.

Balliol's rule

From the beginning of his rule, it was clear that John Balliol was going to struggle to be an effective King of Scots. He probably had not contemplated that he would ever be king – he was the youngest of three brothers – and had had a limited amount of royal training. Not only had he inherited the throne from a very strong king, but a tumultuous ten years had followed the death of Alexander. Even someone with real political skill and knowledge would have struggled to rule Scotland effectively immediately after a succession crisis, threat of civil war and the rule of six Guardians. Further, Balliol would never have had the full support of the other Scottish nobles because families like the Bruces had their own ambitions for the throne.

Balliol's reign began with difficulties that he was never truly able to overcome. This has led many historians to assert that Balliol merely became King Edward's puppet and that he had chosen Balliol because he was the weakest candidate and the easiest to manipulate. But Edward had genuinely followed the rules of primogeniture when choosing Balliol and he was, by this law, the rightful king. However, as we will see, Edward was his superior in kingship and leadership and set out to undermine Balliol's role as the King of Scots from the outset.

Edward's overlordship

Balliol was crowned King of Scots on 30 November 1292. He was crowned upon the stone of destiny at Scone, the traditional crowning place of the kings of Scotland. However, he was also made to pay homage to Edward. This meant that he had to accept Edward as his overlord and as such he would be loyal to Edward. Many had thought that Edward's demands of overlordship had been a temporary arrangement during the succession crisis but this proved otherwise. Edward now very much considered Scotland to be a domain of England.

The first example of Edward undermining Balliol's authority is the case of the burgess of Berwick.

The burgess of Berwick had a legal complaint from the time when the Guardians had ruled Scotland and asked Balliol to rectify it. Balliol told him that the decision still stood as the Guardians had made it and he refused to change it. The burgess went to Edward who then overruled the decision and forced Balliol to change it. This was

Figure 9: *John Balliol pays homage to Edward I.*

humiliating for Balliol – his authority as king had been undermined by Edward, proving Edward's overlordship and that this was acknowledged by the people of Scotland. Balliol tried to use the Treaty of Birgham to uphold Scottish independence in such matters but Edward officially declared the Treaty null and void.

The Macduff case proved the point further. Macduff had been disinherited from his lands and had spent time in prison. He was released when John Balliol came to power but tried to appeal to Edward to try and regain his land ownership. Balliol was forced to go to court at Westminster where he tried to protest that Edward had no business in undermining Balliol's decisions concerning land in Scotland but Edward ignored him and threatened to have him charged with contempt of court if he did not do as he was told. Edward deliberately dragged the case out so as to control and humiliate Balliol.

Edward further stamped his authority by appointing Thomas of Hunsingore as the chancellor of Scotland and Balliol was made to follow English law, practices and customs rather than continue with Scottish traditions and practices. This was effectively English rule in Scotland – it was being ruled by the laws of England. Further, revenues (tax money) raised in Scotland were controlled and spent by the English Crown, something many Scottish nobles resented. However, it must be remembered that not all Scottish nobles would have disagreed with this – many nobles also held land in England as well as Scotland, so may have welcomed English rule as they thought it would increase their own status in Scotland as well as England. This is often a contentious issue with regard to the Bruce family. However, owning lands in England meant they owed homage to the King of England, which may explain why the Bruce's supported Edward at this time.

The Anglo-French war and the Franco-Scottish Treaty

However, the issue that really sparked the rebellion in Scotland was the prospect of a war with France. Edward's ambitions to expand his influence in France were well known and in 1294 he summoned his men to fight. As Edward was Balliol's feudal overlord he was ordered to fight and, in turn, so too were the Scottish nobles. This was a step too far for the Scots. They did not want to fight for England and ruin their trading and political relationship with France and, further, they did not want their tax revenues raised to pay for a war in which they wished to have no part. Considered an emergency, 12 Guardians were appointed. They may have been appointed to take charge of the situation or perhaps simply to offer moral support and political guidance to Balliol. However, they refused to fight for Edward. In 1295 they arranged for a Treaty to be signed at Paris between Scotland and France that stated that Balliol's son, Edward Balliol, was to marry into the French nobility. This Treaty, ratified by the Scottish Parliament in February 1296, guaranteed an alliance between France and Scotland and meant Edward could not have Scottish support for his military campaign. Edward was furious and set about invading Scotland to assert his authority.

The Scottish response

The fact that the nobles were prepared to rebel against Edward in support of Balliol suggests that they were possibly more loyal to him than first thought. The examples of the burgess of Berwick and the

Hint

A burgess was a person who held a position as political head of a town in medieval times. They would be responsible for helping to control the trading of goods in and out of the 'burgs'.

Hint

To disinherit means to exclude someone from the right to inherit land. In medieval times, families would pass on land to their family members when they died. However, the ruling monarch had ultimate control of the land in the realm and could prevent land inheritance taking place, perhaps if the family had betrayed or annoyed the king in any way.

Macduff case may be isolated examples of attempts to undermine Balliol for personal gain, rather than to show any open allegiance for the English throne. Whatever the nobles thought about Balliol's leadership, he was their king by divine right and they wanted to preserve the sovereignty of Scotland.

The subjugation of Scotland

Figure 10: *The Siege and Battle of Berwick, March 1296. It was said that after the attack the river Tweed ran red with blood.*

In 1296 Berwick was in Scotland. Its defences had been boosted and an army of nobles, hired soldiers and tenants were gathered to defend the town.

Edward surrounded Berwick with his troops for three days but the insolent behaviour of the Scots who jeered and insulted the English soldiers encouraged him to attack. An English chronicler, Walter of Guisborough, wrote that 8000 Scots were killed and that the women were spared. However, another English chronicle, the Chronicle of Lanercost, details that 15 000 men and women were killed and the town was sacked and pillaged. Historians agree that the Lanercost account may be more accurate as it is documented that after the siege, Berwick had to be repopulated with people from elsewhere in Northumbria.

Figure 11: *Ruins of Dunbar castle as they are today. Dunbar was an important castle as it held a position with an outlook to the Firth of Forth and the North Sea.*

Hint

In the late thirteenth century Scotland had no professional army. The nobles would certainly have had armed training and many would have been formidable fighters. However, other than the hired soldiers, none would have had formal training. Edward's army, in contrast, were a well-trained, well-equipped professional fighting machine.

Hint

Chronicles are one of the main sources of historical information in the medieval period. They were written by monks who would have been some of the few people trained in how to read and write. We have to be careful with them when considering their historical accuracy as sometimes chronicles were written down as oral accounts that had been passed on and some display bias towards or against certain people or countries.

Make the Link

You will learn more about detecting subjectivity and bias in English and Modern Studies.

The English army then progressed to Dunbar, on the east coast. Edward expected to be able to occupy the castle with no protest, as the Earl of Dunbar had given him the keys to the castle after Berwick. However, the Earl of Dunbar's wife was a Comyn and wished to support the Scottish rebellion, and she gave control of the castle to the Scots. Despite this the English troops, led by Earl Warenne of Surrey, had an easy win when the Scottish troops left the safety of their position on the hill at Dunbar to descend upon the English troops, who they mistakenly thought were retreating. Again, the might of the English army could not be defeated by a smaller, weaker Scottish army. The Scots' death toll was in the thousands and 130 nobles were captured.

This spelled disaster for the Scots. They had tried to defend their lands after Berwick but now it became clear that they were outclassed by Edward and the English army. With so many nobles having been captured, leadership and confidence was low and the survivors began to retreat to their own lands to try to protect them from English attack. The Scots knew that Edward would not stop after Dunbar and that the people of Scotland were about to be subjugated to English rule. Rather than fight a losing battle, most Scots surrendered as the English army approached.

Edward progressed north, taking an eastern route which saw the castle of Roxburgh fall to him within a few days. Jedburgh and Edinburgh held out for longer but Edward had a constant stream of supplies and, when new siege engines arrived, both towns surrendered, knowing that resistance was futile.

Figure 12: *Edward I of England met little resistance as he advanced through Scotland, capturing land and control of the Scots.*

Figure 13: *This medieval map of Scotland shows the importance of Stirling in medieval times – it is right in the centre.*

In the late thirteenth century, Stirling was the keystone to controlling Scotland. But the Scots at Stirling did not even put up a fight – when they saw the English army approaching they handed the keys to the castle caretakers and fled. With Stirling under English control Edward continued his march north and took control of Scone, where the Kings of Scotland were symbolically crowned, then Aberdeen, ending at Elgin in July. John Balliol had put up no real attempt to stop Edward – he did not know what to do or how to do it so offered his surrender on 2 July 1296. Alexander MacDougall, from the west coast, had tried to put up more of a resistance to Edward but without widespread support or capable means, his resistance was not successful.

Balliol was publicly forced to surrender to Edward on 10 July after Balliol had sent Edward a letter asking him to accept his surrender and blaming everything on the bad advice of his nobles. Edward accepted his surrender but made Balliol apologise and renounce his Treaty with France. He was stripped of his royal robes and thus earned the nickname 'toom tabard' or 'empty coat'. It was a denigrating term referring to how gutless Balliol had been.

Edward did not kill Balliol. Instead, he was put under house arrest in England with his son. He eventually went to live in France where he lived comfortably on a pension from the French king. However, despite the fact that the fighting that was to take place in 1297 and 1298 was done in his name, Balliol would never again set foot in Scotland. He refused to fight and anyway was not able to – he was not released from the Tower of London until 1299 and then died in 1314. Although many people tried to persuade him to restore his position on the Scottish throne, Balliol refused.

Edward then tried to remove items of Scottish heritage to get rid of the notion that Scotland should be considered a separate country. This included taking royal documents and the Stone of Destiny, on which Scottish kings were crowned, as well as the Holy Rood of St Margaret. He also took the Scottish crown jewels – a clear indication that the Scottish royal family was no more.

Figure 14: *John Balliol was stripped of his royal robes in July 1296.*

Hint

The Holy Rood of St Margaret was a Christian relic, said to be part of the true cross that Jesus Christ was crucified on. It was brought to Scotland after 1066 from Hungary by Margaret who became Queen of Scotland when she married Malcolm III. Many people made pilgrimages to Scotland to visit the relic. Holyrood Palace is named after the relic. By taking it to England, Edward was symbolically destroying Scotland's divine right as a sovereign nation and quashing its religious independence.

Figure 15: *The Stone of Destiny was where all Scottish kings had been crowned. Taking it away from Scotland symbolised the end of the divine right of kings in Scotland.*

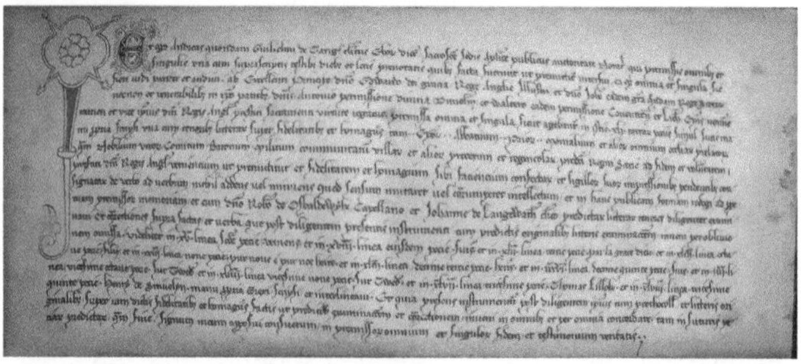

Figure 16: *The Ragman roll was signed by Scottish nobles who swore a personal oath to Edward I.*

In August of 1296 Edward made 1600 leading nobles of Scotland swear fealty to him. The signed document became known as the 'Ragman roll' and shows the power of Edward over the Scots. Scotland was well and truly under English control by August 1296. An extract from the roll shows that the nobles agreed to the overlordship of Edward and to serve him and protect him, under the eyes of God.

> Since we have become faithful and subject to the will of the most noble prince, our well-loved lord Edward … we promise on our own behalf and that of our heirs, upon punishment of body and property and whatever else we can forfeit, that we shall support him; and we shall serve him well and loyally against all mortal men, every time that we are called upon or summoned by our said lord, the king of England, or by his heirs; and that if we shall come to know of anything harmful to them, we shall do all in our power to obstruct it, and we shall make them aware of it. In order to hold to and keep these promises, we pledge ourselves, our heirs, and all our goods. And we have furthermore sworn this upon the holy Gospels. As proof of this matter we have caused these open letters to be written, and sealed them with our seal.

The nobles, no doubt, faced a difficult choice. By signing the roll they effectively signed away Scotland's independence. However, should they have refused, they would have faced punishment from Edward – they would likely have had their lands disinherited and faced imprisonment.

 **Make the Link**

You may learn about the qualities of a leader in Business Management or PE.

GO! Activity 4

1. Write a report explaining the events that led to the subjugation of Scotland. You must include details of the following:
   - The ascension of John Balliol to the throne.
   - The problems facing Balliol at the start of his rule.
   - The demands made by Edward of the Scots.
   - The Treaty between Scotland and France.
   - The Siege of Berwick.
   - The Battle of Dunbar.
   - The capture of other Scottish strongholds.
   - The humiliation of John Balliol.
   - The signing of the Ragman's roll.

   (Higher Scottish unit outcomes: 2.2)

2. In groups of four, take two pieces of A3 paper. On one piece of paper write 'Good leadership displayed by King John' and on the other 'Bad leadership displayed by King John'.

   Take 15 minutes to discuss the leadership of Balliol and write your relevant ideas down on the appropriate piece of paper.

   Share your ideas with the rest of the class.

   Write up an answer to the following question using your evidence:

   Analyse John Balliol's reign as King of Scotland – is it a fair assessment to say he was a bad king for Scotland?

   You can complete this as a collaborative exercise or as an individual exercise.

   (Higher Scottish unit outcomes: 2.3)

GO! Activity 5

Exam style questions

Source E describes King John paying homage to Edward I on 26 December 1292.

> On 26th December at Newcastle-upon-Tyne in the hall of the king of England's palace within the castle ..., the honourable prince John Balliol king of Scotland, did homage in person to the king of England as lord superior of the kingdom of Scotland, for the kingdom and all that belongs to it, saying the words of homage himself in French: 'My lord, Lord Edward, lord superior of the realm of Scotland, I, John Balliol, king of Scots, hereby become your liegeman for the whole kingdom of Scotland with all that belongs to it and goes with it and I hold ... that kingdom ... of you and your heirs, the kings of England; and I will keep faith and fealty to you and your heirs, the kings of England, in matters of life and limb and of earthly honour against all mortal men'.

1. How fully does Source E explain the difficulties which faced John as king of Scots from 1292 to 1296?   **(10)**

   Use the source and recalled knowledge.

   (Higher Scottish unit outcomes: 1.2, 2.2)

Source F is from the chronicle of Walter Bower, the *Scotichronicon*.

> Then after the capture of the town of Berwick by the English and the piteous slaughter of the Scots from Fife became known, the Scots who were sent by King John to help the town of Berwick fought in the same year on 27th April with the English at Dunbar. Where Patrick de Graham and many nobles fell wounded. And very many other knights and barons, on fleeing to the castle of Dunbar in the hope of saving their lives, were received there with ready welcome. But the custodian of the castle in question, Richard Siward by name, handed them all, to the number of seventy knights, besides the Earl of Ross and the Earl of Menteith, to the king of England, like sheep offered for slaughter. Without pity, he handed them over to suffer immediately various kinds of death and hardship.

2. Evaluate the usefulness of Source F as evidence of Edward I's success in the invasion of Scotland in 1296.   **(8)**

   In reaching a conclusion you should refer to:
   - the origin and possible purpose of the source;
   - the content of the source;
   - recalled knowledge.

   (Higher Scottish unit outcomes: 1.1, 2.1)

Source G is from Caroline Bingham, *Robert the Bruce* (1999).

After his inauguration as King of Scots on 30 November 1292 John Balliol travelled south to Newcastle where King Edward was holding his Christmas Court, and there on 26 December 1292 he paid homage to Edward I for his kingdom. Well advised by his kinsmen, the Comyns, John indicated in his first parliament of February 1293 that he intended to build upon Alexander III's achievements. But even as he began to assert his authority it was undermined by Edward's intention to accept appeals from King John's Court. When the case of Macduff of Fife came before the Court of King Edward at the November parliament, John was subjected to the most public humiliation. In the summer of 1294 King John was again in England, and was made to promise Scottish participation in Edward's proposed expedition against Philip IV of France.

Source H is from Michael Penman, *The Scottish Civil War* (2002).

King John must have feared the danger from within his borders from disappointed Scottish nobles who preferred to side with the English King, this of course included the Bruces. For Edward in early 1296 the campaign to Scotland was carried out from the outset by using the full force of England's experienced army. On 30 March his large army made a swift example of the town of Berwick, slaughtering over 7000 inhabitants. When a small Scottish force attempted to relieve the besieged castle of Dunbar, King John was absent. In the ensuing battle at Dunbar on 27 April the Scots were defeated resoundingly by a small English force led by Surrey. Edward then progressed north unhindered. The Scots leaders soon lost all stomach for the fight.

3. How much do sources G and H reveal about differing interpretations of the difficulties faced by John Balliol during his kingship? **(10)**

   Compare the sources overall and in detail.

   (Higher Scottish unit outcomes: 1.3)

4. Explain the reasons why there were difficulties in the relationship between John Balliol and Edward I. **(8)**

   (Higher Scottish unit outcomes: 2.2)

3 William Wallace and Scottish resistance

In this section you will learn about:

- Scottish resistance.
- The roles of William Wallace and Andrew Murray.
- Victory at Stirling and its effects on Scots and on Scotland.
- Defeat at Falkirk and continuing Scottish resistance.

Make the Link

In Modern Studies you will learn about international organisations like the UN that would be involved in such a dispute today.

Figure 17: *The Coat of Arms of Hugh de Cressingham. As treasurer of Scotland, he was hated by most Scots and, we are led to believe, by many English people too.*

Scottish resistance

Many of the Scots did indeed capitulate to Edward but many did not want him as their overlord and, when he put English men in charge of Scotland, it stoked the fires of a resistance movement. There had already been significant resistance to the English occupation from the outset in the west of Scotland.

The Earl of Surrey, John De Warenne, was made Lieutenant of Scotland but left the post early, claiming that he did not like the Scottish weather. However, Warenne was later forced by Edward to command the English army against Scotland, perhaps showing that the English king made no allowances even for his own countrymen. The other Englishmen who were put in charge of Scotland, the judges and lords, had no respect for Scottish customs or laws and no desire to look after the people or lands of Scotland. Naturally, resentment towards the English occupation built up quickly. Hugh de Cressingham had been appointed the treasurer of Scotland and his job was to collect taxes from the Scots. He met with considerable difficulty as Scots refused to pay their dues to the English throne. He wanted to punish the Scots with force for not following English demands.

Open rebellions up and down the country began:

- In the Western Isles, the MacDougall family rebelled against the MacDonald family who had been chosen as Edward's men. This was possibly not so much a rebellion against the English throne and more of a protest at not being Edward's preferred choice for governance of that region.

- In the south west, Bishop William Fraser and the Earl of Carrick rebelled. Fraser was concerned about the level of English control and did not want Scotland's religious freedom jeopardised. The Earl of Carrick would later become known as Robert the Bruce – the Bruce family had its sights firmly set on the Scottish throne. Further, the Bruce family had previously held an allegiance with Edward and had expected to be granted lands and power when he invaded Scotland. When this did not happen, it prompted a rebellion. The rebellion was beaten at Irvine by the superior forces of the English led by Henry Percy.

The failure at Irvine of Bruce and William Fraser to seize control left another gathering rebellion by William Wallace time to organise – the negotiations between the Scottish and English sides continued for weeks.

The roles of William Wallace and Andrew Murray

Figure 18: *Duffus castle, in Morayshire. The Moray or Murray family held strong political positions in Scotland in the thirteenth century.*

The Moray or Murray family was influential in Scotland. Andrew Murray's father had been justiciar of the northern half of Scotland. The family were loyal to King John Balliol. Andrew Murray had been trained as a knight and fought and was captured at the Battle of Dunbar. He was taken as a prisoner to Chester castle after the battle to be held for ransom but managed to escape. When he returned to the north of Scotland he found English garrisons stationed in his home led by William FitzWarin. He began to gather support for a successful rebellion in the north and took the castles of the north such as Inverness, Duffus and Elgin. He joined forces with Wallace in the south in 1297 and in August both groups were successful in the siege of Dundee. From here, Murray and Wallace moved to Stirling to meet the English army led by Warenne which was headed to Scotland from England. Murray's role in the Wars of Independence is often overlooked as he was injured at the Battle of Stirling Bridge and died from his wounds in November 1297. However, without the success of his rebellion in the north, Wallace would not have received the support he needed from Murray in the south and the success at Stirling Bridge may never have happened.

Figure 19: *William Wallace.*

William Wallace is a problematic figure for historians as little is known about him. Before his role in the Scottish resistance, Wallace is not

Figure 20: *Blind Harry's poem 'The Wallace' was the inspiration behind the film* Braveheart.

written about by contemporary chroniclers. In fact, most of the information about Wallace's early life comes to us from the poem The Wallace by Blind Harry. It was written as a piece of entertainment and has Wallace's rebellion as 'an undying vengeance against the English' after the murder of his wife by the Sheriff of Lanark, Sir William Heselrig. However, the role of Marion Braidfute as Wallace's wife seems to have been added in to give Blind Harry's poem a romantic edge as there is no hard evidence that this was Wallace's motivation for rebellion, or indeed that he was even married.

Other chronicles which give us information about Wallace's early life are also problematic because of when they were written. Another work to note is Walter Bower's *Scotichronicon*. Bower was a chronicler who wrote about Wallace in the fifteenth century. John of Fordun also wrote about Wallace in his history of Scotland, *Chronicles of the Scottish People,* although his information is limited.

Therefore, because of the nature of the evidence, Historians find it difficult to determine exactly who Wallace was in his early life. He was a minor nobleman, his family may have owned some lands and it is likely he came from Elderslie in Renfrewshire. He did kill the Sheriff of Lanark, however historians like Fiona Watson argue that it is more likely that, as an outlaw, Wallace was in regular trouble with the Sheriff and wanted to rebel against him. It was probably this that led to the beginning of resistance in the south in the name of John Balliol.

What historians do know about Wallace is that he developed into a leader with a certain amount of military skill. He led the Scottish resistance first in the south then collaboratively with Andrew Murray.

When the rebellion in the South began, Wallace quickly gathered support and, with the help of William Douglas, Robert Bruce (Earl of Carrick), James Steward and Bishop Wishart, had some early success in confronting English occupiers. However, early success was thwarted slightly when Bruce had to surrender to the English at Irvine in July 1297. Nevertheless, even though they had surrendered, their support for Wallace continued and their encounters with the English even allowed Wallace to retreat to Selkirk to plan his next move. He accompanied Andrew Murray at the successful siege of Dundee in August 1297. By this stage, Edward had learned of the rebellion and had sent an army north, led by John De Warenne. Edward himself was campaigning in France, not for a moment anticipating that the rebellion in Scotland would not be defeated swiftly and without difficulty by his garrison. Wallace and Murray decided the best place to fight the English would be to meet them at Stirling Bridge.

wanted to support Edward to advance their own interests and power demonstrable by the fact they made oaths of fealty to Edward.

Figure 26: *The Battle of Falkirk. Note the schiltron formations.*

Wallace knew the strength of the English lay in their heavy cavalry so he set the Scots up in schiltron formation behind a bog – he hoped that the English would find the terrain difficult to manoeuvre. Wallace also positioned the Scottish cavalry away from the front line on the flank. It is likely that Wallace thought to leave the cavalry to charge after the English cavalry had been taken down by the schiltrons – if the Scottish cavalry had been used first they would have been defeated easily because they were outnumbered by the English. The Scots also had some longbow archers who, although skilled men, did not rival the numbers in the contingent of Welsh longbowmen in the English army. Wallace knew the battle would be more difficult than Stirling Bridge and said to his men before the fight: 'I have brought you to the ring – now dance if you can.'

The battle commenced with the English cavalry immediately attacking the Scottish cavalry on the flank. After some unsuccessful fighting, the Scots turned and left. This left the Scottish archers without any protection and they were easily cut down. The schiltrons did what they were supposed to and stopped the English cavalry from making any real progress but, due to the defensive nature of the schiltrons and the lack of archers, they could not mount an attack. The English archers then opened fire on the schiltrons and cut the Scots down where they stood. Lack of mobility was the main reason for the Scottish defeat and, after the archers had taken out hundreds of Scots, the English cavalry came back in and finished off the rest of the Scottish soldiers. The Scots lost most of their men in battle. The Scottish nobles on horseback have been heavily criticised for leaving the battlefield.

However, some historians, such as Fiona Watson think that they knew the cavalry and well-trained nobility was the Scots' best asset and only chance in future of defeating the English, so they chose to preserve themselves to be able to fight another day.

After the defeat at Falkirk, Wallace had to resign as Guardian. John Comyn, who was closely related to John Balliol, and Robert the Bruce became joint Guardians of Scotland. Wallace is rumoured to have travelled to France to try to encourage John Balliol to return to Scotland. There are further rumours of Wallace approaching Pope Boniface VIII to petition him to ask for Balliol's return. In his absence, John Comyn tried to continue the rebellion but was unsuccessful and in 1304 surrendered fully to Edward. Edward had learned his lesson about treating the Scots harshly and did not want to prompt further rebellions so set about giving the nobles special privileges and ruled Scotland with a fairer hand.

By the time Wallace returned, Scotland, although occupied by England, was at relative peace and the first stage in the War of Independence was over. Any call to arms or rebellion by Wallace probably only met with resentment – the nobles had just managed to secure peace with Edward, they did not want to start up the fighting again.

Wallace was handed over to the English by Sir John Menteith and taken to London and put on trial for treason by Edward. However, it was merely a show trial as Wallace's fate had been secured. At the trial, Wallace stated that he could not be guilty of treason because Edward was not the true King of Scotland; Wallace's king was John Balliol. Nevertheless, this stood for nothing and Wallace was sentenced to death. He was hung, drawn and quartered on 23 August 1305. His head was displayed on London Bridge and his body parts sent to northern England and Scotland to serve as a reminder of the consequences to anyone who committed treason.

Figure 27: *Wallace was put on trial for treason in London in 1305. Painting by Daniel Maclise.*

Activity 6

1. In groups of four, create a presentation describing the events in the life of William Wallace from 1297 to 1305.

   Include descriptions of the following:

   - Wallace's early life and career
   - The Battle of Stirling Bridge, 1297
   - The Battle of Falkirk, 1298
   - Capture, trial and execution.

   (Higher Scottish unit outcomes: 2.2)

2. With a partner, analyse the role of William Wallace in the First Scottish Wars of Independence. You can focus on the following questions to help you:

   - Why is Wallace not well known before 1297?
   - Why was Wallace successful at the Battle of Stirling Bridge?
   - Why was Wallace defeated at the Battle of Falkirk?
   - Why did Wallace fail to restart the rebellion against Edward after 1298?

   Discuss the answers to the questions with the rest of your class.

   (Higher Scottish unit outcomes: 2.3)

Figure 28: *Plaque in London that marks the site of Wallace's execution.*

Activity 7

Exam style questions

Source I is from the letter of William Wallace and Andrew Murray to the merchants of Hamburg, 11 October 1297.

> Andrew Murray and William Wallace, leaders of the army of the kingdom of Scotland, and the community of the realm, to their wise and discreet beloved friends, the mayors and common people of Lubeck and Hamburg, greetings and ever-increasing sincere affection.
>
> We have been told by trustworthy merchants of the kingdom of Scotland that you, because of your kindness and not because of what we deserve, are considerate, helpful and well disposed in all cases and matters affecting us and our merchants and we are therefore more obliged to give you our thanks and a worthy repayment: to this end we willingly enter into an undertaking with you, asking you to have it announced to your merchants that they can have safe access to all ports of the Scottish kingdom with their merchandise, because the kingdom of Scotland, thanks be to God, has been recovered by war from the power of the English.

1. Evaluate the usefulness of Source I as evidence of Wallace's role as Guardian. **(8)**

   In reaching a conclusion you should refer to:

   - the origin and possible purpose of the source;
   - the content of the source;
   - recalled knowledge.

   (Higher Scottish unit outcomes: 1.1, 2.1)

(continued)

Source J is from contemporary documents about the surrender of Sir John Comyn on 9 February 1304.

First it was said of Sir John Comyn that it should be granted that his life and limb would be saved. He would be free of imprisonment and of all trespass of his home, nor shall we call on him in times of war and he will pay no ransom and he will keep his family lands, while he is exiled from Scotland for one year. However John Comyn for reverence and honour and to gain the goodwill of King Edward will place all his lands and everything mentioned above into the hands of the king. He will never again hold any of his lands without the king's wish and good will.

The other Scots it was discussed that they be saved life and limb, are free of imprisonment and not disinherited from their lands. For their treason they put their lands under ransom to the king, and keep them only on his good will. All strongholds now in the king's hands are to remain with him till his next parliament, when the king will let it be known what is to happen to them. Prisoners of war will be freed on both sides.

The Bishop of Glasgow is to be exiled for three years for the evil he has done and William Wallace is to be handed over to the king.

2. How fully does Source J give evidence that the Scottish resistance had collapsed by 1304? **(10)**
   Use the source and recalled knowledge.
   (Higher Scottish unit outcomes: 1.2, 2.2).

Source K is from Ranald Nicholson, *Scotland, the Later Middle Ages* (1974).

On 11 September 1297, an English force, under the Earl of Surrey and Treasurer Cressingham, was defeated by the combined troops of Andrew Murray and William Wallace. A mood of optimism appeared in a letter of 11 October 1297, issued by Wallace and Moray, to the merchants of Lubeck and Hamburg informing them that it was once again safe to trade with Scotland, which was now 'recovered by war from the power of the English'. But Murray had been mortally wounded at Stirling Bridge. Within a few months one of the Scottish earls dubbed Wallace a knight. More than that, Wallace was appointed sole guardian of Scotland. In November 1297, Wallace led his army into the north of England and successfully gained vital supplies for their war effort.

Source L is from Alan Macquarrie, *Kingship and Nation* (2004).

William Wallace was probably the son of the laird of Elderslie who had not signed the Ragman Rolls, and was consequently outlawed by the English justiciar. He escaped capture by the English garrison of Lanark with the help of his mistress, who was killed in the process. In revenge, Wallace killed the Sheriff of Lanark and set himself up as head of a band of outlaws. The Battle of Falkirk was a victory for the English mounted knights and the Welsh archers, who wore down the schiltrons by repeated cavalry charges and discharges of arrows. Wallace escaped and rescued the survivors as best he could. He remained at liberty until betrayed by Sir John Stewart of Menteith. After his trial he was dragged for miles at the tail of a horse to Smithfield where he was put to death by being strangled, and dismembered.

3. How much do sources K and L reveal about differing interpretations of the role of William Wallace during the Scottish resistance? **(10)**
   Compare the content overall and in detail.
   (Higher Scottish unit outcomes: 1.3)
4. Explain the reasons why William Wallace made a key contribution to the Scottish resistance.
   (Higher Scottish unit outcomes: 2.2) **(8)**

4 The rise and triumph of Robert Bruce

In this section you will learn about:

- The ambitions of Robert Bruce.
- His conflict with and victory over Scottish opponents.
- His victory at Bannockburn.
- Continuing hostilities.
- The Declaration of Arbroath.
- The Treaties of Edinburgh/Northampton, 1328.
- The significance of the Wars of Independence in the development of Scottish identity.

The ambitions of Robert the Bruce

It was no secret that the Bruce family had ambitions to gain control of the throne of Scotland. Robert Bruce, Lord of Annandale, had tried to persuade Edward I to give the throne to him during the Great Cause and the Bruce family had been responsible for the threat of civil war on more than one occasion. Robert the Bruce, Earl of Carrick, also had these ambitions but his loyalties before 1306 were often split. The Bruce family held lands in Scotland and England, as did many of the Scottish nobles. For this reason, Bruce had been loyal to Edward on several occasions. After he was made Guardian of Scotland (along with John Comyn), following the Battle of Falkirk in 1298, Bruce probably had increased ambitions to take the throne and likely fell out with the Comyn family over this – they were loyal to John Balliol and wished to see him restored to the throne. Bruce continued the campaign against Edward until 1302 and, when the other nobles of Scotland began to accept Edward's terms of peace, Bruce switched his allegiance to Edward.

Figure 29: *A romaticised portrait of Bruce from the 19th century. Robert the Bruce has become a celebrated Scottish hero.*

Edward now took a more carefully considered approach to governing Scotland, mainly because he wished to avoid another rebellion. By the Order for the Ordinance of Scotland of 1305, Edward acknowledged that Scotland should have its own elected representatives and sheriffs and that many of the nobles should gain back disinherited lands. His favourable terms won him support and even John Comyn gave up trying to bring Balliol back to Scotland. However, Edward specifically left the choice of sheriffs up to the Comyns. Bruce was essentially left out of governing Scotland and this may have prompted him to rebel against Edward once more.

The Scottish churchmen were also unhappy with English rule. The church's status as a 'Special Daughter' of Rome was at risk as the English archbishop tried to gain control. In 1304 Bishops Wishart and Lamberton met and agreed to back Bruce on a campaign for Scottish independence. In fact, they were so determined that there was a mutual agreement between the bishops and Bruce that if the loyalty promise was broken by one of them, they would be subject to a £10 000 fine.

Figure 30: *A nineteenth century drawing by Felix Philippoteaux depicting the murder of John Comyn in Greyfriars Kirk, Dumfries.*

The murder of John Comyn

On 10 February 1306, Robert the Bruce murdered John Comyn in Greyfriars Church in Dumfries. There is not much on record to confirm the turn of events but either it was a chance opportunity taken by Bruce to murder his recent rival or a fight that escalated, resulting in the murder of Comyn. The English chronicler, Walter of Guisborough, reckoned that the murder was preconceived, that Bruce had summoned Comyn to the church with a view to murdering him – he wrote that Bruce 'struck him [Comyn] with his sword and went away.' However, John Fordun, a Scottish chronicler, wrote that Comyn and Bruce met in the church where Bruce accused Comyn of treachery for giving up the fight for independence. In retaliation, Bruce and his men stabbed and killed him. There is possibly more evidence for the latter described event as one of Bruce's supporters, Roger Kirkpatrick, is rumoured to have said, after Bruce informed him of stabbing Comyn, 'You doubt! I'll mak siccar (I'll make sure)!' and finished off the job.

Make the Link

You will learn more about Christianity if you study RMPS.

As we have seen, Bruce's campaign for the throne was supported by the key churchmen of Scotland and it may be, as Comyn was the main contender for the Scottish throne, that Bruce was encouraged by these men to kill him. Nevertheless, killing Comyn, especially in a church, meant Bruce was excommunicated by the Pope. Even if Bruce ended English rule in Scotland, he would have to be officially recognised again by the church before he could become King of Scotland.

Figure 31: *Robert the Bruce was crowned King of Scots by the Countess of Buchan, 25 March 1306. This image is from a modern tableau at Edinburgh Castle which charts the history of the monarchs of Scotland.*

Despite Bruce's crime, he was absolved by the leading Scottish churchmen of the time, such as Bishop Wishart of Glasgow. The clergy's main priority was to preserve Scottish independence. Scottish churchmen had always avidly supported Scottish independence from the English Crown as this also guaranteed Scottish religious independence – by submitting to English rule, the Scottish Church would be subject to the commands of the Archbishop of York.

The leading churchmen of Scotland supported the symbolic gesture of crowning Bruce as King of Scotland in March 1306. Bruce immediately began an armed rebellion against English rule in an attempt to restore the Scottish throne.

Bruce's conflict with and victory over Scottish opponents

Now Bruce attempted to regain control of Scotland. He did this by first attacking Edward's strongholds in the south of Scotland. After some early success Bruce's forces were defeated at Methven near Perth and were forced to flee west. Not everyone supported Bruce's rebellion. Bruce was opposed by nobles who had been loyal to John Comyn and was eventually forced to flee to Kildrummy castle in the north east of Scotland. However, Edward's men followed and the castle was successfully besieged. Supporters of Bruce were murdered, his wife was imprisoned in a manor house and his sister was sent to a nunnery in England. The Countess of Buchan and Robert's sister Mary were imprisoned in steel cages at Roxburgh and Berwick and his daughter Marjory was put in a cage in the Tower of London. However, because she was only 12, Edward changed his mind and she too was sent to a nunnery. Bruce's family were targeted in an attempt to get Bruce to halt the rebellion. Indeed, he disappeared for the winter of 1306–07, possibly to the island of Rathlin or perhaps to Orkney. Regardless of his location, he was probably trying to rethink his strategy and raise

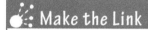

Hint

There is also a legend attached to Robert the Bruce that he took inspiration from a spider during his time in hiding. A spider was having difficulty making a web. He watched the spider persevere time and time again until the web was finished. He decided to persevere with his own struggles. This story was essentially created by Sir Walter Scott and is a creative anecdote only.

Make the Link

In Modern Studies you may learn about the different tactics used in wars and disputes around the world in recent years.

more support for a rebellion. It is during this time that Bruce is given the nickname 'King Hob' – 'King Nobody' – by English chroniclers.

In February 1307 Bruce returned and began to retake castles and strongholds captured by the English. He fought again with Edward's men at Loudoun Hill in May 1307 and won, despite the English force being the better side. Edward I had tried to come up to Scotland to fight one last campaign against Robert. However, he was elderly and ill and died on 27 July at Burgh on Sands in Cumbria. His son, Edward II, had sworn to continue the campaign but made the decision to take his father's body back to York. This rerouted the English army and gave Bruce a significant window of time and an opportunity to take control of Scotland. Bruce set about getting the support of those in the Comyn family. He used force where necessary so that quickly Comyn family members, like the Earl of Ross, surrendered rather than be annihilated. The Comyns made a brief comeback when Robert took ill near Banff and his men worried they might lose him. Edward Bruce, Robert's brother, took over briefly until the king recovered and took over gaining control of the castles in the north. The fighting came to a head with the Battle of Inverurie in May 1308. Here, Bruce rose from his sickbed to defeat the Earl of Buchan and ordered his lands to be destroyed. The 'Herschip of Buchan' meant victory for Bruce and his men – those loyal to the Comyns were killed, houses burned, land and livestock destroyed. The other nobles affiliated with the Comyns soon surrendered to Bruce to avoid similar punishment.

In 1309 Bruce held a Parliament at St Andrews and was officially recognised as king by the Scottish clergy after being forgiven for the murder of Comyn in Dumfries, and support was given by Philip IV of France. The Declaration of the Clergy effectively marked the end of the civil war in Scotland although many nobles still were not entirely loyal to Bruce. Edward II had arrived back into Scotland but Bruce refused to engage in open battle with him, instead preferring to raid in the north of England, forcing Edward II and his men to frequently return to England to defend their lands. This game of cat and mouse bought Robert time, allowed him to build up his men and recapture the remaining castles in the south of Scotland still in the hands of the English. His men employed guerrilla warfare tactics, only attacking when they had the element of surprise and increased chance of success. By 1314 only two strongholds held out: Berwick and Stirling. Control of Stirling would give the Scots the best advantage so they planned to take Stirling Castle first. The commander of Stirling Castle, Sir Philip Moubray, demanded to be relieved by Edward II and his troops by midsummer, or else he would hand over the castle to the Scots. All that would be required would be for the Scots to beat the larger and militarily superior English army to regain control of Scotland.

Bruce's victory at Bannockburn

The Battle of Bannockburn took place on 23 and 24 June 1314. It is a victory that echoes down the annals of Scottish history because of the astonishing accomplishment of the Scottish army when they were vastly outnumbered and outclassed by the English army. The numbers of the English army are estimated to be at 2000 knights/cavalry and 15 000

Figure 32: *The Battle of Bannockburn (1314) is often hailed as one of Scotland's greatest battle triumphs.*

Hint

Scutage is a medieval term that refers to a fee that could be paid so that a knight or noble could avoid presenting themselves in battle and instead send hired fighters, often from foreign lands. Many of the English nobles required to fight at Bannockburn seem to have preferred this option – perhaps they were tired of the constant campaigning on behalf of the English Crown. Whatever the reasons, lack of numbers certainly made Edward's troops weaker.

foot soldiers and the longbowmen possibly numbering 3000. There probably should have been more foot soldiers but many English knights preferred not to fight and had paid scutage to avoid the call to arms.

The Scottish foot soldiers numbered 5000. Most of these men would have been made up of the Common Army of Scotland – ordinary men, most likely tenant farmers. The Scottish cavalry only numbered 500. Their weaponry would have been basic – spikes to use in the schiltrons and a few archers. The nobles would have had more sophisticated armour and swords. Bruce had spent a lot of time training his men and he decided to have the men stand in schiltron formation. However, he had also learned from the mistakes of Falkirk and made them mobile, not just defensive. Bruce knew the land near Stirling well and planned the battle effectively.

Make the Link

In Geography you will learn how to identify the strengths and weaknesses of given areas of land.

Historians point to the leadership of both sides as being a key element in explaining the Scottish victory over the English. Edward II was by no means the soldier or battle tactician his father had been and from the outset made crucial mistakes. The English army was traditionally organised in vanguard, mid-guard and rear-guard, each equipped in a balanced fashion with cavalry, archers and foot soldiers so as almost to act like three separate armies. Commanders would be put in charge who best served each section. However, Edward II decided to give his friends favourable positions instead of selecting who would be best placed to lead the troops. This cost him dearly. Bruce, on the other hand, had proven himself to be a good judge of the opposition and put his most trusted men in charge of the Scottish divisions – his brother Edward, Thomas Randolph and himself. Foot soldiers were placed in front of the schiltrons to act as guides for mobilisation in battle.

On the first day of battle, Bruce positioned himself on the hill in front of Stirling castle. He had prepared the ground with mantraps and calthrops, designed to force the English troops into a position of disadvantage.

Figure 33: *Calthrops were designed to make the terrain difficult for horses, therefore forcing the English to take up a certain position on the battlefield.*

Figure 34: *Bruce kills Henry de Bohun with his axe. This small triumph was a huge morale booster for the Scots.*

Hint

Sma' folk were the ordinary people of Scotland and would have been made up of men, women and even children carrying pots and sticks as weapons. They were supporters of the battle – providing the food and other supplies to the troops.

As the English took up their positions, the Earl of Hereford rode out with the English vanguard to scout out the Scottish position. They met Bruce's troops and a skirmish broke out between them. A knight, Sir Henry de Bohun, took an opportunity to cut Bruce down from his horse but Bruce merely waited while the knight charged towards him and raised his axe at the last moment, splitting Bohun's head.

The rest of the English troops had crossed the Bannockburn to take up their positions and some broke ranks to start fighting with the Scots. This was a big mistake as the Scottish formations could not be broken and the English commander, Sir Thomas Clifford, ordered a retreat. English morale had been crushed before the main battle had even started. On the other hand, Scottish morale had been boosted quite significantly as the English had proven themselves to be disorganised and out-manoeuvrable. The Scots had planned to retreat to Lennox after their early victories but a Scottish knight, Sir Alexander Seton, defected from Edward's troops to the Scots that night and informed Bruce of the low morale of the English troops. Bruce decided it would be worth fighting them in open battle the next day to defeat the English once and for all.

On 24 June, Edward's men were forced to position themselves in the muddy bog close to the Bannockburn and found themselves at the mercy of the Scottish schiltrons. The schiltrons were employed one by one to advance on the English troops who could not manoeuvre their way around the muddy bog nor penetrate the powerful schiltrons. After progress had been made by the main Scottish troops, the 'sma' folk' were commanded to descend from the hill.

The English mistook the sma' folk for being a reserve army and began to retreat. However, it was their numbers that ultimately outdid them. Normally an army's biggest advantage, it turned into the biggest hindrance for the English as they scrambled for safety but got stuck in the mud or in the burn, being trampled and crushed by their own men and horses. Edward II fled to Dunbar and then sailed back to England. The Scots took English knights as prisoners and used them to trade in for the release of Scottish captives like Robert the Bruce's wife, sister and daughter.

The Battle of Bannockburn has been assessed by historians as an astonishing victory, considering that the Scots were outnumbered and outclassed by the English army. However, when assessing why the Scots were able to defeat the English, the following issues must be considered carefully.

- The leadership of the two armies. Undeniably, Bruce's leadership and command of the Scottish army was superior to that of Edward II. Bruce had much more capability in the field of warfare than Edward II and, despite having the larger army, Edward made poor decisions in his appointment of commanding officers and battle tactics.
- The morale boost the killing of de Bohun had and the defection of Alexander Seton. Perhaps if Seton had not passed on that the English morale was so low then Bruce would have retreated. It

must be remembered that Bannockburn was a huge risk for Bruce and his men – he had been used to gaining control of small areas through guerrilla warfare. A battle on such a large scale would have been considered a last resort by Bruce; it was an incredible gamble but really the last opportunity to gain control of Stirling castle and therefore Scotland.

- Bruce's ability to learn from previous mistakes – like the lack of manoeuvrability of the schiltrons at the Battle of Falkirk – meant that he was able to judge the land well, strategically position his men and make the best use of his battle tactics.

- Disorganisation and disaffection by the English army should not be ignored. The fact that Sir Philip Moubray was all but ready to give Stirling castle back to the Scots shows how much power Bruce had already taken back. Further, that many English noblemen were actively trying to avoid the call to arms by paying scutage proves that either they had no interest in fighting for Scotland or that they were resigned to the idea that control of Scotland was all but in the hands of Bruce and it would take more than a win at Bannockburn to regain full control.

The Battle of Bannockburn was won but the War of Independence was not yet over. However, in the short term Bruce gained more loyal supporters for the cause and it looked as if independence was ever more achievable.

Continuing hostilities

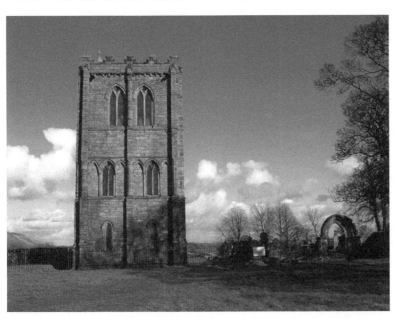

Figure 35: *Cambuskenneth Abbey was the location for the first Scottish Parliament after Bannockburn.*

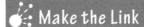

Make the Link

In Modern Studies you learn about the current Scottish Parliament.

After Bannockburn, Bruce held his first Parliament at Cambuskenneth Abbey. This was significant because it forbade Scottish nobility from holding land in England and disinherited the lands of those who had fought with England. Bruce's enemies (the Comyns) had their land redistributed to Bruce and his supporters. Bruce further negotiated the exchange of English prisoners of war, such as the Earl of Hereford, for his own family members who had been held prisoner. Bruce also raided northern England, largely to assert his authority but it gained him valuable supplies that allowed him to extend the campaign to Ireland.

Historians debate why Bruce started a campaign in Ireland. His strategy is thought to have been that an Irish campaign would put pressure on the English by challenging the 'Anglo-Irish', as Edward I had been granted lordship of Ireland 'provided that the land of Ireland shall never be separated from the crown of England'. Also, Irish resources had been used against the Scots. Further, there is some suggestion that successful conquest of Ireland would bring a Kingdom for Edward Bruce.

Edward Bruce had some immediate success and was crowned high king of Ireland in May 1316. After some early success, including the capture of the English stronghold at Carrickfergus, the Scots could not maintain their momentum and failed to capture cities like Dublin. Further fighting ended in disaster in 1318 when Edward Bruce was killed by a common soldier from Drogheda.

The Bruces ultimately wanted Edward II to acknowledge Scottish independence and by campaigning in Ireland they sought to overstretch the English and their soldiers, and threaten more of their lands. This strategy did not achieve its overall aim but did increase fear in England that there might be a Celtic fringe – that Ireland and Scotland would become a united force against England. It definitely meant that time and resources were used up by the English as they had to divert men and weapons to Ireland. However, it did not secure independence.

Therefore, Robert began to raid northern England once again. Initial difficulties gave way to some successes but famine stopped both the Scottish and the English in 1317. However, after this, the English simply paid the Scots to stop raiding their towns – it seemed that Edward II could neither govern his country nor command his army well. Edward II attempted to raid Berwick in 1319 but it was unsuccessful as Scottish troops were deployed to York to stop the English advancing. Further attempts at fighting the Scots were crushed at Newcastle and the Scottish leaders like James Douglas went back to their guerrilla warfare tactics to hit-and-run on the English troops. After the Battle of Old Byland in 1322, which resulted in another humiliating defeat for Edward and the loss of equipment and money, the campaign against the Scots was called off. Bruce ruled the north of England but still Edward refused to grant the Scots their independence.

The Declaration of Arbroath

Figure 36: *The Declaration of Arbroath was submitted to the Pope on 6 April 1320 and is thought to be one of the earliest declarations of independence.*

To be officially recognised as the King of Scotland, Robert had to be de-excommunicated. Pope John XXII opposed Bruce as he had been excommunicated after the murder of Comyn in 1306 and had refused the Pope's orders to cease fighting with England. The clergy in Scotland supported Bruce, however, and it was decided to send written support from the Church and the nobles of Scotland to demonstrate their support for Robert the Bruce as the King of Scots. Only the Declaration of Arbroath, written in 1320, survives. It states the following:

Yet if he should give up what he has begun, and agree to make us or our kingdom subject to the King of England or the English, we should exert ourselves at once to drive him out as our enemy and a subverter of his own rights and ours, and make some other man who was well able to defend us our King; for, as long as but a hundred of us remain alive, never will we on any conditions be brought under English rule.

It is in truth not for glory, nor riches, nor honours that we are fighting, but for freedom – for that alone, which no honest man gives up but with life itself…

May it please you to admonish and exhort the King of the English, who ought to be satisfied with what belongs to him since England used once to be enough for seven kings or more, to leave us Scots in peace, who live in this poor little Scotland, beyond which there is no dwelling-place at all, and covet nothing but our own.

Make the Link

You will learn more about propaganda if you study the Germany topic, and also in English and Modern Studies.

It contains the names of 39 nobles. It is unknown if all genuinely supported the document or even read it, but their seals were added to it anyway. The Declaration of Arbroath is essentially a spectacular piece of political propaganda on behalf of Bruce by which he sought to show the Pope the unequivocal support for Scottish independence – he had to have the support of the Pope and be de-excommunicated to be Scotland's legitimate king.

However, the level of support that Bruce had at this time was questionable – the Soulis conspiracy, which was a plot by supporters of the Balliol family to dispose of Robert, shows that not every noble in Scotland wanted his leadership. Furthermore, Pope John XXII did not shift his position lightly, and further campaigning and changes in leadership in England were required before Robert was officially recognised as the King of Scotland after being de-excommunicated in 1328.

The Treaties of Edinburgh/Northampton 1328

The fighting between the Scots and the English resumed in 1323. Edward II was murdered by his barons, led by his wife, Isabella, and her lover Lord Mortimer. The turmoil over the English throne gave Robert the Bruce the chance to step in and cause more havoc for England – he hoped that extra pressure would mean the English gave the Scots their independence. James Douglas was sent to Northumbria and the new king, 14-year-old Edward III was sent north. Douglas easily defeated the English troops and Robert started up the campaign again in Ireland – reigniting fears of a Celtic fringe. Returning to Scotland, Bruce laid siege to Norham castle and threatened to sack Northumbria. This war of attrition was too much for the English to cope with and Isabella and Mortimer gave in. The Treaties of Edinburgh/Northampton, signed on 17 March 1328, contained the following clauses:

Figure 37: *Robert the Bruce.*

- Bruce to pull out of Northumbria and pay £20 000 compensation.
- Robert officially recognised as King of Scots and independence secured.
- Robert's son David and Princess Joan of England betrothed.

The Treaties of Edinburgh/Northampton signalled the end of the Scottish Wars of Independence. Scotland had won its right to be an independent, sovereign nation with Robert I as its king.

The significance of the Wars of Independence in the development of Scottish identity

Robert the Bruce died on 7 June 1329, having seen Scotland gain its independence and having been officially crowned the King of Scots. Scotland maintained its independence until 1707 when the Parliament of Scotland merged with Westminster to become the United Kingdom.

Historians and social commentators have long discussed the significance of the Wars of Independence in the development of Scottish identity. Some commentators maintain that Edward I, the 'Hammer of the Scots', cemented a nationalist divide between Scotland and England. However, it would be too simplistic to assume that the Wars of Independence should be the defining point for the national identity of Scotland. It is perhaps fair to say that many Scots would identify with the inspirational stories of Wallace and Bruce and fighting the yoke of English rule but a separate Scottish identity had been developing for years prior to this and the Scottish nation was already multilingual and multicultural and continued to be so after 1328. We must not forget that Robert the Bruce himself was probably more concerned with personal gain than achieving independence in order to preserve a Scottish national identity.

Figure 38: *Death of Robert the Bruce.*

In the nineteenth century, it became very popular to celebrate and commemorate the achievements of Wallace and Bruce – the Victorians erected the Wallace monument in Stirling and other tributes to Robert the Bruce, such as the statue at Edinburgh Castle. However, interestingly, historians have pointed to the idea that Scots such as Wallace and Bruce became more celebrated as distinct 'Scottish' heroes in a time where Scotland was firmly placed politically within the United Kingdom and economically within the British Empire. Between the years of 1914 and 1918, Scots fought in the name of the British Empire against German and Central European power expansionism. Following the First World War, the decline of the British Empire and the economic collapse of the 1920s saw Scotland struggle with its place within the Empire and the question of Scottish independence began to emerge.

The question of the development of a Scottish identity therefore cannot solely be attributed to the events of the Wars of Independence. What did emerge at this time is the idea of the Community of the Realm and identity being based on more than following one Lord or another and people of a region. In recent times, the issue of Scottish identity is often linked to the First Wars of Independence which took place over 700 years ago. Further, historical events are often referred to in modern politics. However, this is subjective and should be scrutinised carefully.

Figures 39 and 40: *The Wallace Monument at Stirling and Robert the Bruce at Stirling.*

🟢 Activity 8

1. In groups of three you are going to work together to produce information posters on the following:
    Person 1:
    *   The ambitions of Robert Bruce.
    *   His conflict with and victory over Scottish opponents.
    Person 2:
    *   Robert Bruce's victory at Bannockburn.
    *   Continuing hostilities.
    Person 3:
    *   The Declaration of Arbroath.
    *   The Treaties of Edinburgh/Northampton 1328.
    You must describe each of the events in a maximum of 50 words. On completion, share your descriptions with the rest of the class and see if you managed to describe the salient points.
    (Higher Scottish unit outcomes: 2.2)

2. Class debate: Analyse the reasons for the Scottish success at Bannockburn.

The teacher will split the class into two. One side will argue that Robert the Bruce won an exceptional victory against all odds. The other side will argue that Robert the Bruce won only because of good luck and poor leadership by Edward II.

When preparing your arguments, you can consider the following:

- Size of the Scottish and English armies
- Leadership of the two sides
- Planning and use of land
- Battle tactics
- Day 1 of the battle
- Day 2 of the battle.

As a class, come up with five KEY QUESTIONS that must be answered by each side. Remember to prepare a strong argument in favour of your side and a rebuttal to the potential points made by the opposing side.

(Higher Scottish unit outcomes: 2.3)

GO! Activity 9

Exam style questions

Source M is from Colm McNamee, *Robert Bruce: Our Most Valiant Prince, King and Lord* (2006).

> Moorland, marshland, and hill country, impenetrable to heavy cavalry became his 'favourable territory', where he was safe, and the enemy ill at ease. He relied on ambush and surprise to make the best use of his small force. Choosing his ground carefully, he would suddenly emerge to win a minor skirmish and then retreat once more into the wilderness. He preferred small engagements… He never engaged the enemy unless sure of victory.

Source N is from A.D.M. Barrell, *Medieval Scotland* (2000).

> The opportunity to end the long conflict with a formal recognition by the English crown of Scottish independence came amid the chaos which accompanied the deposition of Edward II in 1327… Dissensions in England gave the Scots a favourable opportunity to renew the war, hence Robert's fresh intervention in Ireland in order to try and force the English to come to terms. In the Borders, an unsuccessful English campaign against a raiding Scottish force in 1327 was followed by an assault on Norham by Robert and rumours that the Scots intended to occupy Northumberland.

(continued)

1. How much do sources M and N reveal about differing interpretations of the rise and triumph of Robert the Bruce? **(10)**

   Compare the content overall and in detail.

   (Higher Scottish unit outcomes: 1.3)

Source O is an extract from the *Lanercost Chronicle*, 1314.

> Upon information that there were Scots in the wood, the king's advanced guard, commanded by Lord de Clifford, began to make a circuit of the wood to prevent the Scots escaping by flight. The Scots did not interfere until the English were far ahead of the main body, when they showed themselves, and, cutting off the king's advanced guard from the middle and rear columns, they charged and killed some of them and put the rest to flight. From that moment began a panic among the English and the Scots grew bolder.
>
> Now when the two armies had approached very near each other, all the Scots fell on their knees to repeat Paternoster (Our Father), commending themselves to God and seeking help from heaven; after which they advanced boldly against the English. They had so arranged their army that two columns went abreast in advance of the third, so that neither should be in advance of the other; and the third followed, in which was Robert…Now the English in the rear could not reach the Scots because the leading division was in the way, nor could they do anything to help themselves, wherefore there was nothing for it but to take to flight.

2. How fully does Source O explain the reasons for the Scottish victory at Bannockburn? **(10)**

   Use the source and recalled knowledge.

   (Higher Scottish unit outcomes: 1.2, 2.2)

Source P is an extract from the Declaration of Arbroath, 1320.

> But from these innumerable evils we have been freed…by our most valiant, prince, king and lord, the lord Robert, who, in order that his inheritance might be delivered out of the hands of enemies, cheerfully endured toil and fatigue, hunger and danger, like another Maccabeus or Joshua. Divine providence, the succession to his right according to our laws and customs which we shall maintain to the death, and the due consent and assent of us all have made him our prince and king.

3. Evaluate the usefulness of Source P as evidence of the strength of Robert I's position in 1320. **(8)**

   In reaching a conclusion you should refer to:

   • the origin and possible purpose of the source;
   • the content of the source;
   • recalled knowledge.

   (Higher Scottish unit outcomes: 1.1, 2.1)

4. Explain the reasons for the rise and triumph of Robert the Bruce. **(8)**

   (Higher Scottish unit outcomes: 2.2)

Summary

In this topic you have learned:

- How Scotland was governed after the death of Alexander III, from 1286–96
- About the succession problem and the Great Cause
- How John Balliol's reign and Edward I's overlordship led to conflict and the subjugation of Scotland
- About William Wallace and Scottish resistance to Edward I
- About the rise and triumph of Robert Bruce
- The importance of the Wars of Independence in the development of Scottish identity.

You should have developed your skills and be able to:

- evaluate the usefulness of a source
- compare two sources
- assess the content of a source and place it in context
- analyse a Scottish historical issue.

Learning checklist

Now that you have finished **The Wars of Independence, 1249–1328**, complete a self-evaluation of your knowledge and skills to assess what you have understood. Use traffic lights to help you make up a revision plan to help you improve in the areas you identified as red or amber.

- Describe and analyse the succession problem following 1286.
- Describe the importance of the Guardians and the Community of the Realm.
- Analyse the importance of the Treaty of Birgham and the importance of the death of Margaret, Maid of Norway.
- Describe and analyse the events of the Great Cause.
- Describe and analyse the rule of John Balliol.
- Describe and analyse the overlordship of Edward I.
- Describe the importance of the Anglo-French war and the Franco-Scottish Treaty.
- Describe the subjugation of Scotland by Edward I.
- Describe the events and the effects of the Scottish resistance.

- Describe the roles of William Wallace and Andrew Murray.

- Analyse the roles of Wallace and Murray.

- Describe the events that took place at the Battle of Stirling Bridge and analyse the reasons for the Scots' win.

- Explain the reasons for the Scots' loss at the Battle of Falkirk and analyse its effect on the continuation of the Scottish resistance.

- Describe the ambitions of Robert the Bruce.

- Describe and analyse his conflict and victory over Scottish opponents.

- Describe and analyse the Scots' victory at Bannockburn.

- Describe continuing hostilities with the English after Bannockburn.

- Analyse the significance of the Declaration of Arbroath.

- Describe the Treaties of Edinburgh/Northampton, 1328.

- Analyse the significance of the Wars of Independence in the development of Scottish identity.

- Successfully evaluate the usefulness of a source, commenting on its origin, content, purpose and limitations.

- Compare how two different sources offer two different interpretations on a single issue, providing evidence from the sources. Use recall to provide further viewpoints on the given issue.

- Successfully analyse a source's content, placing it in context through the use of detailed recalled knowledge.

- Successfully analyse why a significant event in Scottish history took place, evaluating the main factors and coming to an overall conclusion.

- Successfully explain the reasons why a historical event took place or the impact of the actions of a person or people on a historical event.

Studying this topic will provide you with an understanding of the reasons why so many Scots chose to migrate within Scotland and abroad in the period between 1830 and 1939. You will investigate the impact that Scots had on the countries in which they settled and gain an appreciation of how immigrants can influence and shape their new countries or communities. Also, this topic will allow you to explore the experiences of those people who chose to settle in Scotland and the various ways that they have helped to shape aspects of Scottish culture. Finally, you will learn about how Scotland was affected by its role as an integral part of the British Empire and by the migration of people into and out of the country.

This topic is split into four sections:

❖ The migration of Scots.

❖ The experience of immigrants in Scotland.

❖ The impact of Scottish emigrants on the Empire.

❖ The effects of migration and Empire on Scotland, to 1939.

Activities and Outcomes

		Activity												
		1	**2**	**3**	**4**	**5**	**6**	**7**	**8**	**9**	**10**	**11**	**12**	**13**
Outcome	**1.1**				✓						✓			✓
	1.2								✓					
	1.3				✓				✓					✓
	2.1		✓			✓				✓	✓	✓		✓
	2.2		✓		✓	✓		✓	✓	✓		✓		
	2.3			✓			✓				✓		✓	

WE`VE GOT JOBS
WE DON`T WANT

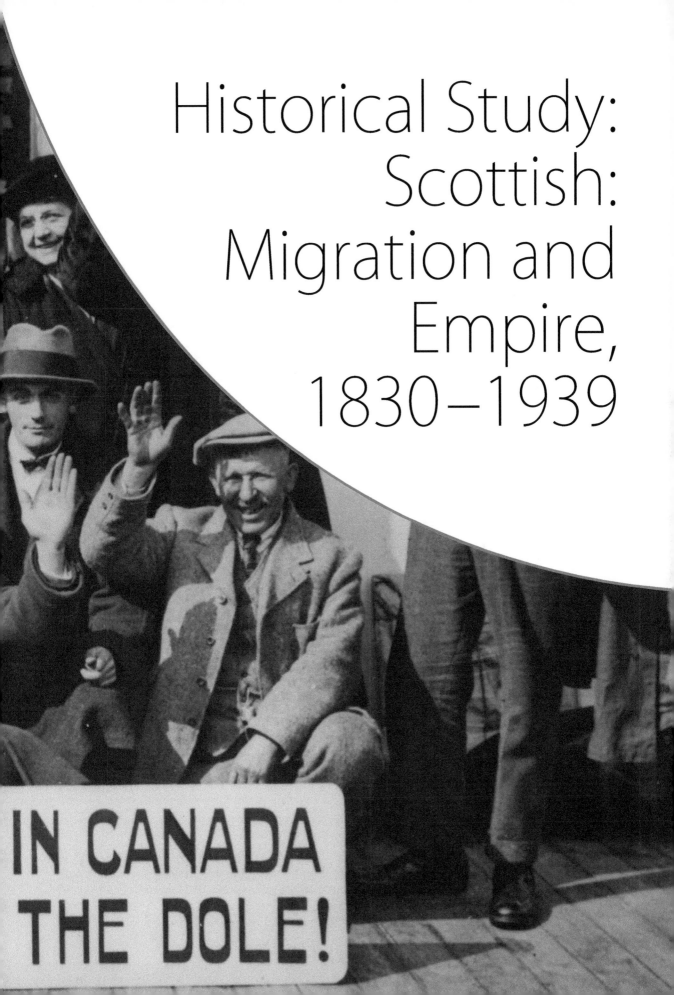

Historical Study: Scottish: Migration and Empire, 1830–1939

IN CANADA THE DOLE!

Background

Scotland has a long history of migration. For hundreds of years, people have chosen to settle in Scotland in the hope of making a better life for themselves, while many Scots have embarked on new adventures abroad for the same reason. Between 1830 and 1939, at the height of the British Empire, there was a significant movement of people into and out of Scotland.

Figure 1: *Between 1830 and 1939 many Scots left to start new lives abroad.*

Between 1830 and 1939 the distribution of the Scottish population changed considerably. There was a significant movement to the cities in the Lowlands that offered employment, better wages and a more varied social life. As we shall see, the motives for those in the Highlands and the southern Lowlands to move were similar in some ways but different in others. Moreover, many of these people also chose to go abroad, as did many Scots living in the cities.

At the same time as Scots were migrating to the cities or abroad, many other people were coming into the country. Irish people, both Catholic and Protestant, immigrated here in significant numbers and were joined by Jews, Lithuanians and Italians. These immigrants came to Scotland for many reasons and their experiences when they arrived were similarly diverse. Some groups were successful in assimilating into Scottish society, while others struggled to maintain their cultural identity. For all groups, relations with the native Scots could be difficult, with religion often a large factor.

 Hint

Scots also emigrated to countries that weren't part of the British Empire, such as the USA.

Scottish emigrants faced challenges too, but many made the most of the opportunities that British-controlled territories offered them, making a significant impact on countries such as Canada, Australia, New Zealand and India. The industry, education and modern-day culture of these countries owe a great deal to the impact of Scottish emigrants, although it is vital that we also recognise the difficult, sometimes violent, relationship they had with the native societies they encountered.

By 1939 Scotland was a very different country to the one it had been in 1830. The population was much more concentrated in the urban centres in the central Lowlands and its ethnic, religious and cultural make-up was much more diverse. Many Scots had also left to seek their fortunes abroad. However, while Scotland had clearly benefited economically from its central role in the British Empire as the 'workshop of the world', some were beginning to question whether Scotland relied too heavily on Empire. As we shall see, the effects of migration and Empire on Scotland were certainly very significant and they helped to shape the nation we know today.

GO! Activity 1

Take a piece of A3 paper and divide it into four sections (you could even create a saltire if you wanted). In each of the four sections, summarise paragraphs 2–5 from the information above. Try to give each section/paragraph a title that best fits. For the whole poster you only have 40 words to work with, so be clever and be prepared to explain your poster to others when you have finished.

Your teacher will give you an appropriate amount of time for the task.

1 The migration of Scots

In this section you will learn about:

- The social effects of the development of the Scottish economy: industrialisation and urbanisation; the importance of the British Empire.
- Push and pull factors in internal and external migration:

  1. Economic factors
  2. Improved transport
  3. Social and cultural factors
  4. Political aspects
  5. Opportunity and coercion.

Between 1830 and 1939 Scots migrated within Scotland and emigrated abroad. They did so during a period of major economic and social change and when the large and powerful British Empire was at its height. These changes created a variety of push and pull factors that saw many Scots migrate to the growing cities of Glasgow, Edinburgh and Dundee and their surrounding areas. Others felt compelled to try their luck abroad.

The social effects of the development of the Scottish economy

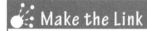
Make the Link

If you study Geography you will learn about the effects of industrialisation and urbanisation today.

Figure 2: *Shipyards on the Clyde in Glasgow were right at the heart of the industrial revolution in Scotland.*

As part of the United Kingdom since 1707, Scotland had benefited from the growth of the British Empire. In the nineteenth century Scotland industrialised quickly and began to produce the resources and products the British Empire needed. As industry boomed, orders flooded in from all corners of the globe. Glasgow became known for producing the best ships in the world, and by 1914 the city's firms were producing one fifth of the tonnage of all ships in the world. The coal, iron and steel industries also boomed, providing the raw materials for Empire and creating jobs in the growing engineering works, mines and factories. As Scotland's industry and economy grew, so the social effects of economic development became clear.

> ## Hint
>
> By the Act of Union of 1707, Scotland became part of the United Kingdom. This gave Scottish companies access to new markets in the British Empire.

Figure 3: *The British Empire was at its height at the turn of the century. All the countries in pink were at one point part of the British Empire.*

Industrialisation resulted in rapid population growth in Scotland. Between 1830 and 1911, the population doubled to 4·761 million. With a shortage of jobs in the areas that relied on agriculture, many Scots flooded into the cities. By 1911, one in three Scots lived in one of the 'big four' cities of Glasgow, Edinburgh, Dundee or Aberdeen. This mass migration of labour to the cities in search of work and accommodation had not been planned and the cities were not prepared for it. Soon, squalor and overcrowding on a massive scale were serious issues in the towns and cities. By 1911 over 60% of Scots were living in one- or two-roomed houses compared with only 7% in England. Also, poverty was widespread, wages were low compared to the rest of Britain and infant mortality rates were high. Many decided to look for a better life abroad, especially during times of high unemployment.

Overall, it is clear that the British Empire was vital to the development of Scottish industry and the economy, and that industrialisation and urbanisation had major social effects on Scotland. All these changes saw unprecedented movement in Scotland between 1830 and 1939.

Figure 4: *As Scots moved to the cities for work, these urban areas became overcrowded and conditions worsened.*

Hint

When someone moves abroad they emigrate.

Make the Link

In Geography and Modern Studies you may learn about why people emigrate or migrate within their country.

Push and pull factors in internal and external migration

Scots chose to migrate within the country and emigrate abroad for a variety of reasons, and these often depended on where they lived. Therefore, it is important to recognise the distinction between Lowland and Highland migration and emigration, as there were often different push and pull factors at play.

Figure 5: *Migration patterns were different depending on whether someone lived in the Highlands or Lowlands in Scotland. This map shows the areas that are considered to be the Highlands and Lowlands.*

1. Economic factors

The Lowlands

Figure 6: *Steam powered machinery, such as the threshing machine above, meant fewer farm workers were required in rural areas and farms.*

The rural Lowland economy was significantly affected by industrialisation. As steam power was introduced on farms in the early nineteenth century, threshing machines began to cut down the amount of time and manpower required to harvest crops. By 1870 most hay and grain were harvested in this way meaning Scots working on these farms were no longer required. What made this situation even more acute was that farm workers rented tied cottages from landowners, effectively tying their accommodation with the job. This meant that when these workers were laid off they also lost their homes. For many, the only choice was to seek employment and accommodation in the growing cities.

Many left the rural Lowlands because, between 1830 and 1911, the population doubled and there simply weren't enough jobs to go round. In the growing industrial centres there were more job opportunities and higher wages on offer.

In the rural Lowlands, farm workers worked long days with few breaks and did not have many holidays. Many were attracted by jobs in the cities that they hoped would require them to work fewer hours and allow them a day off a week.

For those in the cities who were skilled workers, such as handloom weavers, industrialisation meant that their skills were no longer required or economically valuable. As a result, many emigrated to countries where their skills were in demand.

In the Lowlands, in both rural and industrial areas, Scots saw migration as a solution to unemployment and economic depression. Low wages and poor housing conditions convinced many to leave and in times of severe economic depression, when there were few jobs, emigration rates were significantly higher.

The Highlands

In the Highlands, most Scots worked on the land and often struggled to make ends meet. Initially, migration was temporary, as Highlanders

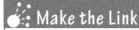 **Make the Link**

In Geography you learn about the effect of machinery on agricultural production nowadays.

Hint

A navvy is someone who helped build the railways. Go online and find out what it is short for.

Hint

A croft is a small piece of land on which many Scots in the north-west Highlands and Islands would live and work. They rented this from landowners and would usually raise livestock on it, as well as planting and harvesting crops. Someone who works on a croft is known as a crofter.

Make the Link

In Modern Studies and Geography you may learn about people nowadays who migrate temporarily for economic reasons. Often they move from less developed countries to more industrial ones.

Hint

The potato famine hit Ireland harder than Scotland and resulted in many Irish coming to Scotland for jobs.

Hint

Highland landlords employed factors to look after their estates. During the Clearances the dirty work of evicting tenants was left to these factors.

sought work to fill in the periods when they could not harvest their crops and supplement their meagre incomes. They did a variety of jobs in the south, including working as navvies in the railway construction boom in the late 1840s and working on farms in the Lowlands. These temporary jobs allowed Highlanders to continue working on their crofts. However, from the mid-1840s onwards temporary migration for many became more permanent due, in the main, to the devastating effects of the potato blight and Highland Clearances.

The potato blight hit the Highlands and Islands of Scotland in 1846, devastating the potato crop and resulting in a terrible famine. Because most Highland Scots were crofters and lived off the land, they relied heavily on the potato crop to survive. With little food to eat many were forced to move simply to avoid starvation. In the Lowlands there was at least the promise of jobs and of food, and many left the land for these very reasons. Some took up positions in the cities in domestic service or as labourers, while others made their way overseas in the hope of working more arable land. For these men and women, migration was permanent, as it was for those affected by the Highland Clearances.

Figure 7: *The Highland Clearances saw many Highlanders leave their land and homes in search of a better life in the cities and abroad. What do you think is happening in this painting? It is called 'The Last of the Clan' and was painted in 1865.*

From the late eighteenth century, well into the nineteenth century, the major landowners in the Highlands began to alter the way they used their land. Previously, they had rented out land to tenants who worked it to produce enough food to survive on and often some to sell on. These crofters and their families had often lived and worked on this land for generations. However, as new methods of farming came into use, including the profitable sheep farming, landlords began to move tenants off their land to enable them to make more money. The Highland economy had been suffering for years and many landlords had actually gone bankrupt in trying to keep tenants working on the land. The eviction of Highlanders from their homes reached a peak in the 1840s and early

1850s, with some landlords' factors employing brutal methods to ensure that people were moved off their land. Highlanders were left without any means of earning a living and many chose to move to the cities or abroad as a result. Those evicted in the Clearances of the 1840s and early 1850s tended to choose Canada rather than Lowland Scotland. Places like Nova Scotia (New Scotland) and Ontario were attractive as they allowed crofters to remain in touch with the land and continue a similar way of life.

By the turn of the century, some crofters remained attached to their land and continued with temporary migration. However, this became increasingly difficult as the use of labour-saving technology increased on Lowland farms and various export markets collapsed in the economic depression of the late 1920s and 1930s. Jobs were scarce all over Scotland and many had little choice but to leave and migrate to the cities or abroad permanently. Between 1911 and 1951 the population of the Hebrides decreased by 28%.

2. Improved transport

With industrialisation came improved transport within Scotland and throughout the developed world. The railway boom in the 1840s made it easier for Scots to move around the country, encouraging temporary and permanent internal migration. Also, the invention of the steamship made travel abroad easier, quicker and cheaper, encouraging Scots to emigrate. For example, in the 1850s it took over six weeks to cross the Atlantic but by 1914 this had been reduced to only a week. Because of this, and the cheaper fares, temporary migration abroad now became a possibility: by 1900, a third of those who had left Scotland had returned. In essence, emigration seemed less risky in the age of the steamship.

> ### ☼ Make the Link
>
> In Geography or Modern Studies you may learn about countries today where agricultural workers are being forced off their land for economic reasons.

Figure 8: *Steamships like this made migration cheaper and quicker than ever before.*

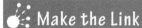

Make the Link

In English you may study books like Lewis Grassic Gibbon's *Sunset Song* or poems by Iain Crichton Smith that describe what life was like in the Highlands in this period.

Make the Link

If you study the Russian topic in Higher History you will learn about the problems peasants there had in gaining control of the land they worked on.

Make the Link

In Modern Studies you may learn why people choose, or are forced, to emigrate nowadays.

Hint

Letters from the time show the importance Scots attached to knowing someone in the place they were emigrating to.

Make the Link

In Business or Graphic Communication you may study how advertising works and how to sell products, ideas and places to people.

3. Social and cultural factors

In rural Lowland areas Scots often lived in basic conditions and lacked the varied social life that city dwellers enjoyed. Many workers therefore left the relative isolation of working alone on the land in the hope of enjoying football games, music halls and cinemas in the cities.

In the south and east Highlands, Scots were pulled to the towns by the promise of jobs but also by better educational opportunities. The Education Act of 1872 gave every Scot between the ages of five and thirteen the right to an education and it was often easier to access schools in larger towns and cities. Also, as with Scots in the Lowlands, Highland Scots recognised that the cities offered a better social life.

In the Highlands living conditions were terrible. These Scots lived in blackhouses, very basic dwellings with stone walls and turfed or thatched roofs. They were without windows and a chimney and, as the name suggests, this caused the interior to become black with soot. Also, living in blackhouses meant having to share space and shelter with animals. Unsurprisingly perhaps, diseases spread easily, with typhus common in some areas. These issues, taken together with the potato famine, the Clearances and the difficulty in surviving off the land, make it easy to understand why so many decided to move to the cities or abroad in the hope of a better life.

4. Political aspects

By the 1880s those Highlanders who remained on the land still had a lack of control over their lives and land. Many began to protest, leading the government to introduce the Crofter's Holding Act of 1886. This gave more rights to crofters, essentially meaning that they could not be removed from their land without good reason. Between 1886 and 1950 over 2700 new crofts were created. However, it did little to ease the difficult living and working conditions for the crofters and between 1911 and 1939 the population of the Highlands fell more steeply than at any point in their history. Clearly, the political solution to the land issue in the Highlands did not discourage migration from the region.

5. Opportunity and coercion

Between 1830 and 1939 there were new opportunities opening up throughout the British Empire, notably in Canada, Australia and New Zealand. The governments in these countries employed emigration agents to convince Scots to emigrate, establishing offices throughout Scotland. They offered various incentives such as free or cheap land and passage for emigrants, which many Scots found hard to resist. Also, as Scottish communities developed in countries abroad some Scots were attracted by the promise of some familiarity in these lands of opportunity.

In this period, newspapers advertised emigration possibilities and, as literacy rates increased in Scotland, more people were able to read these adverts. Also, as education improved in Scotland so Scottish emigrants became a more attractive proposition for countries needing bright and capable individuals to develop their economies.

Many early settlers from Scotland were highly skilled and came from middle-class backgrounds. Some were doctors, engineers and merchants. In the mid-nineteenth century Lowland emigrants were often skilled craftsmen and farmers and by the twentieth century the skilled worker was the largest category of those social groups who had left Scotland. A key reason so many skilled Scots left is because they knew they could command higher wages in countries abroad than they could in Scotland.

For those Scots who had been cleared off their land, there was little choice but to emigrate but some were given assistance in this. Landlords, such as the Dukes of Sutherland and Argyll, often financed emigration schemes to help crofters move abroad. Also, in 1851 the government passed the Emigration Act. This made emigration more freely available to the poorest, with the government providing assistance in their passage abroad. Landlords were able to secure passage to Australia for their crofters for as little as £1. Also, the Highlands and Islands Emigration Society was set up to help emigrants settle abroad. Between 1846 and 1857, 16 533 of the poorest people, mainly young men, were helped to emigrate.

Figure 9: *Adverts like this encouraged Scots to emigrate.*

Activity 2

Use a piece of A3 paper to create each of the tables below. Work your way through the section, picking out the various push and pull factors for internal migration and emigration, and put them in the relevant column. Remember to put in dates and statistics wherever possible. Beside each point you make, consider adding a drawing that will help you remember the factor.

When you have finished, work with a partner to ensure that you have the same points down and add in any points you may have missed.

Internal migration

Push factors	Pull factors

Emigration

Push factors	Pull factors

(Higher Scottish unit outcomes: 2.1, 2.2)

Hint

It is important not to just think of emigrants as poor crofters escaping the Clearances. Scottish emigrants were often highly skilled, choosing to move abroad to better their life chances.

GO! Activity 3

Imagine it is 1939 and you are writing a report/producing a presentation for the government on the main reasons for Scottish migration and emigration. You must analyse and explain why there was such movement in the period after 1830 and pinpoint the main reasons for it, coming to a clear conclusion in your report. Be prepared to explain your conclusions to others or even the class as a whole.

(Higher Scottish unit outcomes: 2.3)

GO! Activity 4

Exam style questions

Source A is from Angus Nicholson, Canada's Special Immigration Agent in the Highlands of Scotland, 1875.

> All the competing Emigration Agencies formerly reported on, are still at work as actively as ever. The New Zealand and Australian authorities are particularly alert, the streets of every town and village being always well ornamented with their bills and posters offering free passages and other inducements to emigrants. Not only so, but nearly all newspapers being subsidised by means of their advertisements, are doing their full share in the same direction. It has to be noted that a considerable number of potential recruits have been diverted from Canada to New Zealand as a result of the latter's offer of free passages. It is extremely difficult for us to attract emigrants when these territories are offering free passages while we expect the emigrants to pay their own fares to Canada.

1. Evaluate the usefulness of Source A as evidence of the reasons for Scottish migration and emigration.   (8)

    In reaching a conclusion you should refer to:
    *   the origin and possible purpose of the source;
    *   the content of the source;
    *   recalled knowledge.

    (Higher Scottish unit outcomes: 1.1)

2. Explain the reasons why so many Scots emigrated after the 1830s.   (8)

    (Higher Scottish unit outcomes: 1.1, 2.2)

Source B is from the *Quarterly Journal of Agriculture*, 1832–1834.

> I have not the slightest hesitation in declaring, that it appears to me as plain as the sun at noonday, that a farmer in Scotland, occupying a farm that does not pay him, distressed as he must be, struggling from morning to night with mental anxiety and worry pressing upon his mind and yet after all quite unable to support his family or better their circumstances—I say that a farmer continuing to remain in Scotland even when unemployed while so much land lies in Canada to occupy, acts the part of an insane person. In a short time there will be no cheap land to be procured about these parts. The best way for my brothers to lay out their money here in Canada is in buying land which is every year rising in value.

Source C is from the *Scotsman*, 20 February 1923, 'Emigration boom in the Hebrides'.

> Great interest is being taken in the scheme of the Ontario government to emigrate young men and women between 18 and 23 to Canada. The Ontario agent finds that he could treble the number he is authorised to enlist owing no doubt to the depressed state of trade in Lewis, the lack of employment generally and the inability of the farmers to satisfy the hunger of the families. Immediately on landing, employment will be found for farmers and the women can find employment in domestic work. The pay is good as experienced men can at the very start earn £5 to £6 per month. The men also have the prospect of becoming owners of their own farms once again.

3. How much do sources B and C reveal about the differing interpretations of the reasons why Scots migrated abroad after 1830? **(10)**

   Use the sources and recalled knowledge.

   (Higher Scottish unit outcomes: 1.3)

2 The experience of immigrants in Scotland

In this section you will learn about:

- The experience of immigrants, their relations with native Scots, and issues of identity and assimilation with regards to:

  1. Irish Catholics

  2. Irish Protestants

  3. Jews

  4. Lithuanians

  5. Italians.

Hint

Cultural assimilation is the process by which a person or a group's culture comes to resemble those of another group. As groups assimilate it can often be difficult for them to maintain their own cultural identity.

Figure 10: *Many Irish immigrants were poor and were encouraged by cheap fares to Scotland.*

Various groups chose to settle in Scotland between 1830 and 1939 and their experiences varied depending on their numbers, their origin and ethnicity, their religion and their interactions with native Scots. Assimilation was often difficult and, as we shall see, certain groups were more successful than others.

1. Irish Catholics

Irish Catholics came to Scotland in large numbers during the Irish Potato Famine of 1845–51, although they had been arriving in smaller numbers before this. They were escaping extreme poverty and poor living conditions, as well as hunger, and most were illiterate and uneducated.

Most Irish Catholic immigrants tended to settle in the areas where their ships disembarked on the west coast, with 29% choosing Glasgow as their new home. A significant number made their way to the industrial areas of Edinburgh and Dundee. By 1851, the Irish formed 7·2% of the Scottish population, a significant increase from the 1841 figure of 4·8%. What they all had in common was their desire for work but, because they were largely uneducated and unskilled, they could only find work in low-skilled manual jobs such as coal mining, textiles or as navvies on the railways and canals. What is more, because of their Catholic religion, they were often discriminated against by Protestant Scots. Scotland was, after all, a Protestant country and religious discrimination became a feature of the Catholic Irish experience in Scotland.

Figure 11: *Many Irish immigrants took on jobs as navvies, helping to build canals and railways in Scotland.*

In the workplace Catholics were openly discriminated against because of their religion. Also, many Scottish workers were worried about the vast numbers of Irish Catholics seeking jobs, which they believed drove down wages and threatened their own positions. Indeed, some Irish were so desperate for work that they did work for less, which obviously confirmed many Scots' suspicions and heightened religious tensions. On the other hand, there is evidence that by the 1870s, Catholic Irish and Protestant Scots were cooperating in the workplace, forming trade unions and going on strike.

The overwhelming majority of Catholic Irish immigrants arrived in Scotland poor and therefore tended to stick together to support one another and settle in the slums where the rent was cheap. As a result, distinct Irish Catholic communities began to develop in the slums of Glasgow and Dundee. Conditions in these areas were terrible, with poor sanitation and overcrowding often leading to outbreaks of typhus and cholera. With poor education and low literacy levels these immigrants had little hope of gaining employment that paid enough to get out of the slums. Some chose to spend part of their wage on drinking or gambling which led some Scots to look down on the Irish and blame them for their poor economic circumstances. For all these reasons, many Scots came to see Irish Catholic immigrants as insular, drunk, poor, uneducated, dirty and disease ridden, and a stereotype was established. The reality was that these immigrants were doing their best to get by, but the stereotype continued and harmed relations with the Scots.

At the heart of these Irish communities was the Catholic Church. It helped to set up clubs, football teams and, of course, schools. In Dundee in the early 1860s there were only two Catholic churches and three schools serving 20 000 people. By 1870 the number of

Make the Link

In RMPS and Modern Studies you may learn about sectarianism in Scotland and around the world today.

Make the Link

In Geography you learn about conditions in modern-day slums.

schools and churches had doubled, largely paid for by the contributions of low-paid workers. In Edinburgh and Glasgow the Irish Catholic communities formed Hibernian and Celtic football clubs in the 1870s and 1880s. The strength of these growing communities was reinforced by high levels of intermarriage. In Greenock in 1851 80·6% of Irish Catholics married people of their own faith. Forty years later, in 1891, it was still high at 72·4%. This often made it difficult for Irish Catholics to integrate and assimilate into the mainstream of Scottish society.

Figure 12: *Celtic Football Club was formed in 1888 by a Catholic priest. It represented the growing number of Irish Catholics in Glasgow.*

Violence and conflict was a part of the Irish Catholic experience in Scotland. Certain areas in Glasgow were out of bounds, depending on your religion, and it was not unusual to see running battles between Catholics and Protestants on the streets of Glasgow in the 1850s and 1860s. Such physical attacks by native Scots were often matched by verbal ones from the pulpit: in 1923 the Church of Scotland published a pamphlet entitled 'The Menace of the Irish Race to our Scottish Nationality'. These attacks obviously made it difficult for many Irish Catholics to feel fully welcome in Scotland.

By 1939, anti-Catholic discrimination still existed in the workplace, especially during recessions when jobs were at a premium. Sectarianism was clearly still an issue in Scotland and it was only later in the twentieth century that Irish Catholic immigrants integrated fully into Scottish society.

2. Irish Protestants

Protestant Irish immigrants began arriving in Scotland in larger numbers in the 1870s. They found life easier in Scotland because they shared the same religion as native Scots and therefore did not experience the discrimination Catholics did. This obviously made assimilation into Scottish society easier.

Hint

Employability in skilled industries is usually dependent on a good education. In this respect, Protestant Irish immigrants had an advantage over Catholic Irish immigrants.

In the workplace, job opportunities opened up for Protestant Irish in ways they did not for Catholics. Although this was partly down to religion, it was also due to the fact that Irish Protestants were often more skilled and educated than their Catholic counterparts. As a result of this, these immigrants moved into better paid, skilled roles, taking on jobs as engineers in iron-making firms like Bairds of Gartsherrie and as train drivers or signal workers in Glasgow.

While the Protestant Irish were certainly much more visible in highly-skilled professions than Irish Catholics, not all were part of what historian Tom Devine calls the 'labour aristocracy'. Many worked in low-skilled jobs too, mixing with and working alongside Catholics.

Although Irish Protestant immigrants found it easier to obtain better paid work and get on well with the native Scots, they also maintained their distinct identity. Perhaps the main way they did this was by forming Orange Orders similar to those found in Ireland. The Orange Order had been founded in Ulster in 1795 and began to develop in Scotland from 1800. It was formed to celebrate the distinct identity of the Protestant Irish, taking its name from the Protestant William of Orange who became King William III in 1688. Orange Lodges were central to the Order, and were places where Protestant Irish would meet with one another. They became important in the community with weddings and funerals often taking place there. By 1835 there were 12 lodges in Glasgow.

The Orange Order may have helped maintain the identity of Protestant Irish immigrants but it often led to conflict with Irish Catholic immigrants. In 1857, 300 Orangemen were attacked by Catholics in Airdrie when they were returning from an Orange march. As a result, marches were banned for a decade in Lanarkshire. Today, Orange marches still take place around 12 July although it is very rare that they result in any open conflict with Catholics.

Figure 13: *Orange Order marches have been a feature of Protestant communities in Scotland for over 200 years.*

🔍 Hint

William of Orange came from the Netherlands (Holland). Today, the Holland football team wears an orange kit as it is their historic national colour.

⚛ Make the Link

If you study the Russia topic at Higher you will learn about the persecution of the Jews under the Tsars.

3. Jews

Jews began to move to Scotland in larger numbers between 1881 and 1911. They did so mainly because of the religious and economic persecution they faced in Russia and because the UK was a good stopover before moving on to the USA. Many, however, chose to stay in Scotland.

Jews tended to settle in Edinburgh, Dundee and, mostly, Glasgow. Indeed, by 1914 there were around 10 000 Jews living in Glasgow alone with most living in the Gorbals area where the accommodation was cheap. Most could not speak English but, as the Jewish community began to grow, so Yiddish was spoken in the streets along with English. Jews opened bakeries and butchers, and were successful in the tailoring trade and cigarette industry. Some Scots accused Jews of paying low wages and operating 'sweatshops' but there is little evidence of this being any more common in Jewish businesses than in

Figure 14: *Garnethill Synagogue in Glasgow.*

Make the Link

In RMPS you may learn about anti-Semitism today.

Hint

In the early eighteenth century in Britain, the Poor Law provided rather limited help to the very poorest in society.

Make the Link

If you study the Germany topic you will learn about the anti-Semitic policies of the Nazi Party.

Hint

Some Jews came to Scotland to escape persecution in Nazi Germany. Many more made their way to the USA, including Albert Einstein who left in 1932 just before Hitler came to power.

Scottish ones at the time. In fact, these accusations are perhaps evidence of anti-Semitism.

Jews did experience some anti-Semitism in Scotland, but it was very rarely violent and was certainly nothing like the persecution that existed in certain areas of Europe in this period. This was down to a number of factors. First, Jews did not compete with Scots in the labour market, being generally self-employed, and they were therefore not seen as a threat. Also, the numbers of Jewish immigrants was relatively small and the communities self-contained, meaning Scots were not concerned about their impact on Scottish culture or society. Lastly, Jews also tended to look after one another and new immigrants meaning that they were not seen as a drain on the Poor Law. As a result of all this, anti-Jewish groups made little headway in this period and Jews were generally left to get on with their lives with little interference.

Figure 15: *Jews in Glasgow produced newspapers, initially in Yiddish, but later also with English words.*

By 1939, Jews had begun to make a significant impact on the legal and medical professions in Scotland and many were moving from the Gorbals to more middle-class, affluent areas of Glasgow. While Yiddish newspapers had once flourished, they were now dying out, and many Jews were making strides in left-wing Scottish political parties, showing that they had assimilated well in Scotland. Jews were still discriminated against in some areas, for example some bowling clubs refused to allow them as members, but on the whole they had managed to maintain their identity, establish strong communities and integrate well into Scottish life.

4. Lithuanians

Lithuanians began to enter Scotland in larger numbers in the 1890s and for many of the same reasons as Jews: persecution in Russia, poverty and the hope of stopping off in Scotland en route to the USA. As with the Jews, many chose to stay and make Scotland their home.

Many Lithuanians arrived in Scotland poor and keen to work. As a result they settled in areas where they could easily find jobs, such as the coal mining areas in Lanarkshire. The town of Coatbridge saw the main influx of immigrants, with a sizeable and flourishing community of 5000–6000 people established there by 1914. Other areas in Lanarkshire and the Lothians also saw Lithuanian immigration.

Initially Lithuanian migrants were not welcomed. They were looked on with suspicion and hostility by Scottish workers who believed that the migrants had been brought in to break strikes and drive down wages in the mines. Indeed, as has been pointed out by Tom Devine, there is evidence to suggest that mine owners did use Lithuanians to do just this. However, this did not last long as Lithuanian miners began to join unions themselves, and in 1912 they even took part in the national strike, thereby assuring their Scottish colleagues of their loyalty. Moreover, Lithuanians became increasingly active in the trade union movement and in left-wing politics. All of this certainly helped to improve relations between Scots and Lithuanians. There were, however, issues with assimilation in other areas.

The overwhelming majority of Lithuanians were Catholic and this sometimes led to discrimination on the part of the native Protestant Scots. Also, some Scots accused Lithuanians of lacking moral fibre and indulging in too much heavy drinking. This stemmed from a misunderstanding of the Lithuanian tradition of having weddings, birthdays and festivals that often went on for days.

Despite the challenges Lithuanians faced, they managed to establish strong distinct communities wherever they settled. They opened businesses and shops, published newspapers in their language, held dances and concerts and attended church. They tended to live in the same cluster of streets as one another, spoke their own language at home and clearly had a strong sense of national pride and togetherness. However, this began to change in the twentieth century as some sought to integrate more firmly into Scottish life by changing their names to Scottish sounding names like Black or Smith. Also, intermarriage with Scots became more common and, as second-generation Lithuanians began to enter higher education, so they left the language and values of the Lithuanian schools in which they had grown up. By 1920 many Lithuanians had returned to Russia and those that had stayed had integrated more and more into Scottish society. This made maintaining a distinct identity increasingly difficult.

Hint

Lithuania was part of the Russian Empire at this time.

Figure 16: *Lithuanians worked mainly in the coal mines of Lanarkshire and the Lothians.*

Hint

Sir Matt Busby, the famous former manager of Manchester United, had Lithuanian ancestry. Busby was from Bellshill in North Lanarkshire and his father was a miner.

Make the Link

In Modern Studies you will learn about the trade union movement and strikes.

Make the Link

In RMPS you may learn about how different cultures and religions celebrate festivals in their own unique ways.

The Great War of 1914–18 also had a major impact on Lithuanians in Scotland. In July 1917 all Lithuanian males aged 18–40 were faced with the decision to remain in Scotland and be conscripted into the British army or to return home to fight for Russia. The majority chose to return to Russia and fight, and few returned after the war. This obviously had a significant effect on the communities to which these men had been central.

By 1939 there had not been a fresh wave of immigrants to keep cultural ties with the homeland alive and many second-generation Lithuanians had fully integrated into Scottish life. This was largely borne out of the desire to fit in and find work in the very competitive labour market of the 1930s. As a result, the previously strong, distinct and vibrant Lithuanian community had clearly diminished by the outbreak of the Second World War, even though some cultural events still remained to show the mark they had made in Scotland.

5. Italians

Between 1891 and 1901 around 25% of immigrants to Scotland were from Italy. These immigrants were escaping poverty and famine in their home country, although many merely saw Scotland as a stopping off point on their way to the USA. As with many Lithuanians and Jews, however, a large number of Italians stayed in Scotland and by 1914 there were around 4500 in Scotland. The largest community was located in Glasgow but Italians also settled in Edinburgh and Aberdeen.

Figure 17: *An Italian café and ice cream parlour on Broughton Street, Edinburgh, 1907.*

The Italian immigrants focused their energies on the catering trade, setting up ice cream parlours and fish and chip shops. In fact, the 'pokey hats' (ice cream cones) were introduced by Italian immigrants as were fish and chip shops; both are now firmly embedded within Scottish culture. These foods became extremely popular among the working class and Italian cafés and ice cream parlours thrived as incomes in Scotland rose between 1880 and 1920. These cafés and ice cream parlours were family run, with new relatives often arriving from Italy to work in them. They were also places where young Scots could meet late into the evening when other businesses had shut. This led some to claim that the cafés were immoral and that they encouraged the young to get together and misbehave. For these Scots, many of whom were religious, the fact that Italian establishments opened on a Sunday also made their existence unacceptable. Others saw the ice cream parlours as a good alternative to public houses, preferring the young to eat ice cream than drink. Italian family-run ice cream parlours like Nardini's and Luca's exist today, as do numerous Italian fish and chip shops.

Hint

In Edinburgh, many Italians settled in the Grassmarket. There are still Italian restaurants there today.

Figure 18: *Nardini's, Largs.*

As well as ice cream and fish and chips, Italian immigrants were also involved in hairdressing in Glasgow. In 1928 they established the College of Italian Hairdressers in Glasgow. Italian barbers can also be found in various towns and cities in Scotland.

Italian immigrants worked long hours that didn't allow them to socialise a great deal with Scots outside of work. Also, at home Italian was spoken, food was Italian and children were expected to marry within the Italian community. Many families sent money home and there was therefore the feeling for some that their futures lay back in Italy rather than in Scotland. Some second-generation Italians may have adapted their names to sound more Scottish, turning Giuseppe into 'Joe' for example, but on the whole Italians maintained a distinct identity in Scotland, maintaining tradition, language and close family ties. Assimilation therefore took place slowly and on their own terms.

From the Scottish perspective, the Italians were not a threat in the labour market because they, like the Jews, were generally self-employed. Also, the Italians ran popular cafés, shops and restaurants which Scots clearly enjoyed. However, there is evidence of some discrimination and prejudice due to Italians being Catholic and individuals had to endure name-calling in the streets and at school. This perhaps reached its peak after 1940 when Mussolini declared war on Britain, but before this there is little evidence of the discrimination that the Catholic Irish experienced. This is arguably because the Italians did not migrate in such large numbers as the Catholic Irish and were therefore not viewed by Scots as being of a similar threat to their jobs.

Hint

Immigrants often bring their cuisine to the countries they settle in. Can you think of any other examples of this in Scotland?

Make the Link

If you study the Italian topic you will learn about Mussolini's Fascist Party in more detail.

GO! Activity 5

Split into five groups. Your teacher will number each group 1–5 (see the start of this section for the immigrant group to which each number relates). Each group is responsible for creating a lesson on their immigrant group. This lesson must clearly explain, in your own words where possible:

1. The experience of your immigrant group.
2. Their relations with native Scots.
3. Any issues of identity and assimilation.

Each lesson must feature a presentation to your class and an A4 information sheet that can be photocopied and handed out to the class. Every person in each group must be able to deliver the lesson to another person/group.

Your teacher will give you an appropriate amount of time for this activity.

(Higher Scottish unit outcomes: 2.1, 2.2)

GO! Activity 6

Why did different groups of immigrants have different experiences in relation to assimilation and maintaining their identity?

Write a balanced paragraph that answers the above questions, making reference to all the immigrant groups.

(Higher Scottish unit outcomes: 2.3)

GO! Activity 7

Exam style questions

1. Explain the reasons why immigrant groups in Scotland had differing experiences.   (8)

(Higher Scottish unit outcomes: 2.2)

GO! Activity 8

Exam style questions

Source D is from *The Ayr Advertiser*, 1849.

> The Irish have been driven by the increasing poverty in their own country to emigrate to Scotland. By their hard work railways have been formed and new and important sources of wealth opened up. However, the Irish, during the past ten years, have absolutely inundated this country. They have also swallowed up our rapidly increasing Poor Rates, have directed charity away from its proper channels, and have filled our jails. By their greatest numbers they have lessened wages or totally deprived thousands of the working people of Scotland of that employment which legitimately belonged to them. Lastly, there can be no doubt that their contact with the Scotch has not been for the benefit morally or intellectually of the latter. Let us redouble our efforts not to keep Scotland for the Scotch, for that is impossible; but to keep Scotland—Scotch!

Source E is from *Images, the Irish and the history of violence in Scotland*, an online article written by Professor Richard McMahon (31 May 2016).

> Irish workers in the nineteenth century often joined with their Scottish counterparts in strikes, trade union activities and in wider political movements. Although there were areas of concentration, Irish migrants also lived, in the main, alongside the Scottish working class. On a more intimate level, there was also intermarriage between Irish Catholics and Scottish Protestants. Irish migrant labour also made a considerable contribution to the success of the economy in the west of Scotland in the nineteenth century. Even some of the good of Glasgow occasionally commented on the better habits of the Irish. For Henry Houldsworth, who employed large numbers of Irish migrants in his spinning mill in the 1830s, migrants, were, on their arrival, 'in general very decent and respectable in their appearance and manner'. This was diminished somewhat by their encounters with the 'lowest dregs' of Glasgow's working class population but still the Irish remained 'equal to the standard of the population employed in factories' in the city. Houldsworth was also by no means alone in praising, albeit in often highly patronising tones, the work and habits of Irish migrants.

1. How much do Sources D and E reveal about differing interpretations of the experience of Irish immigrants in Scotland in the nineteenth century? **(10)**

   Use the sources and recalled knowledge.

   (Higher Scottish unit outcomes: 1.3)

Source F is from Martin J. Mitchell, 'Irish Catholics in the West of Scotland', in his *New Perspectives on the Irish in Scotland* (2008).

> The prevailing view about Catholic Irish in nineteenth-century Scotland is that they were despised by the bulk of the native population, and as a result formed separate and isolated communities in the towns in which they settled in significant numbers. Yet, there is considerable evidence that members of Catholic Irish communities were involved—often in significant numbers—in strikes, trade unions and trade union campaigns. Moreover, this participation was both welcomed and sought by Scottish workers. Some historians have highlighted sectarian riots and disturbances in Scotland in the nineteenth century as proof that there was considerable Protestant working class hostility towards the Catholic Irish community. However, if these incidents are looked at more closely, most of the incidents did not involve Scottish workers, but were instead 'Orange' and 'Green' disturbances involving Protestant Irish and Catholic Irish immigrants. The available evidence states or suggests that most Scottish workers were not participants—they remained aloof and let the two immigrant groups continue their old battles.

2. How fully does Source F illustrate the experience of immigrants in Scotland? **(10)**

   Use the source and recalled knowledge.

   (Higher Scottish unit outcomes: 1.2, 2.2)

3 The impact of Scottish emigrants on the Empire

In this section you will learn about:

- The impact of Scottish emigrants on the economy and enterprise, culture and religion and native societies in the following countries in the British Empire:

  1. Canada
  2. Australia
  3. New Zealand
  4. India

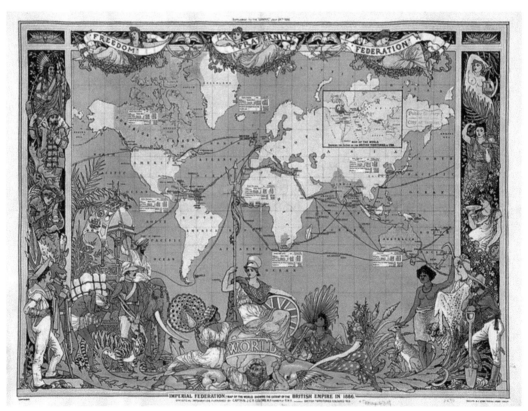

Figure 19: *This elaborate map from 1886 shows, in red, the extent of the British Empire at this time. Look closely and it shows some of the routes that Scots took to the colonies abroad.*

With the British Empire at its height in the nineteenth and early twentieth centuries, hundreds of thousands of Scots made their way across the globe, settling as far afield as Australia, New Zealand, India and Canada. Between 1830 and 1939 their impact on these countries was significant.

1. Canada

Between 1900 and 1939 alone, around half a million Scots migrated to Canada, following thousands who had arrived in the nineteenth century. These Scottish emigrants made a huge impact on Canada, helping it to grow into the successful, modern country it is today.

Economy and enterprise

Scots dominated the Hudson Bay Company, whose trading posts stretched for thousands of miles into what was to become known as Canada. Trading mainly in furs, many Scots made their fortunes in the Company, including Orcadians who were often recruited because of their experience and skill in trapping animals.

Scots were also dominant in textiles, furniture making, paper, sugar, oil, steel and iron, and bakery products. By the end of the nineteenth century, one third of the Canadian business elite was of Scottish origin despite the fact that first-generation Scots only made up 16% of the population. Clearly, Scottish emigrants punched above their weight when it came to business and enterprise.

Most Scots, many of them Highlanders forced off their land during the Clearances, made their way to Canada for the land and agricultural opportunities. There were vast plains on which to raise crops and cattle and the skills they had learned in Scotland stood them in good stead.

Perhaps the biggest impact on the Canadian economy in this period was the construction of the Canadian Pacific Railway. It spanned almost 6000 km (3700 miles) and connected areas of Canada that had previously been cut off from each another. George Stephen, a Scottish financier who became Lord Mount Stephen, was the driving force behind the railway and the chief engineer on the project, Sandford Fleming, was also a Scot. When Stephen and Fleming's project was completed on 7 November 1885, the Prime Minister of Canada, a Scot by the name of John MacDonald, attended the ceremony. Scots were right at the heart of Canadian Pacific Railway.

Hint

Orcadians are people from Orkney. Living and working conditions in Orkney were often similar to those encountered in the Hudson Bay area.

Make the Link

In Geography you learn about the agrarian economy.

Figure 20: *Nova Scotia is Latin for New Scotland and this is its flag. The Scottish influence couldn't be more obvious!*

🔍 Hint

Scotland has a long tradition of banking and finance: the Royal Bank of Scotland and Bank of Scotland are still two of the largest banks in Britain.

Many of Canada's banks were established by Scots. Canada's first bank, the Bank of Montreal, was established in 1817 by wealthy Scots. In 1832, the Bank of Nova Scotia opened its doors. It was managed and dominated by Scottish immigrants. This is perhaps unsurprising considering that Nova Scotia was first settled by Scots.

Culture and religion

Scots had a major impact on Canadian culture, especially its politics. Canada's first Prime Minister was John MacDonald. Along with seven other Scottish 'founding fathers' of Canadian democracy, he guided Canada to independence in 1867. His successor as Prime Minister, Alexander MacKenzie, was also Scottish.

🔍 Hint

Even though some of the dates mentioned here are before 1830 you can still use them in your answers as they help prove an overall point about the impact of Scots on Canadian education.

In education, Scots helped to establish various schools and universities, as well as greatly influence their curricula. In 1818, the Scot, George Ramsey, 9th Earl of Dalhousie, established Dalhousie University. In 1821, McGill University was founded using the money from the estate of James McGill, a politician and merchant who had emigrated from Glasgow. Six years later in 1827 the University of Toronto was established by the Scot James Strachan.

In terms of religion, Queens University was founded in Kingston, Canada, by the Church of Scotland. Its first principal was the Scot Reverend Dr Thomas Liddell. Also, Scots took their Protestant and, to a lesser extent, Catholic faiths to Canada, establishing many churches and charities that became the centre of their communities.

Figure 21: *Scottish emigrants took with them various pastimes and sports, such as curling, when they settled in Canada. This photo shows a group of men curling in Ontario in 1907.*

Make the Link

In Music you may learn how to play Scottish instruments and in PE you may have tried Scottish Highland dancing.

Scottish emigrants brought their pastimes and sports to Canada and these have become part of Canadian life. Even today, Highland Societies exist where bagpipe playing, whisky tasting and ceilidhs are enjoyed every weekend. Games like curling are also popular. Many Canadian army regiments still wear the kilt and play bagpipes.

Native societies

Along with their fellow European immigrants, Scots first met the native peoples of Canada when they worked in the Hudson Bay Company. Through trade, the native peoples developed close relationships with Europeans, which soon led to intermarriage between the two groups. The subsequent generation of people with an immigrant parent and a native parent were known as the Metis people.

The Metis people helped trade flourish, being able to speak and deal with both Scots and native tribes easily. However, not all Scots were respectful towards the Metis or the natives, seeing them as savages or as inferior. Some Scots forced these people off their lands, even though many had experienced that misfortune themselves in Scotland. The irony may have been lost on them, but it is a pattern that Scots repeated wherever they settled, as we shall see later.

Native Canadians and the Metis people did fight back against the encroaching immigrants, many of whom were Scots. In 1885 the Metis staged a rebellion but their leader, Louis Riel, was executed. The government continued to take land on which generations of native peoples had worked and lived, and many Scots were the beneficiaries.

2. Australia

It is thought that before 1900 over a quarter of a million Scots had made the long journey to Australia. Their impact was considerable.

Economy and enterprise

Scots made an immediate impact in Australia, working in remote settlements to establish farms and towns. They exported new agriculture techniques honed on Lowland farms and Highland crofts in Scotland and soon had successful businesses and farms of their own.

Many Scots tried their luck in the gold rush of the 1850s. Although not all struck gold, many chose to settle in these areas and work in coal mines and other growing industries.

Scots were also dominant in various other industries and businesses, from finance, engineering, shipping and coal mining, to sugar and manufacturing. Indeed, in the 1850s the Scots James and Alexander Brown set up large coal mines in Newcastle, New South Wales. By 1914 their mines were producing 8% of all coal in the region.

John Buncle, born and schooled in Edinburgh, recognised the need for good tools in the atmosphere of increased agricultural and industrial production and established the Melbourne Iron Works in 1852. He became wealthy and even founded a School of Design in Hotham, Melbourne.

Scots also made an impact in the brewing industry. Robert MacCracken, born in Girvan, Ayr, established a brewing industry in Melbourne in 1851. By 1884, his brewery was producing approximately 100 000 barrels per year.

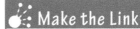

Make the Link

In Geography you learn about how agricultural techniques have developed in recent years.

Hint

Some Scots also tried their luck in the Californian gold rush of the 1850s.

Hint

Many Scottish immigrants to Australia had the education, skills and experience required to succeed in industries like mining, shipping and engineering.

Hint

The man who 'discovered' Australia and claimed it for Britain was Captain James Cook. He was the son of a Scottish ploughman.

In finance, the first Australian bank was founded in 1817 with the encouragement of Lachlan Macquarie, the Scottish Governor. Around a quarter of chief executives of the bank, up until 1900, were Scots. Also, the government of Andrew Fisher, three times Australian Prime Minister and a Scot, founded the Commonwealth Bank.

Culture and religion

Scots have made a considerable impact on modern Australian culture. There are numerous Scottish societies and Burns clubs and some regions of Australia even have their own tartan. Also, and quite significantly, two of Australia's national songs, 'Waltzing Matilda' and 'Advance Australia Fair' were written by Scots.

Catherine Helen Spence was born in Melrose, Scotland, and went on to become Australia's first female political candidate and first female journalist. During her lifetime she was called Australia's Greatest Woman for her political efforts and writing, and even today is remembered for her efforts to advance democracy in Australia. Her actions undoubtedly advanced the cause of women's rights in Australia.

In education, Scots helped create the modern Australian school system. The head of Queensland's teacher training between 1874 and 1892 was the Scot James Semple Kerr. Scots also set up schools throughout the country, notably Melbourne Academy, a secondary school in Melbourne that, due to its Scottish foundations and links, became known as Scotch College.

The Scottish Kirk helped to set up schools in Australia. By 1842 there were 42 parish schools in New South Wales. Elsewhere, Scottish ministers were influential in governing primary and secondary schools, many of which focused on the importance of helping the community as well as formal academic training.

The impact of the Scottish influence in education is important to recognise because these schools helped to produce the next generation of political, economic and educational leaders in Australia.

Native societies

Figure 22: *The Western Australia Police Pipe Band at Bridge of Allan Highland Games in Scotland.*

Hint

Australian women first gained the right to vote in 1902, a full 16 years before women in Britain enjoyed the franchise.

Hint

In the nineteenth and early twentieth century the Scottish education system was seen by many as one of the best in the world.

Make the Link

In Modern Studies or RMPS you may learn about conflicts today over land, as new people and companies move into territories that are already occupied.

Figure 23: *Some Scots were responsible for brutal attacks on Aborigines.*

Those Scots who arrived in Australia intent on working on the land often came into conflict with the native population, the Aborigines. Aboriginal tribes had moved freely throughout the Australian outback for thousands of years and resented being told where they could and could not go. This often had dire consequences for all involved, but especially the Aborigines, as the Hornet Bank Massacre showed.

In 1854, the Fraser family from Scotland established a sheep and cattle farm at Hornet Bank in Queensland. As their farm expanded it encroached into Aboriginal territory. Aborigines in this area had previously been attacked and murdered by European settlers trying to move them off the land and they were not prepared for that to happen again. As a result, in 1857 a group of Aborigines killed eight of the Fraser family and three other white Europeans. In retaliation, William Fraser, who had been away at the time, killed around 100 Aborigines himself and in the years that followed the tribe that had attacked the Frasers was hunted down. It is thought that they were eventually wiped out and with them went their unique language and culture.

There are examples of good relations between Scots and the Aborigines. Francis Armstrong learned the language and culture of local Aboriginal people and John and Alec Mortimer stood up for the rights of the Aborigines. Some Scots married Aboriginal women and in New South Wales surnames like Cameron and Campbell exist in Aboriginal communities.

3. New Zealand

Many Scots made the long journey to New Zealand in the hope of establishing Presbyterian settlements, as well as taking up the opportunity of cheap or free land. By 1920 one in three immigrants to New Zealand was Scottish.

Economy and enterprise

Many Scots who migrated to New Zealand had some experience of agriculture and this stood them in good stead. Dr David Munro introduced the first sheep from Australia in 1842 and within 20 years he had 14 000 sheep on his farm. Within years there were hundreds of sheep, cattle and mixed farms in New Zealand, with Scots working on many of them. One such Scot, Donald Reid, arrived in New Zealand in 1849 and purchased his own land three years later. When he died in 1919 he was a wealthy man with an estate of 6300 acres.

Scots also moved into frozen meat and dairy exports. The Scot, Thomas Brydone, helped found the New Zealand and Australia Land Company which in 1882 sent the first ever consignment of frozen meat from New Zealand to London on the appropriately named *Dunedin*.

Make the Link

In Art you may study the unique and beautiful paintings and drawings of Aboriginal people in Australia.

Hint

You will notice that there is a theme developing with regard to how Scots treated native societies. When answering a question on this, be sure to have clear, detailed examples to make your point.

Make the Link

In Geography you learn about the different types of farms that exist throughout the world.

Hint

Before the development of refrigeration, it was almost impossible to transport fresh produce internationally.

Figure 24: *The Dunedin was the first ship to transfer refrigerated meat. It was charted by the Scot Thomas Brydone.*

Figure 25: *The logo of the Dunedin Highlanders rugby team clearly shows the pride the city has in its Scottish heritage.*

Culture and religion

When they arrived in New Zealand in the 1840s, many Scots settled in Otago province. The settlement in Otago was originally developed by the Free Church of Scotland as a Presbyterian colony and was led by the Reverend Thomas Burns, the nephew of Robert Burns. It had a distinctly Scottish feel, and still does. Its capital is Dunedin, which means Edinburgh in Gaelic. Dunedin even has some of the same street names as Edinburgh, such as Princes Street and George Street. Moreover, the Dunedin rugby team is called the Highlanders in homage to the city's Scottish roots.

Scots set up schools throughout New Zealand, including in 1871 New Zealand's first school for girls. James MacAndrew, originally from Aberdeen, played a significant role in establishing numerous schools in Otago as well as helping to found the University of Dunedin. It is estimated that over 100 schools were founded because of him and, as a result, he is often viewed as one of the 'founding fathers' of New Zealand. It should also be noted that MacAndrew had a lively, long and often controversial career in the politics of the region.

All over New Zealand the cultural impact of Scots is clear in the many Caledonian societies, clubs and pipe bands that exist today. What is more, two of the most common surnames, Campbell and MacDonald, are Scottish.

Native societies

Scots had a mixed relationship with the Maori in New Zealand. Initially it was friendly, with Maoris helping Scottish settlers during the harsh winters of 1848 and 1849. Indeed in some areas in the south, many Maoris converted to Christianity and freely sold land to Scots. However, this changed as more Europeans arrived looking for land.

In 1840 the British government signed the Treaty of Waitangi with the Maori, ultimately to protect Maori land and allow the British government to rule New Zealand. However, the Treaty did not work as intended as it was often unclear who owned what, and the British and Maori had different ideas as to what constituted ownership. Scots sometimes took advantage of the situation by moving onto land that was not necessarily theirs, which led to conflict with Maoris between 1845 and 1872. These Maori Wars were uneven affairs because British troops were drafted in to suppress the Maori who were often armed only with spears. Once again, issues over land ownership soured relations between Scots and native societies.

As in Australia, there were Scots who treated the native peoples of New Zealand with respect. Some, like Donald Maclean from Tiree, learned the Maori language and tried to foster better working relationships with them. There is also evidence of intermarriage between Scots and Maoris, which obviously helped foster more positive relations between the groups.

4. India

From the eighteenth century thousands of Scots migrated to India in the hope of making their fortune as part of the powerful East India Company. When India was formally taken over by Britain in 1857 Scots played an integral role in governing and controlling the country.

Economy and enterprise

As part of the East India Company, Scots were heavily involved in exporting jute, timber, coal, sugar, indigo and cotton. Many made their fortunes this way, although it is questionable as to how much of this money made its way back into the Indian economy as Scots often sent money home.

Scots also became involved in the lucrative tea trade and helped India overtake China as the leading distributor in the world. Perhaps the biggest beneficiary of the tea trade was Thomas Lipton, a Glasgow merchant whose company came to dominate the market in the late nineteenth century.

The infrastructure in India in the nineteenth century was so dire that the local economy struggled. James Ramsey, Marquis of Dalhousie, who served as Governor-General of India between 1848 and 1856, helped to change this. He oversaw the creation of a massive railway network that connected remote areas of India to the large cities, as well as building new roads and canals to allow easier transport of goods and people. Dalhousie also introduced the telegraph and cheap postage, which improved communication. His focus on the building of schools also helped to improve literacy, which had the knock-on effect in the long run of improving the economy. Lastly, through large irrigation projects he brought water to areas that needed it, stimulating the agrarian economy. Essentially, Dalhousie's impact was significant because he helped to modernise Indian infrastructure.

Figure 26: *The East India Company was so powerful it even minted and issued its own coins. Scots played a central role in its administration.*

Figure 27: *James Ramsey, Marquis of Dalhousie, made a considerable impact on India, economically, educationally and culturally.*

⚫ Make the Link

In Business you may learn about the importance of a modern infrastructure in creating a thriving, successful economy.

Culture and religion

Dalhousie also made an impact on Indian culture. First, he banned Suttee, the Hindu practice where a widow would throw herself on the funeral pyre of her dead husband. Dalhousie believed it to be barbaric and wrong, especially as widows would sometimes be forced to do it. He did the same with Thuggee. Thuggee was a term used to describe an organised group of killers who would attack travellers and strangle them with rope or cord. The English word 'thug' comes from this. Dalhousie hanged hundreds of Thugs and in doing so made travelling in India safer.

Figure 28: *Dalhousie banned the Hindu practice of Suttee.*

Dalhousie's views of these practices as immoral and uncivilised may strike us as being fair and reasonable today, but at the time they were part of his overall view that India needed to be civilised. While Dalhousie may have believed he was doing what was best for India, many Indians resented his, and some of his fellow Scots', interference and superior attitude.

In education, Reverend Alexander Duff established a school in Calcutta in 1830 that taught English. Within a week of opening, it had over 300 applicants and was used as a model for other schools throughout India. Duff was also important in the founding of the University of Calcutta, the first medical school in India, as well as the first girls' schools in India.

Native societies

In 1857 there was a mutiny in India, when Indian troops serving in the East India Company army rebelled against their British officers. They were unhappy with British rule and felt that their Islamic and Hindu faiths were not respected by British officers. The Indian Mutiny was crushed by British soldiers, many of whom were commanded by Scottish officers such as General Colin Campbell. What is more, during the mutiny Scottish soldiers had exacted brutal revenge for the massacre of British civilians in the town of Cawnpore (now Kanpur).

Hint

There are many examples of Indian words that have entered the English language, such as 'avatar' and 'bungalow'.

Make the Link

In RMPS you learn about the importance of respecting other people's cultures and belief systems.

Hint

Following the Indian Mutiny the British government took formal control of India. Ninety years later, in 1947, India became independent.

Some had captured innocent Indian civilians and forced them to lick up the blood of the dead British. In the British army this may have resulted in the Scottish soldier gaining a reputation for being a fierce and brutal warrior, but it did little to improve the image of Scots in India.

 ## Activity 9

You are going to complete a piece of work that relies on you working well on your own and then explaining your work to those in your group. You therefore rely on one another to work well.

Get into groups of three and number yourselves 1–3. Each person in the group is responsible for creating a detailed, interesting piece of work on their topic:

Person 1: **Economy and enterprise:** Scots in Canada, Australia, New Zealand and India.
Person 2: **Culture and religion:** Scots in Canada, Australia, New Zealand and India.
Person 3: **Native societies:** Scots in Canada, Australia, New Zealand and India.

You must read over the sections for each country and focus on producing a piece of work on your topic. Your piece of work could be a video, a poster, a storyboard or an illustrated mind map. You should ensure that you get at least **seven separate points** in your piece of work and that you can explain them clearly to your group. Once you have finished you will explain them to one another and take notes on each.

(Higher Scottish unit outcomes: 2.1, 2.2)

 ## Activity 10

Exam style questions

Source G was written by David Laing to his sister in Scotland, 19 February 1873. Laing emigrated from Edinburgh and settled in Canada after he left the army.

> Dear Sister, I have read your letter 20 times over since I received it. I am prospering in life now but I am so lonely. My health has not been so good since I arrived on these shores as part of our army all those years ago, but still I must work. The boys are all grown up men and are working on the same railway I do. I was promoted on the first of April, am foreman of a gang of 20 men receiving all the stores and material. We have 86 locomotive engines to keep in repair and 400 miles of rails to keep in good repair so that the produce of this land can reach the ports and then across the world. Our foremen are nearly all Scots and many of the working men also. I fear that without these men there would be no railway, no prosperity and no trade in this part of the world.

1. Evaluate the usefulness of Source G as evidence of the impact of the contribution of Scots to the growth and development of the Empire. **(8)**

   In reaching a conclusion you should refer to:

   • the origin and possible purpose of the source;
   • the content of the source;
   • recalled knowledge.

   (Higher Scottish unit outcomes: 1.1, 2.1)

(continued)

Source H is from Ian Donnachie, *Success in the 'Lucky' Country* (1988)

There were many fields of Scottish achievement in Australia. Scots were early and successful pioneers in sheep farming and the wool trade, which became big business, centred in places such as Melbourne and Adelaide. Scots also invested heavily in mining, at first in coal and later in copper, silver and gold. The Gold Rush of the 1850s brought to Australia a considerable number of Scottish miners, many of whom stayed after the initial gold fever died down and prospered. Shipping and trade were other areas of enterprise in which Scots excelled. Two later shipping firms were both fiercely Scottish, McIllwraith McEachan and Burns Philp. The profits of Burns Philp were built on the northern Queensland sugar boom of the 1880s in which Scots played a large part in creating the profitable business. Politics and government was another sphere in which the Scots made a sustained contribution to Australian life.

2. How fully does Source H show the contribution of Scots to the economic growth and
   development of the Empire? **(10)**

   Use the source and recalled knowledge.

   (Higher Scottish unit outcomes: 2.3)

4 The impact of migration and Empire on Scotland, to 1939

In this section you will learn about:

- The contribution of immigrants to Scottish society, economy and culture.
- The impact of Empire on Scotland.
- The significance of migration and Empire in the development of Scottish identity.

Today, Scotland is a vibrant, multicultural country with a rich history. There is little doubt that migration and Empire have played significant roles in shaping modern Scotland and the Scottish identity. Indeed, without the flow of people into and out of Scotland in the nineteenth and twentieth century, the country would look and feel very different today.

The contribution of immigrants to Scottish society, economy and culture

Impact on Scottish society

Immigrants have helped to shape Scottish society in various ways. The establishment of Catholic schools by Irish immigrants, and the subsequent support of them by the government, has helped to foster in Scots a tolerance of other religions from a young age.

Jewish immigrants have also contributed in terms of education, valuing its importance since they arrived in Scotland. Many Jews have forged successful careers in medicine and law, further enriching, and making a valuable contribution to, Scottish society.

In the twentieth century many Irish Catholics and Lithuanians were active in the Labour Party and trade union movement. The Irish also produced important political leaders like John Wheatley who was born in Ireland and moved to Scotland when he was seven. Wheatley would go on to be a Labour MP and Minister of Health in the British government of 1924. He was responsible for taking forward a scheme that built 500 000 affordable houses for working-class people.

Impact on the economy

Economically, immigrants have made a huge contribution to Scotland. The influx of Irish immigrants helped to power the industrial revolution in Scotland. These immigrants were so vital, mainly because they were a mobile labour force, willing and able to go where their labour was required and thus keep Scotland's economy and industry moving forward. As navvies, dock workers, shipbuilders, labourers and jute

Hint

When answering questions on this issue you can obviously bring in anything relevant you learned in section 2, The experience of immigrants in Scotland.

Hint

In some countries, like France, denominational schools are banned, as is the teaching of religion in the classroom. What do you think about the issue?

Make the Link

In RMPS you may discuss the pros and cons of denominational schools.

Make the Link

In the Higher topic Britain, 1851–1951, you learn about the post-war house-building programme.

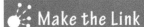 Make the Link

In Modern Studies you may learn about the debate surrounding the economic impact of immigrants in Britain today.

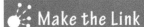 Make the Link

In the topic USA, 1918–68, you learn about the impact immigrants made there.

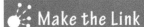 Make the Link

In Health and Food Technology you may have made foods from some of the countries mentioned.

🔍 Hint

In the nineteenth and twentieth centuries the vast number of Italian and Irish immigrants to the USA made a massive impact on its economy and culture.

and cotton mill workers, the Irish were right at the heart of Scotland's economic and industrial development and their importance is hard to overstate.

Jewish immigrants contributed a great deal to the Scottish economy, albeit on a smaller scale than the Irish. They established successful businesses as tailors and cobblers, as well as playing a prominent role in the development of the cigarette industry in Scotland. These Jewish immigrants were also successful shopkeepers. Goldberg's, for example, started off as a simple shop selling material to wholesalers; by 1980, there were 135 stores nationwide. These businesses also provided jobs to many Scots.

Italians made a valuable contribution in the retail and food industry, as was outlined in section 2. These businesses have provided Scots with jobs for many years and made an invaluable contribution to the Scottish economy. What is more, the success of Italian immigrants in the food and retail industry laid the groundwork for Chinese and Indian immigrants in the 1940s and 1950s to establish their own restaurants and takeaways. These have now, along with fish and chip shops, become part of Scottish society and culture.

Impact on Scottish culture

Immigrants have made a substantial contribution to Scottish culture. In sport, Irish Catholic immigrants were responsible for founding the football teams Celtic, Hibernian and Dundee United. At times, the rivalries these clubs developed with their Protestant counterparts are still a negative feature of Scottish football. However, the development of football into Scotland's national sport and its central role within Scottish culture owes much to the actions and passions of Irish immigrants.

Irish Protestant immigrants founded the Orange Order which, through its annual parades and Orange Lodges, is part of our rich and diverse Scottish culture, especially in West and Central Scotland. It must also be acknowledged, however, that there is a clear sectarian element to these parades and marches that can lead to tension between those marching and Catholic bystanders.

Irish immigrants, both Catholic and Protestant, have also enriched Scottish culture with their music, whether it be marching bands or more traditional Celtic music. Irish pubs can often be found playing the latter, with groups of enthusiastic revellers joining in.

Italian immigrants have helped to develop a café culture in Scotland as well as having made fish and chip shops seem as Scottish as Irn Bru and bagpipes.

The impact of Empire on Scotland

Scotland benefited in many ways from its role in the British Empire, but also suffered because of it.

The social and cultural impact: pros and cons

The Empire provided various destinations and opportunities for Scots who wished to escape their lives in Scotland and try their luck abroad.

Also, as Scotland's population grew rapidly during the industrial revolution such emigration to the colonies helped to deal with overcrowding. In some respects, those who emigrated actually helped to improve conditions for those who remained in Scotland.

On the other hand, this emigration to the colonies resulted in what has been called the 'brain drain'. Various historians and observers, including Tom Devine and Edwin Muir, have argued that the most talented and skilled Scots left their home country and became successful abroad, rather than in Scotland. These Scottish emigrants, it is argued, utilised their skills and education to enrich countries in the Empire at the expense of their own.

Figure 29: *Many of Scotland's brightest and best chose to make their fortunes abroad, thus denying Scotland of their talents and skills.*

Being part of the Empire encouraged people from Britain's colonies to settle here. As we have seen, large numbers of Irish immigrants settled in Scotland and in doing so enriched its culture. Indian, African and West Indian immigrants did the same later in the century arguably compensating for the brain drain.

The economic impact: pros and cons

On an economic level, the Empire helped make Scotland a wealthy country. Glasgow became the workshop of world and industries throughout Scotland, such as shipbuilding, coal, steel and jute, thrived on trade with the colonies. Edinburgh became the banking and commerce centre of Scotland, where money flowed in from all corners of the globe. Many Scots clearly relied on the Empire for their jobs.

Numerous Scottish firms made their fortunes because of trade with the Empire. For example, William Weir made his money in the coal and iron industries and was said to be worth around £2 million before 1914.

Moreover, the Empire provided some of the raw materials necessary for Scottish industry, the most obvious example being imported jute from Bengal. Dundee's factories used this raw jute to create packaging that was then sold to all corners of the world. Dundee boomed as a result, earning the nickname 'Juteopolis'.

> **Hint**
>
> Some social commentators believe that new, IT-literate economies such as India are seeing a brain drain, with many of the best and brightest making their way to Europe and the USA in search of better pay.

> **Hint**
>
> Dundee historically relied on the three Js: jute, jam and journalism.

The other side to this story was that some Scottish industries became over-reliant on trade with the colonies and, as a result, they became complacent and failed to modernise. Heavy industries like shipbuilding and steel were so successful largely because the Empire provided an almost unlimited market. However, when these markets contracted during recessions, these industries struggled and the effect on the Scottish economy was devastating. This happened after the First World War and unemployment rose sharply. What is more, Scottish industries had become complacent in their success and had failed to invest and modernise their techniques and equipment. This meant that they struggled to compete with other countries that had modernised, such as Germany and the USA. Essentially, trade within the Empire had propped up a structurally weak Scottish economy for many years but, when there was a worldwide economic downturn in the 1920s and 1930s, it could no longer do this and Scotland suffered massively as a result.

Figure 30: *In the 1920s Scotland's industries struggled, the economy flatlined and unemployment rose. The over-reliance on exports to the colonies was partly to blame. Desperate for food and work, people queued outside workhouses.*

As the Empire grew in the nineteenth century, so competition from colonies adversely affected many industries in Scotland. Scottish emigrants had helped industries in the colonies grow but these eventually came to compete with Scottish firms. The jute industry in Bangladesh, for example, overtook Dundee as it could produce jute cheaper due in part to wage levels being much lower there. Indian cotton firms were also able to beat the prices of Scottish cotton mills, essentially finishing off the industry in Scotland. As well as this, many wealthy Scots saw in these growing colonial economies a better investment opportunity than in Scotland. For example, by the 1880s 40% of investment in the Australian economy came from Scotland. The lack of investment in Scotland contributed to the lack of modernisation in Scottish industries.

Make the Link

In Business Management you may learn about the importance of industries adapting to cope with the changing economic environment. By the 1920s Scotland was unable to do this.

Make the Link

In N5 History you may have learned about the economic problems Scotland experienced after the Great War.

Make the Link

In Business Management you may learn about the importance of investment for industries and economies to grow.

Hint

It is ironic that the success of Scots abroad contributed to problems in the Scottish economy in the twentieth century.

Scotland's urban landscape

The money that flowed in from the Empire helped to build new, impressive buildings and factories throughout Scotland. The urban landscape of Scotland changed as large town houses and mansions were built in Glasgow, Edinburgh, Dundee and Aberdeen.

Scotland's martial tradition

Scottish soldiers played an integral role in the conquest, expansion and maintenance of the Empire, suppressing revolts and mutinies and helping to control belligerent locals. Having taken on the Highland traditions of wearing kilts and tartan, and playing bagpipes before battles, these Scottish regiments were highly visible within the army. As a result, people around the world came to identify the kilted Scottish soldier with the power of the British Empire. What all this did was help to create a popular image in Victorian Britain of the fierce Scottish warrior, which in turn created a strong martial tradition in Scotland whereby young men were attracted to the army in large numbers.

Figure 31: *In Victorian Britain, and throughout the Empire, the Scottish soldier was seen as a ferocious warrior in Highland dress.*

The development of the martial tradition in Scotland meant that many Scots were involved in British conflicts between 1830 and 1939, the most notable being the Great War of 1914–18. Various historians have pointed out that in this conflict, Scots appear to have signed up in proportionately larger numbers than men from England, Wales and Ireland and that around 25% of Scottish soldiers were injured or killed, a much higher proportion than the British army as a whole. It is important to note that there remain some disagreements amongst historians as to whether these figures are wholly correct. Those who agree with the figures explain them by pointing out that Scots were

 Hint

Even today there is a strong martial tradition in Scotland. For example, there are four British army units currently based in Scotland.

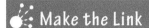

Make the Link

In English you may study poetry from the Great War.

often sent over the top into the line of fire as 'shock troops' because they were seen as ferocious warriors. The development of the proud martial tradition in Scotland, therefore, may have led to a disproportionate number of Scottish casualties in the Great War.

The significance of migration and Empire in the development of Scottish identity

Migration has certainly been significant in the development of Scottish identity. Scottish identity has in many ways been bound up with the Highlands for the last 200 years and this is partly down to migration of Scots.

We just need to look at what Scots do on formal occasions to see how Highland traditions have taken hold of the Scottish national consciousness: tartan, kilts, ceilidhs and bagpipes all often feature at weddings and celebrations across the land. Arguably, this fixation on Highland traditions as being synonymous with Scottishness is a consequence of three factors: firstly, the large scale migration of Highlanders in the nineteenth century that was then romanticised in Victorian novels – particularly Sir Walter Scott's – which captured the Scottish public's imagination; secondly, the desire of Scottish emigrants to identify with a heroic, distinct image of Scotland and carry it forth into their new lives abroad; and lastly, the image of the Scottish soldier, clad in Highland regalia, that was projected throughout the Empire. Scottish identity, at the very least on the face of it, owes a lot to the Highlands.

Many Scots are also proud of the fact that Scots have influenced and shaped so many nations and within the Scottish national identity there is a clear pride in the apparent adventurous spirit that led these emigrants abroad. Again, it is a simplified view of the historical reality but it stems from the basic truth of emigration and the impact Scots made in the Empire.

Finally, one could also argue that, with regard to immigration, many Scots are proud that they have historically welcomed people from abroad and that these people have generally assimilated successfully into Scottish society. Although this is, again, a simplified history, it shows the significance of migration on the development of the Scottish identity.

The Empire also helped to shape Scottish identity. Scots recognised the economic importance of the Empire and many had jobs in industries that relied heavily on exports to the colonies. Also, in terms of the military, many Scots joined the British army and helped to maintain the Empire, buying into the martial tradition and continuing the idea of the kilted, Highland warrior. Scottish civilians enjoyed the fact that Scotland was part of the most powerful Empire on earth and the prestige and opportunities that the Empire afforded them. Many Scots voted for political parties that stressed the importance of maintaining the Empire, recognising its importance to them individually and collectively. Indeed, the historian Tom Devine suggests that 'every nook and cranny of Scottish life, from culture to identity, from economy to politics was shaped by this experience of Empire'. It is hard to argue with this. For most Scots, being proud of Scotland, Britain and the Empire was the norm, and talk of Scottish independence was rare indeed before 1919. It was only after the economic devastation of the 1920s that Scots began to question their role in the Empire, and an identity that had been shaped by it.

Overall, it is clear that Scottish identity in the period in question, and even today in many respects, was largely shaped by migration and Empire. As the nation goes forward, it will be interesting to see how Scottish identity develops and what makes it do so.

Post-script: On 18 September 2014, Scotland went to the polls to decide whether the country should be independent. The build-up to the referendum had seen Scots from across all classes and backgrounds engage in the debate about Scotland's future. For many, the debate raised the interesting question of what it meant to be Scottish today and what it should mean moving forward. For others, it provided the opportunity to assess what benefits Scotland had gained from the Union in the past and whether they were still valid today. When the results came in they showed that 55% had chosen to remain in the Union, with 45% voting for independence. With these statistics in mind one might argue that a majority of Scots identified themselves as primarily British and voted accordingly. However, this would be too simplistic a position to take, as many people cast their ballots for a variety of social, political, historical, economic and emotional reasons. Indeed, for the 45% who voted for an independent Scotland, nationalist sentiments were not necessarily at the forefront of their minds on polling day. Perhaps the most important statistic, however, was the high voter turnout of 85%. Clearly, Scots had engaged with the issue much more so than in normal elections. Arguably, therefore, the clearest victor in the referendum was democracy itself and Scots, whether they voted Yes or No, can surely agree on this. Moving forward, it may well provide the foundations on which Scotland can grow and prosper, and, as in the days of Empire, make the most of its greatest resource: its people.

GO! Activity 11

Working alone, make at least five bullet-point notes under each of the following headings:

1. The contribution of immigrants to Scottish society, economy and culture.
2. The impact of Empire on Scotland.
3. The significance of migration and Empire in the development of Scottish identity.

Leave space underneath each in case you need to add more in.

Once you have finished making notes, compare them with a partner so that you can add in any points he or she has that you have missed.

(Higher Scottish unit outcomes: 2.1, 2.2)

Activity 12

Do you think migration and Empire have contributed positively to Scottish society, culture, economy and identity?

Imagine it is 1939 and you are writing a letter to a relative living in Australia. In a previous letter she asked you the above question. You must answer the question in a balanced manner, using facts to support your overall argument and conclusion. Discuss the issue with a partner before you begin and consider jotting down notes on the pros and cons of migration and Empire up until 1939.

(Higher Scottish unit outcomes: 2.3)

GO! Activity 13

Exam style questions

Source I is from an interview given by Mrs Aitken, a Glasgow resident, talking about Jewish settlement in the Gorbals in the early twentieth century, quoted in *The Complete Odyssey: Voices from Scotland's Recent Past,* edited by Billy Kay (1996).

> It was nearly all Jewish shops and Jewish firms in the Gorbals. There was Fogel's at the corner of Hospital Street and Cleland Street; there was the Jewish bakery at the corner of Dunmore Street. Gleicken, the tailors were there and the Ashers as well. The Gerbers, the Woolfsons, them that had all the jewellers, the shops in the Trongate, they came from there. There were small cabinet-making businesses and upholstery work right up Cumberland Street. They could get their customers everything. They all opened little shops, just doing alterations and repairs to suits and everything. People always helped each other out. Everyone knew someone who would give credit if times were hard. It was a great place the Gorbals!

1. Evaluate the usefulness of Source I as evidence of the contribution of immigrants to Scottish society.
    (8)

    In reaching a conclusion you should refer to:

    *   the origin and possible purpose of the source;
    *   the content of the source;
    *   recalled knowledge.

    (Higher Scottish unit outcomes: 1.1, 2.1)

Source J is from W. Ferguson, *Scotland, 1689 to the Present* (1968).

> The developing economy of Scotland proved very attractive to the poverty-stricken Irish. In some ways they were an economic asset, providing a hard working mobile force of unskilled labour. Gangs of Irish 'navvies' did excellent work in all sorts of construction projects, particularly canal and railway building. They also provided a supply of seasonal labourers. However, they also acted as cut-price labour in the mines, where they were frequently employed as strike-breakers. Economic rivalry gave rise to bitter resentment, especially in the coal fields of Lanarkshire, although seasonal harvesters, both Highland and Lowland, also had grievances about losing work to the Irish workers.

Source K is from Tom Devine, *The Scottish Nation* (2007).

> Young Irishmen, some of whom were only working in Scotland to earn enough to cover their passage to the land of real opportunity across the Atlantic, formed a great mobile army of navvies, moving across the length and breadth of the country, completing the harbours, railways, canals, bridges and reservoirs which became the physical sinews of the new economic order. At the time, however, the Irish did not receive much credit for helping to sustain the Scottish economic miracle. They were 'strangers in a strange land', alien in religion, speech and culture, massed at the bottom end of the labour market, often attracting vociferous criticism for burdening ratepayers and the poor law.

2. How much do Sources J and K reveal about the differing interpretations of the contribution of immigrants to Scotland? **(10)**

   Use the sources and recalled knowledge.

   (Higher Scottish unit outcomes: 1.3)

Summary

In this topic you have learned:

- Why Scots chose to migrate in such large numbers
- About the experiences of different immigrant groups in Scotland
- How Scottish emigrants made an impact throughout the Empire
- How migration and Empire helped to shape Scottish identity.

You should have developed your skills and be able to:

- evaluate the usefulness of a source
- compare two sources
- assess the content of a source and place it in context
- analyse a Scottish historical issue.

Learning checklist

Now that you have finished **Migration and Empire, 1830–1939**, complete a self-evaluation of your knowledge and skills to assess what you have understood. Use traffic lights to help you make up a revision plan to help you improve in the areas you identified as red or amber.

- Describe the push and pull factors that led Scots to migrate within Scotland.

- Describe the push and pull factors that led Scots to emigrate abroad.

- Evaluate the main reasons for the migration of the Scots in this period.

- Describe the different experiences of the five immigrant groups focused on.

- Describe their relations with native Scots.

- Evaluate how well these groups assimilated into Scottish society.

- Describe the impact Scottish emigrants made on the economies of four different countries: Canada, Australia, New Zealand, India.

- Describe the impact Scottish emigrants made on the cultures of the four different countries.

- Describe the impact Scottish emigrants made on the native societies of the four different countries.

- Describe the contribution of immigrants to Scottish society, economy and culture.

- Evaluate the impact of the Empire on Scotland.

- Explain the significance of migration and Empire in the development of Scottish identity.

- Successfully evaluate the usefulness of a source, commenting on its origin, content, purpose and limitations.

- Successfully compare two sources and come to a conclusion on the main issues they agree or disagree on.

- Successfully analyse a source's content, placing it in context through the use of detailed recalled knowledge.

- Successfully analyse why a significant event in Scottish history took place, explaining the main reasons it occurred and coming to an overall conclusion.

Studying this topic will provide you with an understanding of how and why Great Britain evolved into a modern democracy between 1851 and 1951, and of the development of the role of the state in the welfare of its citizens. You will examine all the factors that motivated political change, as well as evaluating the successes of such changes in meeting their aims. By the end of this topic you will have a detailed and firm understanding of a period in British history that saw major political, social and economic changes, the results of which we are still living with today.

This topic is split into six sections:

❖ An evaluation of the reasons why Britain became more democratic, 1851–1928.

❖ An assessment of how democratic Britain became, 1867–1928.

❖ An evaluation of the reasons why women won greater political equality by 1928.

❖ An evaluation of the reasons why the Liberals introduced social welfare reforms, 1906–14.

❖ An assessment of the effectiveness of the Liberal social welfare reforms, 1906–14.

❖ An assessment of the effectiveness of the Labour social welfare reforms, 1945–51.

Activities and Outcomes

		Activity																	
		1	2	3	4	5	6	7	8	9	10	11	12	13	14	15	16	17	18	19
Outcome	1.1			✓		✓			✓	✓		✓		✓					✓	
	1.2			✓		✓			✓	✓		✓		✓					✓	
	2.1		✓		✓			✓		✓	✓	✓	✓		✓	✓	✓			✓
	2.2		✓		✓			✓		✓	✓	✓	✓		✓	✓	✓			✓
	2.3		✓	✓	✓			✓		✓	✓	✓	✓		✓	✓	✓			✓

Historical Study: British: Britain, 1851–1951

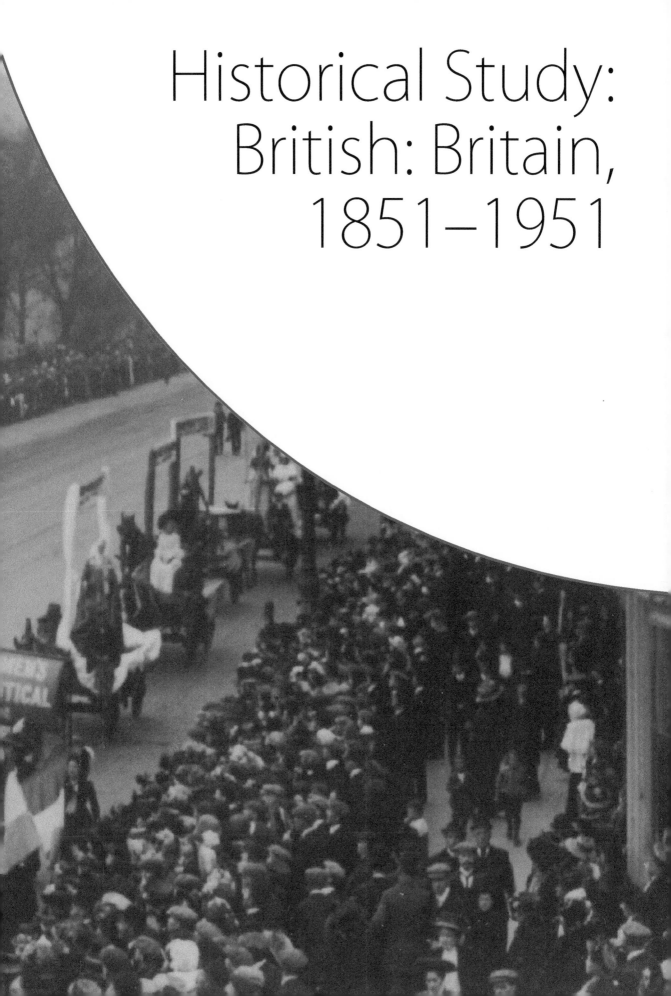

Background

Britain was perhaps the most powerful nation on earth in 1851. The British Empire ruled over hundreds of millions of people and controlled resource-rich areas throughout the world. The **Industrial Revolution** was in full swing and Britain's economy was growing rapidly. As it did, the make-up of British society changed, so much so that politics often struggled to keep up. The political leaders of the day soon passed Acts that made Britain more **democratic**, although their reasons for doing so are still argued about. However, as Britain evolved into a democracy and Britain's wealth increased, many remained extremely poor and without any real power to improve their lives. This was a period when **laissez-faire** politics ruled but poverty became an issue that could no longer be ignored by the government. Its role in the lives of its citizens had to change, and it did.

Hint

An 'Act' refers to an Act of Parliament. This is when a new law or rule is put in place by the government of the time.

Figure 1: *In the late nineteenth century women began actively to campaign for the vote. It was not until 1928 that they were able to vote on the same terms as men.*

Fast-forward one hundred years to 1951 and Britain was considered by many to be one of the most modern democracies in the world.

What is more, the **government** had just put into place radical and far-reaching welfare reforms that had impacted on the lives of every Briton. Progress indeed. At the heart of these changes were the three political parties that dominated British politics in this period: the Conservatives, the Liberals and Labour. Indeed, some argue that the rivalry between these parties lay at the heart of many of the Acts that were passed.

The **Conservative Party** and the **Liberal Party** dominated British politics in the years before the First World War. The Conservatives generally believed in maintaining tradition and preserving the power of the aristocracy and monarchy. Most Liberals were in favour of reducing the powers of the aristocracy and monarchy and introducing some sort of social reform. Some also wanted a limited extension of the **franchise**. Before 1906 both parties believed in taking a limited role in the lives of British citizens. The rivalry between these two parties was intense.

The **Labour Party** was formed in 1900 and rose to overtake the Liberals in popularity by the mid-1920s. The Labour Party formed two minority governments in the 1920s and 1930s, and in 1945 was elected to government with a large majority. It held power until 1951.

In summary, between 1851 and 1951 politicians passed various Acts that made Britain more democratic and increased the role of the government in the lives of British citizens.

🔍 Hint

The Conservative Party was, and still is, often called the Tory Party or the Tories.

🔍 Hint

Before 1870, those politicians who identified themselves as Liberals were known as Whigs and Radicals.

🔍 Hint

Labour means 'to work'. The Labour Party chose their name to show that they represented the working classes.

Activity 1

Read the information above. Create a poster/illustrated mind map/ presentation that summarises what each paragraph says. Also, your poster must explain what each word in **bold** means. You may need to do some internet research to find out the meanings of some of the words or phrases. You should use words and pictures in your piece of work.

1 An evaluation of the reasons why Britain became more democratic, 1851–1928

In this section you will learn about:

- The effects of industrialisation and urbanisation.
- Popular attempts to gain the franchise and pressure groups.
- Changing political attitudes, including developments abroad.
- Party advantage.
- The effects of the First World War.

Between 1851 and 1928 Britain became more democratic. By 1928 men and women over 21 could vote, corruption had been effectively addressed and the political system was fairer than ever before. Historians have long debated why these changes occurred, pointing to a variety of factors to explain them.

The effects of industrialisation and urbanisation

> ### Make the Link
>
> If you study Geography you will learn about urbanisation.

Figure 2: *The Industrial Revolution changed Britain in many ways and had a major impact on the politics of the time.*

In the nineteenth century Britain went through the Industrial Revolution. This saw new ideas, inventions and manufacturing techniques improve the production of goods, leading to the growth of factories and textile mills in towns and cities. It also saw hundreds of thousands of roads, canals and railways built all across Britain. Soon people from rural areas in Britain were flocking to these growing urban centres in the hope of finding work. This process is known as urbanisation and it had a significant political impact on Britain.

In 1871, the population of Britain was 31·8 million, and by 1911 it had increased to 45·3 million. Also, by 1911 80% of people lived in cities. Britain's cities had become rather crowded, rather quickly. The workers who were at the heart of industrialisation experienced terrible living and working conditions in these overcrowded, unsanitary towns. As socialist ideas spread, demands for a greater voice for the working class increased. Indeed, trade unions emerged to fight for better working conditions and pay and, from 1900, the Labour Party offered workers a political party that represented their interests.

Middle-class businessmen, factory owners and entrepreneurs also began to call for more political power. They argued that they should have more power and influence in the running of the country because it was they who were truly creating the wealth in Britain. Economic changes had clearly changed society in Britain, and this in turn had created pressure for political change. This pressure was made more acute by changes in education and technology.

Figure 3: *The Forth Rail Bridge under construction (it was completed in 1890). The development and then rapid growth of the railways contributed to an increased political awareness among Britons by the turn of the century.*

The introduction of the 1870 Education Act (1872 in Scotland) meant that more people than ever before were receiving a basic education and as a result literacy rates improved. These education acts were necessary to ensure that, in an industrialised Britain, the growing urban workforce needed to be better educated for the urban workplace. The increase in the number of public libraries in Britain after the Public Libraries Act of 1850 also contributed to increased literacy rates. With the invention of the locomotive and the rapid spread of the railways network from the 1840s, people, ideas and news could travel much faster around the country. National newspapers reached large areas of Britain, meaning the increasingly literate population could now

---

🔍 **Hint**

Socialism is the political idea that all the world's resources should be owned in common by the world's population.

Make the Link

If you study the Russian history topic you will learn about socialism.

🔍 **Hint**

The political decisions in Britain are made in Westminster, London, in the Houses of Parliament. People therefore often refer to 'Westminster' or 'Parliament' when discussing political decision making.

Make the Link

If you study Modern Studies you will learn about the decisions made in Westminster and the Houses of Parliament today.

consume news from all across the country. As a result a national political identity began to develop, with Britons becoming more interested in how Britain was run and by whom.

With so many social and economic changes in Britain in this period the government arguably had little choice but to keep pace politically. The Second Reform Act of 1867 recognised the expanding, skilled working class by giving them the vote and the 1885 Redistribution of Seats Act ensured that the growing towns had the right to send more MPs to Parliament. In short, the growth of democracy in Britain owes a lot to the effects of industrialisation and urbanisation.

📖 Historiography

'Parliamentary reform was largely a reflection of changes in the economic and social structure of the country.'

D.G. Wright

'Gradual social and economic change combined to make further political reform not only desirable, but inevitable.'

Morrison, Morrison and Monaghan

Make the Link

If you study Modern Studies you will learn about the role of pressure groups in politics today.

Popular attempts to gain the franchise and the role of pressure groups

Throughout the nineteenth century various pressure groups formed in the hope that they might convince and, indeed, pressurise the government into making Britain more democratic. In the 1860s groups like the Reform League and Reform Union had been active, calling for major reforms and changes to the British political system. They held marches and rallies, brought petitions to Parliament and kept the issue of political reform in the headlines. These groups held large-scale meetings, with one such gathering resulting in the famous Hyde Park riots of 1866. These cannot have failed to gain the attention of the politicians of the time. The influence and impact of these pressure groups on the growth of democracy in Britain is difficult to assess, although it could be pointed out that the Second Reform Act was passed in 1867, only a year after the Hyde Park riots and major demonstrations elsewhere in London and Glasgow. On the other hand, the much bigger Chartist movement that had peaked in 1848 had not won any concessions from government.

Figure 4: *The Hyde Park riots of 1866. Riots by pressure groups hoping to force change may have influenced politicians to consider reforms to the political system.*

After 1867, pressure groups continued to make themselves heard, notably in 1884 when the Reform League, the Reform Union and trade unions held a franchise demonstration outside Parliament. However, by this stage most reform campaigners were using contacts within Parliament to get their points across rather than demonstrations. Indeed, Radical MPs, such as John Bright, played a part in putting pressure on government from within Westminster.

Figure 5: *A women's suffrage march along Princes Street, Edinburgh, 1909.*

In the twentieth century perhaps the most notable pressure groups were those that campaigned for women's suffrage. The Suffragists and Suffragettes certainly had a significant role in women gaining the vote in 1918, as we shall see later, although other factors also played a part in this.

🔍 **Hint**

For more information and analysis on the reasons why women got the vote in 1918, turn to pages 113–120.

📖 Historiography

Royden Harrison argues that there was a revolutionary spirit in the 1860s and that this, combined with popular pressure groups, was a major factor in influencing the government to pass the 1867 Reform Act.

Changing political attitudes, including developments abroad

In the 1850s and 1860s politicians in Westminster began to recognise that the skilled, more literate and educated working class were becoming more politically aware, and that perhaps they and the middle classes could be trusted to use the vote responsibly. The fear of the 'revolutionary mob' that had existed previously had declined, and many politicians began to argue for the extension of the franchise. Indeed, following the death in 1864 of the anti-reform Prime Minister, Lord Palmerston, many Conservatives and Liberals felt that they could now truly pursue political reform. Palmerston's death has been seen by some as a turning point in British politics, as old ideas gave way to new, more progressive ones. Events abroad also played a part in the changing political attitudes of the time.

🔍 **Hint**

The ruling classes in most European countries had long been worried about the potential power of the sizeable lower classes and often referred to them using patronising and pejorative terms, such as the 'revolutionary mob', or the 'rabble'.

The historian Gertrude Himmelfarb argues that Disraeli passed the 1867 Reform Act because he wanted to embrace the idea of democracy and was keen to move with the times.

Hint

A civil war is a war fought within a country between two or more different groups.

Between 1862 and 1865 there was a civil war in the USA, between states in the North and those in South. The North were fighting, among other things, to ensure that slavery was abolished throughout the USA and this fight for liberty and equality struck a chord with people in Britain who shared similar ideals. Many among the skilled working class supported this cause, even going so far as to boycott cotton produced in the South. Such political awareness impressed the ruling classes. What is more, many middle- and upper-class people supported the North and there developed a growing feeling in these circles that it was therefore only logical to support the growth of liberty and equality in Britain also.

In 1848 there was a series of revolutions in Europe that threatened France, Austria and the German states. Workers were beginning to demand more of a say in how their countries were run, and the political classes in Britain cannot have failed to take notice. However, the fact that the Second Reform Act wasn't passed until nearly 20 years later perhaps indicates that concerns about the 1848 revolutions were not acute enough to prompt any real changes in Britain at the time. What they did do, perhaps, was help to change attitudes towards giving the working classes more political power.

📖 Historiography

The historian Brent E. Kinser argues that widespread support for the North in the US civil war encouraged the forces in Britain that demanded more democracy.

Party advantage

In the nineteenth century the Conservatives and Liberals competed with one another to win the votes of the electorate. As we shall see, this played a part in the passing of various Acts that made Britain more democratic.

At the beginning of 1866 the Liberals were in power but they were split on the issue of reform, and who the vote should be given to. The Liberal Prime Minister, Lord John Russell, wanted to extend the franchise but was forced to resign when his party didn't back him on the issue. His successor was the Conservative leader, Lord Derby. Derby and his Chancellor, Benjamin Disraeli, wanted to stay in power because the Tories had been out of office for 20 years, and so they decided to adopt the Liberals' idea of electoral reform to make them more popular. Benjamin Disraeli reasoned that if his party gave the vote to working-class men in towns then these men would cast their vote for the Conservatives in the future. The result of all this was the Second Reform Act of 1867 which actually went further than even Lord John Russell had argued for, granting the vote to 1.5 million men who lived in urban areas. Disraeli and Derby had effectively stolen the ideas of the Liberals in the hope of gaining a political advantage for their party!

Whether this actually worked is open to debate because in the general election of 1868, the Liberals were elected, with William Gladstone becoming Prime Minister. That being said, in the 1874 election, Disraeli seized back control for the Conservatives, making it unclear as to whether political advantage was gained by the Tories when passing the 1867 Reform Act. What is certainly clear is that the real winner was democracy, and in particular those men who gained the vote.

THE DERBY, 1867. DIZZY WINS WITH "REFORM BILL.

Mr. Punch. "DON'T BE TOO SURE; WAIT TILL HE'S *WEIGHED*."

Figure 6: *This Punch cartoon from 1867 shows Disraeli beating Gladstone in the 'race' to pass the Reform Act. Was it a race to gain an advantage for their respective parties?*

📖 Historiography

F.B. Smith and Maurice Cowling both argue that party advantage was a decisive influence in the passing of the 1867 Reform Act.

⚫ Make the Link

If you study Modern Studies you will learn about how different political parties in Britain and the USA compete to gain votes.

The 1867 Reform Act is not the only example of politicians acting to ensure party and political advantage. In 1872, Gladstone's Liberals passed the Secret Ballot Act and then in 1883 passed the Corrupt and Illegal Practices Act. Together, these Acts meant that voting now had to be conducted in secret, therefore making the bribing of voters much more difficult, and the amount of money that could be spent on elections was limited. Gladstone was well aware that the Conservative Party was able to use its superior wealth to buy votes and dominate election campaigns and hoped that these Acts would reduce their advantage. Also, by placing the Corrupt and Illegal Practices Act of 1883 and the 1884 Third Reform Act close to the next election, Gladstone hoped his Liberal Party would be seen by voters as the true party of reform.

📖 Historiography

'… governments had their own motives for reform [and] it can be argued that political advantage was at the heart of much of the change.'

Kerr and McGonigle

🔎 Hint

Historians often refer to the First World War as 'World War One' or the 'Great War'.

⚫ Make the Link

If you study the Scottish unit, The Impact of the Great War, 1914–28, you will learn all about how the Great War changed Scottish politics.

The effects of the First World War

When the First World War began in 1914, women and many men could not vote in British elections. However, just over four years later when the war ended, the Liberal government had passed the 1918 Representation of the People Act which granted the vote to all men over 21 and women over 30 who owned property. It is worth considering the importance of the war in making this happen.

When conscription was introduced in 1916, calls for all males to have the vote became louder. It was argued that the government could not order men to fight and kill on its behalf and then not allow them a chance to choose the government. In the 1919 election all men over 21 were given the vote, with those who had served in the armed forces being allowed to vote at 19.

When men went off to war in 1914, women took on their jobs and in the process earned the respect and admiration of men from all classes. After the war, some women were given the vote. This issue is dealt with in more detail in section 3 but it is fair to say that the Great War did have an impact on women gaining the vote, thereby making Britain more democratic.

🔎 Hint

It was not until 1928 that men and women were able to vote at the same age (21). In 1967, the age was lowered to 18. In 2014 in Scotland 16- and 17-year-olds were allowed to vote in the Independence Referendum.

📖 Historiography

'The experience and response of the mass of people during the First World War were of major importance in shaping the pattern of British politics.'

Martin Pugh

Activity 2

There are five different factors that we can argue led to the growth of democracy in Britain. You must be able to say how important each factor is by referring to evidence to back up your point.

Take a double page in your jotter/use an A3 piece of paper and complete the table below. The completed table will be ideal in helping you to structure and write your first essay.

If you have access to ICT you could turn this into a presentation, but just make sure it is totally clear and well laid out. Your teacher will give you an appropriate amount of time to complete this.

Factor	Description or summary of factor.	Evidence: Acts or changes in society that the factor led to, which made Britain more democratic.	Evaluation: Summary of the argument judging how important the factor is.	Historiography: Show your awareness of alternative interpretations.
The effects of industrialisation and urbanisation.				

(Higher British unit outcomes: 2.1, 2.2, 2.3)

 Activity 3

Which arguments are strongest and why?

Get into groups of three. Using five scrap pieces of paper, write one factor on each. Your challenge is to negotiate with others in your group and then rank the factors in order of importance, from most important to least. Crucially, you must be able to justify why certain factors are more/less important than others.

Now that you have constructed your argument, locate at least four historians' arguments to either support or contradict your argument. You are now going to write a paragraph explaining your overall argument, introducing historiography to show an awareness of alternative interpretations.

(Higher British unit outcomes: 1.1, 1.2, 2.3)

Hint

Adding historiography to your essay answers will show your awareness that there are alternative interpretations of the issue you are writing about. Using quotes and arguments well will certainly help you pick up marks.

 Activity 4

Exam style questions

How far were social and economic changes responsible for the growth of democracy in Britain after 1851? **(22)**

(Higher British unit outcomes: 2.1, 2.2, 2.3)

2 An assessment of how democratic Britain became, 1867–1928

In this section you will learn about:

- The widening of the franchise, 1867–1928.
- Fairness in the electoral system.
- Increasing choice for voters.
- The accountability of Parliament.

A democracy can be best defined as a political system where the people have the right to elect representatives who then govern the country. In a modern democracy there should exist the basic principle of one person, one vote; one vote, one value. Gender and wealth should have no say in whether someone can vote or not. Also, the electoral system should be fair and free from corruption, with a clear choice of parties to vote for. Finally, the government should be accountable to its electorate. In 1867 Britain could not be considered a democracy. By 1928, however, many changes had been made and Britain was closer than ever to being a modern, functioning democracy.

The widening of the franchise, 1867–1928

Hint

When historians talk about groups gaining the franchise, they simply mean getting the right to vote in elections.

In 1866 very few people in Britain could vote. The franchise was restricted to the wealthiest men, meaning only one in seven males had the vote. Also, women were completely disenfranchised. However, between 1867 and 1928 various Acts of Parliament were passed that widened the franchise.

In 1867, the Second Reform Act was passed. Most skilled working-class men in towns were given the vote as long as they rented or owned property valued at £10 or more a year. Also, in the countryside agricultural landowners and tenants with very small amounts of land were enfranchised. The Act increased the electorate massively, from 1·3 million to 2·45 million. Now around one in three adult males could vote. On the one hand, it was a significant step forward for democracy in Britain because it enfranchised some working class men for the first time and arguably got the ball rolling in terms of the widening of the franchise. On the other hand, it did not give women the vote and also meant that there were different voting rights depending on whether you lived in a town or the countryside.

📖 Historiography

Martin Pugh argues that the 1867 Reform Act 'greatly accelerated the democratisation of British politics' because it paved the way for the Third Reform Act of 1884.

In 1884 the Third Reform Act granted the same voting rights to men living in the countryside as the Second Reform Act had given to those living in towns. In effect, it levelled the playing field for male voters in terms of property qualifications. The number of voters increased from 3·1 million to 5·7 million.

Arguably, the biggest advances in widening the franchise occurred in the twentieth century. The 1918 Representation of the People Act abolished property qualifications for men and also extended the vote to all men aged 21. Also, for the first time ever women were given the vote, albeit not on the same terms as males. Only women over 30 who met a property qualification were given the vote. However, ten years later, in the Equal Franchise Act of 1928, property qualifications for women were removed and the age limit for males and females was made equal. This Act completed the process of widening the franchise, meaning that all men and women over 21, regardless of wealth or where they lived, could now vote. It is clear that the right to vote for all, one of the main democratic principles, had been achieved by 1928. This was a massive step towards Britain becoming a democracy.

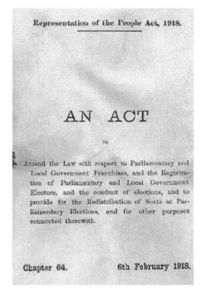

Figure 7: *The Representation of the People Act extended the vote to some women for the first time.*

Fairness in the electoral system

A true democracy needs to have a fair electoral system, free from corruption and bribery. Before 1872, voters would cast their ballot in public, declaring openly who they were voting for. Also, there were no fixed or clear rules about bribery or intimidation. This system of voting meant that candidates, or people working for them, could bribe or intimidate voters to vote for them. However, in 1872 the government passed the Secret Ballot Act. This Act meant that votes would now be cast in secret. This discouraged candidates from bribing or intimidating voters as they could not be sure how that person would cast their ballot. However, the 1872 Act did not eradicate corruption or make Britain totally fair. Further Acts were required to do this.

The 1883 Corrupt and Illegal Practices Act clearly detailed how much money candidates could spend during election time, meaning that richer candidates had no advantage over their poorer counterparts. Also, it banned activities such as the buying of food or drink for voters and put a limit on the number of carriages that political parties could use to carry voters to the polls. By 1883 the voting system was undoubtedly fairer but issues remained with regard to the unequal value of votes in Britain.

> **Make the Link**
>
> In Modern Studies you may learn about the voting process in Britain, as well as who is and isn't eligible to vote in elections nowadays.

📖 Historiography

Morrison, Morrison and Monaghan argue that the 1883 Act 'plugged the gaps' in the 1872 Act.

Hint

In politics, a Member of Parliament (MP) is said to hold a 'seat' if they have been elected to represent a constituency.

Before 1885, small rural towns that had once been large could still elect two Members of Parliament (MPs), whereas new industrial towns that had once been small might not even have one MP. The number of seats given to each town had simply not caught up with the changes in Britain that had seen many people move from the countryside to the growing industrial towns. In effect, this led to small towns and their voters wielding a disproportionate amount of power. The system was clearly unfair and unequal. To combat this, the Redistribution of Seats Act was passed in 1885. This Act did exactly what its title suggests, redistributing seats more fairly based on the number of people living in towns. It had the effect of creating constituencies of approximately equal size. This meant that votes in Britain now had a similar value.

📖 Historiography

Malcolm Pearce and Geoffrey Stewart argue that the Redistribution of Seats Act 1885 meant that for the first time there was 'something approaching fair parliamentary representation'.

Despite the advances made in making the British political system fairer and therefore more democratic, by 1928 problems remained. Plural voting still existed at this point, meaning that a person could vote more than once if they owned property in different constituencies. Also, as universities still elected their own MPs in 1928, graduates were able to vote twice, once at university and once in their home constituency. In one election, a man was able to vote 23 times! In 1911 plural voting counted for 7% of votes. Plural voting clearly made a mockery of the notion of one vote, one value and meant that Britain's democracy was not as fair or equal as it could have been in 1928.

Increasing choice for voters

Make the Link

In Modern Studies you may learn about countries around the world with different political systems that mean people have a very limited choice in who they can vote for.

It is vital in a democracy that voters have a real choice when they cast their ballot. In a true democracy, people should be able to choose to vote for the party that best reflects their own politics and ideas. In nineteenth century Britain this was not the case, because the electorate could only vote for Liberal and Conservative candidates who generally represented the middle and upper classes. However, in 1900 the Labour Party was formed, created to represent the concerns of the working class. Now, for the first time in Britain, there was real choice for working-class voters, making the system more democratic in the process.

📖 Historiography

John Kerr and James McGonigle argue that 'the creation of the Labour Party provided choice, an essential ingredient in a democratic society'.

Before 1911 MPs were not paid a salary. This meant that only rich individuals who did not need to rely on a salary could afford to run for Parliament. In response to this, the 1911 Parliament Act was passed. MPs were now to be paid, therefore making Britain fairer and providing a real choice to those interested in entering national politics.

The accountability of Parliament

Ideally, in a democracy, the most important decisions must be taken by the elected representatives in that country. This means these representatives are clearly and directly accountable for the running of the country. The 1911 Parliament Act ensured that this was the case in Britain. For the first time, the unelected House of Lords lost its power over budgets and could no longer veto (reject) bills passed by the elected House of Commons. This certainly made Britain more democratic because it meant that those representatives in the House of Commons who had been elected by the people of Britain were now more directly accountable for the laws passed, and the power of unelected members in the Lords had been curbed. That being said, the unelected House of Lords still exists today, and can still influence bills and delay them. Arguably, this could be seen as not being democratic because the voters have no say over who sits in the Lords and they are not directly accountable to the electorate. That being said, some would argue that the House of Lords performs an important function in that it acts as a check on the House of Commons.

Figure 8: *In 1928, as today, the House of Lords was unelected. Its power was curbed by the 1911 Parliament Act, however.*

Another important aspect of the 1911 Parliament Act was the fact that it reduced the maximum length of time between elections from seven years to five years. Interestingly, this still fell well short of the Chartists' demands in 1848 for annual elections. This meant that MPs could be voted out of power more quickly if voters were not happy with them and their policies. This made MPs more directly accountable to those who elected them as they knew they had to perform and represent their constituents or they risked being voted out in the next election.

📖 Historiography

Martin Pugh argues that the 1911 Parliament Act was 'an immense triumph for parliamentary democracy'.

GO! Activity 5

Analysing a source

Source A was written by a modern historian.

> Britain was in many respects a fully functioning, modern democracy in 1928. Men and women over 21 had the vote, property qualifications no longer existed, and the voting system was, by and large, fairer and less corrupt. Clearly, the political system had moved with the times and adjusted accordingly. However, by 1928 Britain was not fully democratic. Crucially, the House of Lords continued to be unelected and exercise power over bills, and the head of state was unelected.

Use at least four pieces of information from Source A and at least two points from your own knowledge to explain how democratic Britain was by 1928.

(Higher British unit outcomes: 1.1, 1.2)

GO! Activity 6

How democratic was Britain by 1928?

Get into groups of four and number yourselves 1–4. As there are four themes in this section, number 1 takes the first factor, number 2 the second, and so on. Each person must produce a poster or presentation on their factor explaining how Britain became more democratic. Each pupil will explain their topic to the rest of the group as they listen and take notes.

Rules for the piece of work:

1. Feature historiography and clearly relate it to your point.
2. Show both sides of the debate wherever possible (the progress towards democracy and any limitations that existed in 1928).
3. No more than 50 words can be used. It should contain pictures to help you explain it.
4. Take your time explaining it to ensure everyone understands.

Once you have all your written notes in front of you, highlight all the ways that Britain was perhaps not a democracy in one colour, and the ways it was in another colour. Lastly, using a third colour, highlight all the historiography you have collected.

GO! Activity 7

Exam style questions

To what extent could Britain have been called a democracy in 1928? (22)

(Higher British unit outcomes: 2.1, 2.2, 2.3)

3 An evaluation of the reasons why women won greater political equality by 1928

In this section you will learn about:

- Changing attitudes to women in society.
- The women's suffrage campaigns: the NUWSS and WSPU.
- The example of other countries.
- The part played by women in the war effort, 1914–18.

In 1928 women were given the franchise on equal terms with men. This was the culmination of years of campaigning by women's suffrage groups, but was also the consequence of changing attitudes to women over the preceding 50 or so years, not only in Britain but throughout the world. Also, the Great War certainly had a part to play in changing attitudes towards women. While most historians agree that the above factors all played a part in women winning greater political equality by 1928, they often disagree on the relative importance and significance of each factor, as we shall see.

Changing attitudes to women in society

In the mid nineteenth century women were generally seen as being intellectually inferior to men. Legally, women had few rights and socially, women were expected to fulfil the role of the dutiful wife or devoted mother. Moreover, the vast majority of men, and some women, firmly believed that women were simply different in character to men. However, as the century wore on, attitudes and laws concerning women's role in society changed.

In 1857, a law was passed that allowed women to divorce husbands who were cruel to them or husbands who had left them. Women gained more financial independence in 1870 as they were now legally allowed to keep the money they earned, and the 1882 Married Women's Property Act gave women rights over property. Also, in 1891 women could not be forced to live with husbands unless they chose to. All these laws meant that women had more rights, and can be seen as an important shift in the way society perceived women.

In the mid to late nineteenth century, women became increasingly active in public affairs. Between 1870 and 1894, women gained the right to vote for and stand for election to school boards, county councils, the Boards of Guardians for poor houses and Parish and District Councils. Also, women became members of political organisations.

Historiography

Martin Pugh argues that 'their participation in local government made women's exclusion from national elections increasingly untenable'.

In education, more opportunities slowly opened up to women. For example, in 1870 the first university college for women, Girton College, was set up. In 1879, women's colleges were founded at the renowned and highly respected Oxford University. A year later the 1880 Education Act was passed which meant all five- to ten-year-olds, including girls, had to attend school. As more and more opportunities emerged for women in education, so new professions opened up to those who had degrees.

By the turn of the century women had trained and were successfully practising as teachers, lawyers and social workers. Also, the number of women doctors increased. By moving into roles previously dominated by men, women were challenging and changing centuries-old stereotypes. Indeed, when we consider all the changes discussed it is clear that attitudes towards women's roles in society had altered. Millicent Fawcett, a leading campaigner for women's suffrage at the time, argued that these social changes were vital in the eventual winning of the franchise. That being said, these changes had not seen politicians even come close to granting women the franchise and it was clear to many that a forthright and active campaign on this issue was necessary.

 Historiography

With regards to various legal, educational and professional advancements that were made by women in Britain, John Kerr and James McGonigle argue that 'the overall effect of these developments was to erode male prejudices'.

The women's suffrage campaigns: the NUWSS and WSPU

 Hint

In politics, pressure groups often 'lobby' politicians in an attempt to influence their decision. Lobbying involves presenting politicians with facts, figures and arguments in an attempt to convince them of a particular point of view.

Campaigners for women's rights recognised that unless women had the vote their ability to influence and effect real change was extremely limited. With this in mind, the National Union of Women's Suffrage Societies (NUWSS) was formed in 1897. They were later nicknamed 'the Suffragists' and were led by Millicent Fawcett.

The Suffragists believed that the best way to convince politicians and those in power to grant the franchise to women was to gain their respect through peaceful, moderate tactics. They held meetings, distributed pamphlets, organised petitions and lobbied politicians to introduce parliamentary bills on the issue of women's suffrage. The Suffragists were certainly successful in gaining some publicity for their cause, but perhaps not as much as they would have hoped. Their peaceful, moderate tactics did not gain headlines in newspapers. That being said, the Suffragists were successful in convincing many MPs to support their cause and in 1910, 1911 and 1912, Parliament heard arguments for and against a bill for limited female suffrage. Many MPs voted for it again and again, and it could be argued that they did so partly because of the campaigning by Suffragists. Indeed, when women did gain the vote in 1918, it was passed into law by many politicians who had been lobbied by Suffragists over the previous 20 years.

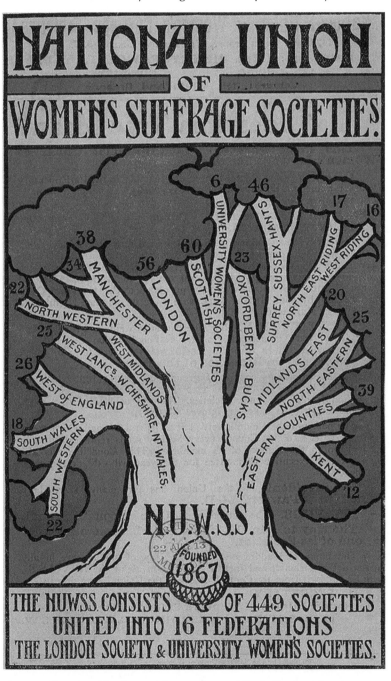

> **Make the Link**
>
> In Modern Studies you may learn about the role and influence of lobbyists in modern-day politics.

Figure 9: *The NUWSS, who were later nicknamed the Suffragists, played a significant part in women winning the vote in 1918.*

📖 **Historiography**

Paula Bartley argues that an important reason women were given the vote in 1918 was because 'several suffragist MPs were promoted to the cabinet' in the preceding years.

Sandra Stanley Holton argues that the Suffragists were vital in women gaining the vote 'especially … in securing the strong position enjoyed by their cause at the outbreak of war'.

Despite historians now recognising the success of the Suffragist campaign in influencing politicians, at the time many women felt that the NUWSS was not doing enough to get their points across. In 1903, Emmeline Pankhurst broke away from the NUWSS and formed the Women's Social and Political Union (WSPU). They would later be nicknamed 'the Suffragettes' and would have an explosive impact on the campaign for the vote.

The Suffragettes believed that direct action was needed to gain publicity for their cause and re-focus the media and politicians on it. Their motto was 'Deeds not Words'. Suffragettes would heckle MPs at politics meetings, chain themselves to railings, organise large rallies, marches and petitions and even engage in illegal activities such as setting postboxes on fire and slashing expensive paintings in art galleries. These illegal activities often landed Suffragettes in prison, where many went on hunger strike in protest at not being considered political prisoners. The government responded by instructing prisons to force-feed the Suffragettes. When this became widely reported, there was considerable sympathy for the Suffragettes from both men and women. Again the government responding by putting an end to force-feeding and putting in place the Prisoners (Temporary discharge for ill-health) Act 1913. This meant that any women who went on hunger strike were released until they became well again, at which point they were re-arrested and put back in jail. It was dubbed the 'Cat and Mouse Act' for obvious reasons.

Figure 10: *Suffragettes were made fun of and criticised heavily in the media.*

Source B was written by a modern historian.

The Suffragettes' militant tactics certainly gained plenty publicity for their cause but very rarely in a positive way. Newspapers and cartoonists made fun of them and it led some Suffragists to claim they were doing more harm than good to the cause. Some men said the actions of the Suffragettes simply proved that women should not have the vote. The Suffragists disapproved of the tactics and there was an obvious split in the women's suffrage movement as a result. It is interesting to note that as the Suffragette campaign became increasingly violent in the years before the war, so membership of the NUWSS grew as disillusioned women left the WSPU. Also, the Suffragettes made few friends among the political class who saw them as dangerous terrorists, especially when attempts were made to blow up or set on fire politicians' houses.

Overall, it is clear that the Suffragettes mobilised opinion for and against the suffrage campaign. Perhaps without the publicity they raised, politicians may have ignored the issue of votes for women. However, for opponents of women's suffrage, the Suffragettes' actions simply provided proof that women could not and should not be trusted with the vote.

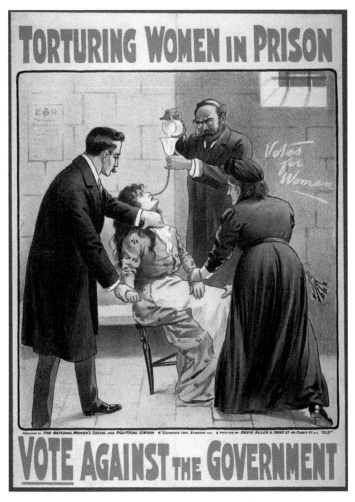

Figure 11: *The Suffragettes used the force-feeding of their members to gain sympathy for their cause and foster anti-government feeling.*

Martin Pugh argues that the only positive impact the Suffragettes had was to increase the membership of the Suffragists.

Midge Mackenzie believes the Suffragettes were the 'remarkable women who fought for, and won, the battle for the vote'. She also argues that it was the Suffragettes who 'revitalised the question of votes for women' before 1914.

The example of other countries

The women's suffrage movement was not limited to Britain and it had in fact been very successful all across the globe. By the time the USA entered the war in 1917, many states had given women the vote. Also, years before this, in 1906, Finland granted women the vote. What is more, countries in the British Empire, such as New Zealand (1893) had given the vote to women. No disasters had occurred in these countries and the political systems had remained stable, despite warnings from anti-suffrage campaigners. British politicians often saw themselves as being in charge of the greatest democracy and Empire on earth and were perhaps keen to demonstrate that they could keep up with this next great reform in politics. With this in mind, perhaps the example of other countries did influence some politicians to be more open to the idea. Also, the fact that women in other countries had the vote cannot have failed but provide hope for the British suffrage campaigns and instil in them a determination to see their cause through to the end.

📖 Historiography

Paula Bartley argues that politicians were influenced by the fact that women elsewhere had already gained the vote: 'It would have been a peculiar embarrassment if the mother of democracy, Britain, lagged behind other countries'.

Figure 12: *Women took on many new roles during the war.*

The part played by women in the war effort, 1914–18

When Britain declared war on Germany on 4 August 1914 it only took the NUWSS two days to decide to suspend its political campaigning for the vote. As men flocked to recruiting stations to sign up, so women filled the void they left. Throughout the war women took on roles in government departments, the post office, as clerks in business, public transport and as land workers. Perhaps the most famous role that many women took on during the war was that of the 'munitionette': a worker in the many munitions factories creating weapons for war. Indeed, by Armistice Day munitions factories were employing 950 000 women.

The fact that women stepped ably into these roles certainly gained them a lot of respect and admiration from men across all classes. Politicians were also quick to praise the efforts of women. The war certainly did see a change in the way women were perceived and was important for this reason.

Figure 13: *Women moved into roles which previously would have been considered too dangerous or too 'male' for them, such as munitions factory workers.*

When women were granted the vote in early 1918, it was easy for politicians to claim, rather patronisingly, that women had 'earned' it for all their hard work in the war. In fact, while war work certainly played a part in women gaining the vote, it is a rather simplistic explanation. The fact that the vote was only given to women over 30 who owned property or were married to someone who did meant that most of the young, working-class women who had gone into work during the war were still without the vote. The war had clearly not benefited them politically. Also, there had been significant moves towards female enfranchisement before the war, with an increasing number of MPs supporting the idea. Therefore, it could be argued the war simply sped up a process that was already underway. It is important to also remember that women did not gain the franchise on the same terms as men until 1928, ten years after the war. On balance, the efforts of women during the war were of course important in them gaining the vote, but it would be naïve to ascribe too much weight to this one factor when so much had occurred before it.

📖 Historiography

A.J.P. Taylor argues that 'War smoothed the way for democracy – it is one of the few things to be said in its favour'.

Constance Rover argues that the war was important because it saw women being openly praised and a change in public opinion become clear: 'Public opinion became overwhelmingly favourable towards women'.

GO! **Activity 8**

Analysing a source

Use at least four pieces of information from Source B on page 117 and at least two points from your own knowledge to explain the impact of the Suffragettes on the campaign for the vote.

(Higher British unit outcomes: 1.1, 1.2)

GO! **Activity 9**

Why were women more equal politically by 1928?

This activity involves you working in groups of three. Using all the information in this section, your challenge is to create a piece of work that:

1. Describes the main reasons women got the vote.
2. Explains each factor's importance.
3. Shows an understanding of the limitations of at least one factor's importance.
4. Features brief interviews with at least four historians.
5. Clearly explains which factors your group believes are the most important and why.

You can produce anything (a video, a booklet, large posters, a presentation) as long as it fulfils the criteria above.

(Higher British unit outcomes: 1.1, 1.2, 2.1, 2.2, 2.3)

GO! **Activity 10**

Exam style questions

How important was the Suffragist campaign in women gaining the vote in 1918? **(22)**

(Higher British unit outcomes: 2.1, 2.2, 2.3)

4 An evaluation of the reasons why the Liberals introduced social welfare reforms, 1906–14

In this section you will learn about:

- Concerns over poverty – the social surveys of Booth and Rowntree.
- Municipal Socialism.
- Fears over national security and national efficiency.
- The rise of the New Liberalism.
- Party advantage and the rise of Labour.

At the beginning of the twentieth century Britain was arguably the most powerful, wealthiest nation on earth. Despite this, poverty was a massive problem that affected many Britons, and those in power were beginning to recognise that something needed to be done to combat it. Between 1906 and 1914, the Liberal government brought in many reforms that were designed to address some of the major causes of poverty in Britain. However, historians have long argued as to the main reasons why these reforms were introduced.

Concerns over poverty – the social surveys of Booth and Rowntree

In nineteenth century Britain, poverty had long been seen as an affliction that the poor brought on themselves. Books like Samuel Smiles' popular *Self Help* articulated what many already believed about poverty, notably the idea that people should look after themselves, work hard and improve their own lot in life. However, attitudes towards poverty slowly began to change as the extent of the problem became known.

Figure 14: *Poverty was a major problem in Britain at the turn of the century.*

Charles Booth was a London businessman who didn't believe claims by socialists that a quarter of London was in poverty. He set out to investigate the issue in London's East End, using solid, scientific methods and trained researchers. His aim was to provide, for the first time, real, hard evidence about poverty in London. The result was his 1889 book *Labour and Life of the People*. It conclusively proved that 35% of London's population were living in extreme poverty. Booth's findings sounded a warning bell for the government. Not only did they highlight the extent of poverty in London, but his recommendations clearly stated that the government needed to intervene or they could face a backlash from the poor working class.

> ### ☀ Make the Link
>
> In Geography and Biology you may well undertake fieldwork to gather data in a scientific manner, just like Charles Booth and his researchers did.

Figure 15: *Charles Booth.*

Figure 16: *Seebohm Rowntree.*

Make the Link

In Business Management you may learn about successful business people who carry out independent research into issues in which they are interested.

Make the Link

In Modern Studies you will learn about the powers that local governments have nowadays.

Seebohm Rowntree was a successful businessman who carried out investigations into poverty in York. In his study of 1901, *Poverty, a Study of Town Life*, Rowntree showed that 30% of York lived in extreme poverty. Clearly, he concluded, high poverty levels were not just limited to large cities like London. He also showed that problems such as illness, old age and unemployment were often at the root of poverty and that the poor could do little to improve their situation in life.

Like Booth, Rowntree had provided a wealth of statistical evidence about the state of poverty in Britain with clear conclusions about what the government needed to do. Also, it is very interesting to note that Rowntree met the Liberal MP David Lloyd George in 1907 and they became close friends. Lloyd George, a New Liberal and Chancellor of the Exchequer from 1908, was behind some of the most forward-thinking Liberal reforms that addressed many of the problems identified in Booth and Rowntree's studies.

📖 Historiography

Graham Goodlad and Richard Staton argue that Booth and Rowntree 'focused attention on the deep-seated reasons for deprivation, about which poor people could do little unaided: low wages, sickness, old age, raising children'.

'New Liberalism was given a powerful impetus by the revelations of Booth and Rowntree.'

Peter Murray

Overall, the social surveys of Booth and Rowntree were crucial in the eventual passing of the Liberal reforms. They highlighted the extent of poverty in Britain, and proved for the first time that no matter how hard some people tried, they could not escape poverty. MPs and those in power began to talk about the 'deserving poor', those who were poor through no fault of their own and therefore needed government assistance. This theme ran through the Liberal reforms and it is hard not to overstate the importance of these surveys in influencing the politicians of the day.

Municipal Socialism

By the second half of the nineteenth century the public had become more used to local (municipal) authorities taking an increased role in their lives. Some local authorities carried out improvements that were paid for by local taxes taken from residents, with taxes based on an individual's wealth. For this reason local authority action came to be known as Municipal Socialism.

The most famous and most successful example of this was in Birmingham where the Liberal Mayor, Joe Chamberlain, made various improvements to the city, paid for by local taxation. Chamberlain bought the waterworks and gasworks in Birmingham to ensure that its citizens always had a ready supply of both. He also cleared many of the worst slums and built better houses in their place. The fact that Municipal Socialism was successful and popular in Birmingham raised the possibility that it could work on a larger, national level. Municipal Socialism can be considered a factor in laying the groundwork for the Liberal reforms as it proved that government intervention (albeit local government) could benefit citizens.

Fears over national security and national efficiency

At the start of the twentieth century Britain was the most powerful nation on earth and had the strongest economy and industry. Clearly, the government wanted the status quo to remain unchanged. However, events abroad and the rise of competing nations meant that British politicians had to think very hard about how to maintain their place as the pre-eminent power in the world.

Figure 17: *Boers fighting the British in 1899. Note how they are dressed and how this might differ from how British soldiers at the time were dressed and kitted out.*

Between 1899 and 1902 Britain was engaged in the Boer War in the colony of South Africa. The British army was fighting to keep the colony in British hands, and was up against Dutch farmers (Boers) who wanted independence. When volunteers were brought in to the army to boost numbers, it was discovered that 25% had to be rejected because they were unfit for service. Politicians and the public began to question whether Britain could hold on to her Empire if its 'fighting stock' of young men were not fit enough to fight and defend it. As a result, in 1904 an Interdepartmental Committee on Physical Deterioration was created to look into the problem of ill health in England and Wales and a similar investigation took place in Scotland. The reports suggested that many adult males were in poor health and they clearly stated that diet and overcrowding were contributing factors that needed to be addressed. The reports recommended school meals be given and that medical inspections be carried out in school. It is important to note that these points were actually carried through to the Liberal reforms and became Acts of Parliament, so it is clear that the concerns over national security did influence the Liberal reforms.

Hint

In the nineteenth century many wealthy, upper-class politicians were very wary of socialism in any form as they felt it threatened their interests.

Make the Link

In the Higher History topic Migration and Empire, 1830–1939, you learn about how Scots helped the British Empire develop.

Hint

Maintaining a large empire is a difficult and costly business. Britain's many colonies throughout the world provided pride and wealth for the nation but were often difficult to administer and control. A strong military was therefore vital to Britain.

Concerns over national efficiency were very much at the forefront of politicians' minds at this time. Germany and the USA were beginning to become stronger industrially and economically, and were posing a serious threat to Britain's position and wealth. It was believed that Britain needed to have fit, strong workers to compete with these other nations, and that there needed to be a better way to ensure that all jobs available were filled quickly and efficiently. These concerns prompted calls for labour exchanges (like early job centres) to be created and for workers to be better looked after, both when in work and when unemployed. Again, the Liberal reforms directly addressed these concerns, showing the influence of concerns over national efficiency in their creation.

> ### 🔍 Hint
>
> In Business Studies you may well study why some countries are more economically efficient than others.

📖 Historiography

Eric Evans has argued that 'arguably, the single most important precondition for the spate of social reforms between 1906 and 1914 was fear of the consequences of an unfit and debilitated population'.

Peter Murray points out that concerns over national efficiency were reinforced by the findings of Booth and Rowntree. Indeed, Alan Sykes argues the same point with regard to concerns over national security.

New Liberalism

Figure 18: *Lloyd George (on the left) and Churchill (on the right) were two of the most influential New Liberals.*

Traditional Liberal politicians firmly believed in laissez-faire. They argued that the individual should look after him or herself. However, toward the end of the nineteenth century a new brand of Liberal emerged. These New Liberals believed that the government should get involved to help the poorest in society. They were certainly influenced by the findings of Booth and Rowntree and believed that the state had a duty to help the poor help themselves. The most important of these New Liberals were Herbert Asquith, who became Prime Minister in 1908; David Lloyd George, who was Chancellor of the Exchequer; and Winston Churchill, who was President of the Board of Trade. They came to prominence after 1906, and were at the forefront of the Liberal reforms. They proposed bills and pushed the reforms through Parliament. Had it not been for the New Liberals, it is unlikely that there would have been any of the Liberal reforms at all.

> ### 🔍 Hint
>
> It is not unusual for political parties to change direction as new, younger MPs exert their influence upon party policy. A similar situation occurred in the Labour Party in the 1990s when Tony Blair took over as leader and re-christened the party 'New Labour'.

📖 Historiography

'It was Lloyd George and Churchill in partnership who carried Asquith's Government forward into a progressive and active social policy.'

Derek Fraser

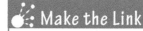

Make the Link

In Modern Studies you may learn about how and why political parties develop distinct ideologies.

Party advantage and the rise of Labour

After 1884 most working-class men had voted Liberal but with the emergence of the Labour Party in 1900 the Liberals had to find a way to keep these working-class voters. Some historians believe that it was the desire of Liberal politicians to gain an advantage over Labour that led them to introduce the reforms.

Figure 19: *The Labour Party, founded in 1900, was a real threat to the Liberals.*

The Liberal reforms that came into effect between 1906 and 1914 undoubtedly helped the poorest in society who overwhelmingly came from the working classes. Because of that, it has been easy to argue that the Liberals introduced their reforms to make them popular among the working classes and to combat the rise of Labour. This argument, however, has its limitations.

In the election campaign of 1905 very little was said about helping the poor and New Liberalism was not guiding Liberal policy yet. Therefore, in 1906 working-class voters were not casting their ballots for the Liberals in the hope of far-reaching reforms that would help them the most. Also, it was only in 1908, when the Prime Minister Henry Campbell-Bannerman died, that New Liberals truly came to the fore and the Liberal reforms proceeded with more pace and urgency. On the other hand, it could be claimed that by 1908 the Liberals had one eye on the next election and ensuring that their party appealed more to working-class voters than Labour.

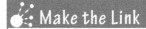

Make the Link

In the previous section on the growth of democracy in Britain, you learned that politicians sometimes passed Acts that they felt would provide their party with an advantage.

Overall, the rise and threat of Labour cannot have failed to motivate the Liberals when they were in power to introduce new reforms. In this respect, gaining a political advantage over Labour and, indeed, the Conservatives, can therefore be seen as a contributing factor in their decision to introduce the more radical reforms after 1908.

📖 Historiography

Graham Goodlad and Richard Staton have argued that 'some reforms ... can be directly traced to Labour Party pressure. Fear of "socialism" may well have encouraged the Liberals to bring forward their own reforms, so that there would be no need for the masses to turn to Labour'.

GO! Activity 11

Why were the Liberal Reforms passed?

Working on your own, your challenge is to create a lesson on the above issue, which you will deliver to someone else. You must do the following:

1. Produce an information sheet that summarises the main facts, dates, statistics, individuals involved and historiographical arguments in relation to the reasons why the Liberal Reforms were passed.

2. Create a card sort activity to go with it.

3. Present your analysis of the issue in a short (1–2 minute) presentation.

Your teacher will give you an appropriate amount of time for this task.

(Higher British unit outcomes: 1.1, 1.2, 2.1, 2.2, 2.3)

GO! Activity 12

Exam style questions

To what extent did the Liberal government of 1906–14 introduce social reforms due to the social surveys of Booth and Rowntree? (22)

(Higher British unit outcomes: 2.1, 2.2, 2.3)

5 An assessment of the effectiveness of the Liberal social welfare reforms, 1906–14

In this section you will learn about:

- The effects of the reforms on the young.
- The effects of the reforms on the old.
- The effects of the reforms on the sick.
- The effects of the reforms on the in and out of work.
- Areas the reforms failed to address.

The Liberal social welfare reforms of 1906–14 saw the most significant intervention of a government into the lives of its citizens up until that point. They were designed to help the poorest in society find a way to escape poverty and improve their lives. Winston Churchill, one of the architects of the reforms, said, 'If we see a drowning man we do not drag him to the shore. Instead, we provide help to allow him to swim ashore.' The reforms focused on four main groups that the investigations of Booth and Rowntree had identified as being particularly vulnerable and that the Liberals felt were most in need of assistance to escape poverty: the young, the old, the sick and the in and out of work. As you will see, the reforms helped the poor in Britain in various ways but they also had their limitations.

⌕ Hint

Much like the Reform Acts that made Britain more democratic, the Liberal reforms were Acts of Parliament that had to be voted on and passed into law.

The effects of the reforms on the young

The Liberals recognised that in British society the poorest children had no real chance of escaping poverty or any of the problems associated with it. With this in mind, they set about creating a series of reforms aimed at improving the health of children, as well as the rights they enjoyed in society.

Figure 20: *The Education (Provision of Meals) Act 1906 ensured children had at least one full meal a day during the term.*

Make the Link

In PE and Health and Food Technology you may have learned about the importance of a good diet when you are growing up.

Hint

The National Health Service did not exist in Britain until 1948. Before this, people had to pay for any medical services.

The Liberal government first passed the Education (Provision of Meals) Act of 1906. Recognising that many poor children could go a whole day without a proper meal, this Act provided school children with one school meal a day during term time. This was clearly beneficial to many children. However, critics have pointed out that because it was down to local governments to pay for these school meals, many chose not to because of the cost. By 1911 less than a third of all education authorities were providing school meals. Also, as the meal was only provided during term time it meant that many children were still going without during school holidays.

As was mentioned in the previous section, various reports had confirmed the poor health of young Britons. Indeed, the Royal Commission of 1904 clearly stated that: 'Provision should be made for regular inspection of school children.' The Liberals decided to address this by passing the Education (Administration of Provisions) Act 1907. Through this, medical inspections at school were made compulsory. However, initially they simply diagnosed problems and didn't treat them, which was obviously of limited use. However, this changed in 1912 when free medical treatment for school children was brought in. From this point onwards medical inspections served to highlight and address problems children had with their health.

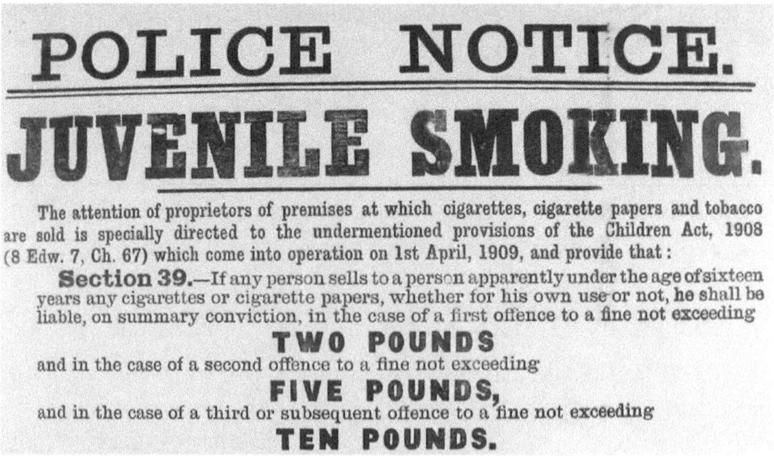

POLICE NOTICE.

JUVENILE SMOKING.

The attention of proprietors of premises at which cigarettes, cigarette papers and tobacco are sold is specially directed to the undermentioned provisions of the Children Act, 1908 (8 Edw. 7, Ch. 67) which come into operation on 1st April, 1909, and provide that:

Section 39.—If any person sells to a person apparently under the age of sixteen years any cigarettes or cigarette papers, whether for his own use or not, he shall be liable, on summary conviction, in the case of a first offence to a fine not exceeding

TWO POUNDS

and in the case of a second offence to a fine not exceeding

FIVE POUNDS,

and in the case of a third or subsequent offence to a fine not exceeding

TEN POUNDS.

Figure 21: *The Children Act of 1908 banned certain activities that children should not engage in, such as smoking.*

Seebohm Rowntree's investigations had found that children were extremely vulnerable and that there were very few laws to protect them. The Liberals addressed this by introducing the Children Act 1908. This was designed to protect and shield children from abuse and neglect, as well as any activities that were unsuitable for them to engage in. It banned children under 16 from smoking, drinking alcohol and begging. Also, it set up specialist juvenile courts and borstals to keep children away from adult criminals. The Act was clearly a massive step in the right direction and was important in establishing what young people could or could not do. However, critics have pointed out that those parts of the Act concerning age limits were often hard to enforce. Also, some parents resented the government intervening in the parenting of their children. The result was that the Act only helped improve the lives of some of the poorest and most neglected children during this time.

📖 Historiography

Martin Pugh has argued that 'Much of the State's activity in connection with children … was resented by parents as an infringement of their role'.

The effects of the reforms on the old

Being old and poor in Britain at the turn of the century was very difficult. There was little real support for those who were too old to work and these people often became homeless, sometimes forced to beg to get by. The Liberals tried to address this problem by introducing the Old Age Pensions Act 1908. In practice this Act provided single men and women over 70 up to 5s a week, and married couples 7s 6d. Once a person over 70 had an income over 12s a week their entitlement to a pension stopped. The Act was understandably popular among the elderly working class. As well as the obvious benefits of an income, they also liked the fact that no individual contributions were required. Much to the annoyance of richer taxpayers, pensions were to be funded from general taxation. Another popular element was the fact that pensions were paid at the Post Office, removing the stigma of the hated Poor Law that had required people to claim help at a poorhouse. Indeed, pensions were so popular that by 1914 nearly a million people had claimed theirs. Despite these positive aspects, many criticisms have been aimed at the Act.

> **🔍 Hint**
>
> Until 1971, money in Britain was divided into pounds (£), shillings (s) and pence (d).

> **⋮ Make the Link**
>
> In Modern Studies you may look at different benefits and entitlements that the state provides to its citizens today.

First, Rowntree had identified that 7s a week was required to keep an individual out of poverty but a pension did not provide this. Further, the pensionable age of 70 was high, especially as the average life expectancy in 1901 was around 45 for men and 48 for women. In practice, many people simply did not live long enough to claim a pension. Moreover, by their mid-50s many people working in industrial areas were too old to continue hard physical work and therefore had to languish in extreme poverty until they were old enough to get their pension at 70.

Figure 22: *An elderly man claiming his pension in 1909.*

Make the Link

In Modern Studies you may learn that in Britain, the age at which pensions can be claimed has changed recently, due in part to increased life expectancy and an ageing population.

It is clear that the Old Age Pensions Act was limited in its reach and effect. However, many elderly Britons benefited from it and a precedent had been set for the government providing some sort of financial help for the elderly. In that respect, it was a significant step forward in helping the poor in Britain.

Historiography

Peter Clarke has argued that the reforms were skilful in bypassing the Poor Law and winning popular appeal. The Pensions Act arguably did both these things.

A.J.P. Taylor has stressed the limitations of the Act, pointing out that 'The state provided a meagre pension for the needy over 70'.

The effects of the reforms on the sick

In the nineteenth century, those who suffered from ill health and could not afford treatment had little choice but to suffer their illness and hope to get through it. More often than not they would be laid off because they were unable to work. These individuals were, for obvious reasons, extremely vulnerable to falling into poverty and being unable to then get out of it. The National Insurance Act 1911 (Part I) was designed to help these individuals.

Figure 23: *A leaflet promoting the National Insurance Act 1911.*

The National Insurance Act Part I 1911 was essentially a social security system that provided all workers aged between 16 and 60, and earning less than £160/year, an income when they were off work ill. They would receive 10s per week for 26 weeks. It covered 15 million workers and required weekly contributions from the workers, employers and the government. Workers would contribute 4d, the employer 3d and the government 2d. Lloyd George called it the 'ninepence for fourpence', as workers would get 9d worth of benefits for contributing 4d. As well as receiving an income, workers were entitled to free medical treatment including medicines when they were off ill. Workers who needed time off due to ill health clearly benefited from this Act and it was a major step forward in the government taking an active, positive role in the life of the worker. However, upon closer inspection the Act is limited in scope. After 26 weeks there was no benefit paid, meaning that the long-term sick could fall back into extreme poverty. It also did not cover the worker's wife or children if they became ill and did not provide hospital treatment. Further, many workers disliked paying the weekly contributions, seeing it as a wage cut, and employers disliked having to contribute.

Overall, the Act was a very good start in addressing the problems ill health caused workers, but it had significant limitations, not least the fact that it ended after six months. Indeed, Lloyd George himself recognised its limitations but argued that his government could afford to do no more at the time.

📖 Historiography

Martin Pugh argues that the National Insurance Act Part I was significant because it 'began the process of getting medical and material assistance to those members of the community who most needed it'.

Malcolm Pearce and Geoffrey Stewart call the National Insurance Act 1911, 'perhaps the single most important piece of social legislation of the twentieth century'.

The effects of the reforms on the employed and unemployed

Unemployment was a key factor in causing poverty, and politicians had come to recognise that workers enjoyed fewer rights in the workplace than in other modern economies such as Germany. The Liberals therefore passed reforms designed to help these workers in the hope that more people could find work and then be productive and happy in it.

For those struggling to find work, the Liberals passed the Labour Exchange Act 1909. Labour exchanges were places where workers could find a job, a sort of early job centre. The exchanges were a real improvement from the previous, informal situation where people would have to search for work themselves. By 1914 around 3000 people were finding work every day in labour exchanges. Despite such apparent success, labour exchanges were not without fault. For example, workers were not required to register and employers did not have to notify the exchanges of vacancies.

Labour exchanges may have provided a place to find work but they did not address the very real problem workers faced of how to get by when unemployed. Previously, being unemployed meant that no income came into the household. The Liberals changed this by introducing the National Insurance Act Part II 1911. This worked in a similar way to Part I of the Act, in that it required contributions from workers, employers and the government in return for protection when the workers found themselves out of work. When employed, workers contributed 2½d/week, employers matched this and the government contributed 3d/week. It was limited to trades that were known to be susceptible to seasonal or cyclical unemployment, such as shipbuilding, building and construction. When a person became unemployed they would receive 7s/week for up to 15 weeks in any one year. The obvious limitation is that the payment only lasted for 15 weeks, after which point a person was expected to have a job and, if not, fend for him or herself. Also, some workers resented the money coming out of their wage each week and some were unhappy knowing that if they were sacked they could not claim the benefit. Despite this, around 2·3 million people were insured against unemployment by 1913 and it proved such a success that, by 1914, the government was planning to extend it to other trades.

The reforms also dealt with those who were in work. The Workers' Compensation Act of 1906 was actually inherited from the previous Conservative government and ensured that workers could now claim compensation for injury or disease resulting from working conditions. Further, in 1908 the Coal Mines Act was passed. This limited a miner's working day to eight hours. As well as this the Trade Boards Act of 1909 established minimum wage protection for workers in sweated trades, and the Shops Act of 1911 limited working hours and provided workers with a half day off every week. Clearly, these reforms were designed to improve the lot of the working man and woman and were largely successful in doing so. Despite this, some employers were unhappy with some of the changes as they meant increasing workers' rights, conditions and wages, which they felt undermined their drive for profit.

Make the Link

In Business Studies you may learn about some of the laws that businesses have to abide by today in relation to their workers.

Historiography

Morrison, Morrison and Monaghan argue that, taken together, the reforms aimed at the in-work 'constituted a significant improvement for millions of workers, many of whom had no one to speak up for them'.

What areas did the Liberal reforms fail to address?

Source C is from Malcolm Pearce and Geoffrey Stewart, *British Political History, 1867–2001* (2002).

> Many national disaster areas had been left untouched. The slums of the cities had to wait until the 1920s and the 1930s for a real assault and the Burns Housing Act of 1909 was more of a hindrance than a help to planning. State education, although modestly encouraged by the Liberals, remained markedly inferior to that of Germany. Only £250000 went from the public purse to British universities in 1914 … and the British working man remained the inferior of his German contemporary in secondary schooling. Despite these areas of neglect, social service spending had roughly doubled since 1906.

 Activity 13

Analysing a source

Use at least four pieces of information from Source C and at least two points from your own knowledge to explain some of the limitations of the Liberal social welfare reforms, 1906–14.

(Higher British unit outcomes: 1.1, 1.2)

 Activity 14

How successful were the Liberal reforms in helping the poorest in society?

You have been asked by a history website to produce a page on their site that clearly answers the above question. They want you to present your information on A3 sheets of paper. First, they want you to create a large table/diagram that shows:

1. The ways that the reforms helped the poorest in society.
2. The limitations to each reform.
3. Historiography to support points you have made.

Secondly, they want you to write:

4. A clear evaluation of the question above that shows balance. It should be no longer than one paragraph.

Your website page will have to be detailed, accurate and fulfil the criteria above. You may be asked to 'pitch' your webpage design to your teacher, another pupil, a small group or even the class.

Your teacher will give you an appropriate amount of time to complete this.

(Higher British unit outcomes: 2.1, 2.2, 2.3)

 Activity 15

Exam style questions

To what extent did the Liberal reforms of 1906 to 1914 make a significant improvement to the lives of the British people? **(22)**

(Higher British unit outcomes: 2.1, 2.2, 2.3)

6 An assessment of the effectiveness of the Labour social welfare reforms, 1945–51

In this section you will learn about:

- The aims of the welfare state and the five giants.
- The extent to which Labour's welfare reforms dealt with:

  1. Want (Poverty)
  2. Disease (Health)
  3. Ignorance (Education)
  4. Squalor (Housing)
  5. Idleness (Employment)

Make the Link

You may study the modern-day welfare state in Britain in Modern Studies.

In 1945, having emerged victorious from a lengthy and costly war against Nazi Germany, Britain may well have been expected to vote for their current war leader and national hero, Winston Churchill, and his Conservative Party. Instead, the public overwhelmingly cast their ballots in favour of Clement Attlee's Labour Party. Labour had been elected on the back of their promise to create a new, fairer society, one in which the government truly looked after the welfare of its citizens. Between 1945 and 1951 the Labour government passed a series of reforms aimed at creating a welfare state. There was, and continues to be, much debate as to whether Labour were successful in achieving their aims and, if so, to what extent.

The aims of the welfare state and the five giants

In 1942 Churchill's coalition government commissioned a senior civil servant named William Beveridge to produce a report detailing what was necessary to make Britain a better place in which to live and work. The resultant Beveridge Report was mainly concerned with dealing with the issue of poverty but also identified four other main issues that together came to be known as the five giants. These five giant problems that Britain faced had to be dealt with, he argued. First, Beveridge argued that **want** must be dealt with by creating a scheme of social insurance. Secondly, the giant of **disease** was to be tackled through the creation of a new national health service. Thirdly, **ignorance** was to be dealt with by reforming the education system to make it fairer and more modern. Next, the issue of **squalor** was to be addressed by improving housing provision in the country. Lastly, Beveridge believed that **idleness** needed to be tackled by creating more jobs. The Beveridge Report became the blueprint for the new Labour government when they came to power in 1945. By 1951, all five giants had been addressed by Labour in one way or another, with varying degrees of success.

Figure 24: *The Beveridge Report detailed how the five giants could be tackled.*

The extent to which Labour's welfare reforms dealt with want (poverty)

The Beveridge Report had focused primarily on how to deal with want in Britain, and had recommended that a system of social insurance be set up to allow all British citizens to access state help when they needed it. In fact, the wartime government produced a White Paper that recommended a system of compulsory national insurance which Churchill even went so far as to say would provide care for all from 'cradle to grave'. When Attlee came to power his Labour administration essentially took the idea and ran with it, creating the National Insurance Act in 1946 and then the National Assistance Act in 1948. As well as this Labour passed the National Insurance (Industrial Injuries) Act 1946.

The National Insurance Act extended the Liberal Act of 1911 to include all adults and established a comprehensive system of social security. It provided unemployment, sickness, maternity and widow's benefit, as well as pensions for men over 65 and women over 60. All workers had to pay into a national insurance scheme run by the government and there would be a flat rate contribution for everyone. In keeping with this, there would be a flat-rate benefit for all. Clearly, this was a significant improvement on what had gone before as every Briton was now entitled to help from the government, regardless of wealth, age or gender. Despite this, it faced criticism because sickness benefits were only available to those who had made 156 weekly contributions. Many people, therefore, were not eligible and fell through the cracks. To address this, Labour passed the National Assistance Act of 1948. This Act was designed as a safety net to catch those not covered by the National Insurance Act. National Assistance Boards were set up to help citizens whose resources were insufficient to meet their needs. This system, while certainly helpful to the poorest in society, was not perfect though, mainly because it was 'needs tested' which many people disliked.

The National Insurance (Industrial Injuries) Act 1946 was inherited from the coalition government. By passing it, Labour ensured that workers were now entitled to benefits if they were injured at work. Not only that, but benefits would be paid at a higher rate than those paid for sickness. All workers and employers had to contribute payments into the scheme.

> ### 🔎 Hint
>
> In politics, a White Paper is a report or guide produced by the government on a particular issue. Its production and publication usually shows that there is some support for its implementation.

> ### 🔎 Hint
>
> You may hear people talk about 'cradle to grave' care when discussing the welfare state. Be prepared to see this phrase come up in an exam question on the issue.

> ### ⁂ Make the Link
>
> In Personal and Social Education you may be learning about the world of work. When you leave school and enter full-time employment you will have to make national insurance payments.

Overall, the system of social security that had been established by Labour clearly addressed the problem of want to a large extent, alleviating poverty for many, but not for all. A survey by Seebohm Rowntree in 1951 found that poverty levels had fallen significantly since 1936. While recent academic studies of Rowntree's findings has found them to over-estimate the fall in poverty levels, they did find that the welfare reforms had reduced poverty levels by up to 10% in York, by 1951. That being said, the average welfare benefits in 1948 were only 19% of the average industrial wage, showing that the social security system was not sufficient to completely pull people out of poverty. Taken together, it is therefore clear that want still existed in Britain when Attlee left office in 1951, but that the giant had at least been brought to its knees.

📖 Historiography

Kenneth Morgan stresses the positive angle, arguing that the introduction of the social security system 'provided a comprehensive universal basis for insurance provision that had hitherto been unknown'.

Pat Thane argues that 'social security was 'to the real advantage, especially, of many women and also those of the lower middle class who had previously been excluded from most social insurance benefits'.

The extent to which Labour's welfare reforms dealt with disease (health)

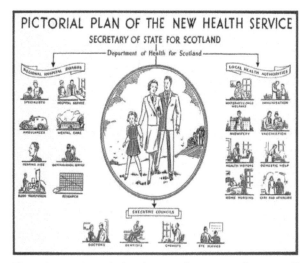

Figure 25: *A pictorial plan showing the services the NHS offered in Scotland. It was the same all over the UK.*

Perhaps the biggest achievement of the Labour government was the creation of the National Health Service (NHS). Created in law through the National Health Service Act of 1946, it came into effect two years later on 5 July 1948. Funded through general taxation and national insurance, it fundamentally revolutionised medical services in Briton, establishing the notion of universal health care for all, free at the point of use. What this meant in practice in 1948 was that individuals could visit a doctor, hospital, dentist or optician and be treated without having to pay any money at all. Prescriptions, too, were free in 1948. The government was totally unprepared for the number of people who needed to access the NHS, and it was not unusual to see queues forming outside doctors' and dentists' surgeries in 1948. The number of prescriptions issued by September 1948 was almost double the number issued before the NHS. Also, in the first year of the health service, eight million dental patients were treated and five million pairs of spectacles were issued. Clearly, these were services that the British public needed. It is easy to see why many historians believe the NHS to be the crowning glory of the Labour welfare reforms. However, critics of the NHS have been quick to point out that it was not without its problems or failings.

 Historiography

R.C. Birch argues that the NHS was 'the greatest single achievement of the story of the welfare state'.

> **☀️ Make the Link**
>
> In Modern Studies you may learn about the NHS in Britain today, and possibly health care systems in other countries too.

The NHS was created to provide free health care for all but by 1950 cracks were beginning to show. The costs were enormous. By 1950 the NHS cost £358 million, far outstripping the £140 million that the government had budgeted for each year. It was because of this that charges were brought in for prescriptions, spectacles and dental treatment in 1951 and 1952 and, although modest, they undermined the basic principle of free health care for all. As well as this, the NHS had failed to eradicate the use of private beds in hospitals, meaning that richer patients could afford to buy care quicker than those without money. These criticisms have often been dismissed by those who point to the fact that Britain was struggling financially at this point, paying off war debts and putting into place other important but costly welfare reforms. They argue that by 1951 the NHS may not have been perfect, but it was still a huge leap forward in addressing the giant of disease that Beveridge had identified. This argument certainly has its merits. Other historians, however, have argued that the NHS was not only not as effective as it claimed to be in the short term, but that its creation had a long-term negative effect on Britain's economy. As you can see in the historiography section below, it has been argued that Britain should have concentrated more money on improving her industry after the war, rather than ploughing money into an expensive, inefficient NHS. Indeed, the debate surrounding the cost of the NHS rages on today. What remains clear, however, is that the NHS was a remarkable achievement that many Britons still feel proud of today.

 Historiography

Alan Sked and Chris Cook argue that the NHS was 'almost revolutionary ... since it improved the quality of life of most of the British people'.

Charles Webster argues that the NHS benefited the middle classes over the lower classes, especially after charges were brought in.

Correlli Barnett argues that Britain should have focused on its industrial and economic regeneration, like Germany did, rather than on expensive reforms like the NHS.

Sidney Pollard rejects Correlli Barnett's arguments, noting that in 1950 Britain was still one of the richest and technologically advanced nations in the world, as it had been post-war. He rejects the assumption that the welfare reforms crippled Britain economically or somehow put her on the back foot.

The extent to which Labour's welfare reforms dealt with squalor (bad housing)

Figure 26: *Following the bombings of World War II, house building was a key feature of Labour's election manifesto.*

During the war, German bombing raids had destroyed around 700 000 houses in Britain and prevented new houses being built. Even before this, housing provision for Britons had been inadequate and clearly needed to be addressed. Labour set about addressing these problems by building more houses and passing the New Towns Act 1946.

To tackle the housing shortage, Labour planned to build 200 000 homes a year and, to combat homelessness, easy to assemble pre-fabricated houses were introduced. Between 1945 and 1948, 157 000 'pre-fabs' had been put up. However, Labour's record in house building was not, in the main, as successful as it would have hoped. In 1946 only 55 000 homes were built. Labour continued to struggle to hit its targets, although in 1948 around 280 000 houses were built, exceeding the self-imposed target. Although the Labour administration has been criticised for not building enough houses during their time in government, they were responsible for building council houses that provided communities with high quality accommodation. These houses were more spacious than people were used to and had a separate kitchen, bedrooms and a living room. They also had electricity, gas, hot and cold water, and indoor toilets. For many, these houses improved their lives considerably.

Figure 27: *Pre-fabs were cheap to make in factories and assembled on site.*

The New Towns Act 1946 was designed to do exactly what it said: create new towns. This Act created 14 new towns including Glenrothes and East Kilbride. The Act also gave the government the power to decide where to build new towns and to ensure that towns were created that were well planned, spacious, and pleasant to live in.

Overall, while Labour's record in addressing squalor has been attacked as being inadequate, one must bear in mind that this was a time when basic raw materials for house building, such as timber, were both expensive and in short supply. Also, after the war there was a sharp rise in marriages and the birth rate, and Britain was of course still recovering from wartime damage. On the other hand, homelessness was higher in 1951 than it had been in 1931, and in 1951 there was still a serious housing shortage as well as long waiting lists for council housing. It is widely believed that Labour's inability to deliver the homes they had promised was a key factor in them losing the 1951 election but whether this can be fully blamed on the government is up for debate.

 Historiography

Morrison, Morrison and Monaghan note that 'given the scale of social and economic problems facing the government in 1945, historians have tended to judge Labour less harshly than the voters did in 1951'.

The extent to which Labour's welfare reforms dealt with ignorance (education)

The wartime coalition government first addressed the giant of ignorance in 1944. The Education Act 1944 created a new system of education, one that the Labour government chose to continue with when they came into government.

First, this Act raised the school leaving age to 15 and made the provision of school meals and milk compulsory. Attendance at primary and secondary school was also made compulsory. For these elements alone, the Education Act should be praised. However, the Education Act also created a new system of secondary education that many have since criticised and which is deserving of closer inspection.

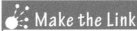 Make the Link

In Modern Studies you may study the housing policy of the government today.

Hint

The Education Act 1944 is sometimes referred to as the Butler Act after R.A. Butler, the President of the Board of Education at the time. Remember this if you are doing research online and see the Butler Act referenced.

Figure 28: *Children drinking their free milk in school in 1955.*

🔍 **Hint**

In Scotland the eleven-plus was also known as the 'qually', short for qualification exam.

The Act created a three-tiered education system that saw children sit a test at 11 (12 in Scotland) to determine whether they would attend a grammar, secondary modern or technical school. This 'eleven-plus' exam essentially determined a child's academic ability and the school they went to reflected this.

Those children who excelled in the exam went to a grammar school. Grammar schools were in the business of successfully preparing pupils for exams and their pupils would generally be expected to move on to university and a professional job thereafter.

Those children who did not do so well in the eleven-plus were sent to secondary moderns or technical schools. In the former, academic subjects were still taught but with less focus on moving on to university; in the latter, less 'academic' pupils were encouraged to learn a trade to prepare them for the world of work.

The idea was that each school would have equal status and funding but in reality grammar schools and secondary moderns were seen as better places for learning and subsequently received higher funding from the government. This therefore helped create a situation where technical schools were not respected, few wanted to go there to learn or teach, and those who did go there had a sense of failure from the beginning. Also, deciding a child's academic future at the age of 11 was, and is, seen by many as being too early and too deterministic. After all, we now know that children learn and mature at different ages. Critics have also argued that the system favoured middle-class children whose parents could afford tutors to prepare them for the exam. The result was a system in which technical schools were often working class in composition, and grammar and secondary moderns, middle class. This system, one might say, perpetuated the class system in Britain, and completely went against the basic socialist notion that educational opportunities should be the same for all. Because of this, Labour's decision to continue with the Education Act – which was introduced by a Conservative in the wartime National Government – and not amend it is certainly questionable. Arguably, as the party of the working class, this Act could be seen as working against this group.

Indeed, a later Labour government would abolish the 11-plus. However, it could be argued that the 11-plus actually provided a clear route to various professions for many working-class people.

📖 Historiography

Morrison, Morrison and Monaghan argue that 'the Labour government did little for the educational welfare of the working class'.

Martin Pugh notes that 'For Socialists it was also a matter of regret that the reforms failed to eliminate … private education, which continued to offer advantages to the wealthy'.

The extent to which Labour's welfare reforms dealt with idleness (employment)

Beveridge had clearly identified that as many people as possible needed to be employed in post-war Britain but didn't believe that unemployment could be brought down below 3%. However, Attlee's government was fully committed to the policy of full employment and had a clear vision as to how this could be achieved: nationalisation of industries.

Nationalisation is essentially when a government takes over the country's major industries and runs them for the benefit of the people. This is precisely what Attlee's government did between 1945 and 1951, taking control of the Bank of England, coal, railways, gas, electricity, long-distance transport and steel. The idea was that profits from these industries would be put back into the country rather than filling the pockets of private owners. Also, the government wanted to control industry to ensure that jobs could be provided. Indeed, during Labour's time in power near full employment was achieved, something that left-wing historians often point to as proof that nationalisation worked. As well as this, the average real wage in 1949 was 20% higher than in 1938. People were better off.

However, while nationalisation certainly contributed to full employment, the boom in private investment and building after 1945, as well as Marshall Aid, also contributed to falling unemployment. Critics of the policy of nationalisation have also argued that it did little to improve working efficiency in the industries the government took over. Supported by taxation money, these industries had little incentive to be profitable. These critics argue that by 1951 Britain's industries were beginning to lose their competitive edge and had fallen behind countries that still had competitive, private industries, keen to maximise profits. Therefore, in the short term Labour did address the giant of idleness, but some would argue that nationalisation harmed Britain's economy in the long term.

📖 Historiography

Stephen Brooke argues that 'The single most important domestic achievement of the Labour government was the maintenance of full employment after the war'.

Paul Addison argues that 'Full employment was the result of … the boom in private investment after 1945'.

GO! Activity 16

How well did Labour deal with the five giants?

Get into groups of five. Draw lots to decide who is going to work on each area of the Labour welfare reforms. Once you've done this, each person will produce a poster, using pictures and no more than 50 words, that clearly shows:

1. The ways in which Labour were successful in this area.
2. The limitations and criticisms aimed at Labour's actions.
3. An evaluation of Labour's actions in this area.

Once all posters have been produced, you must teach one another, all the while taking notes from what you are learning. You will have completed the activity when everyone has notes on all of the five giants.

(Higher British unit outcomes: 2.1, 2.2, 2.3)

GO! Activity 17

Evaluating the success of Labour in this period

You are going to debate the following issue:

The motion: The Labour government 1945–51 was successful in creating a welfare state that catered for the needs of the British people.

Your teacher will divide the class into two groups: for and against the motion. You must come up with the strongest arguments to support your side. You will be expected to argue against the other side, using facts and historiography to support your argument. Your teacher will decide whether this is a whole class debate or if you should get into opposing pairs.

GO! Activity 18

Draw up two columns in your jotter: SUPPORTIVE and CRITICAL. You are going to summarise all the historiographical arguments and put them into the correct columns, based on whether the arguments are supportive of or critical towards Labour's welfare reforms. Beside each argument, write the giant it refers to in brackets.

SUPPORTIVE   CRITICAL

Brooke thinks that Labour was
largely responsible for achieving
full employment after the war
(squalor)

(Higher British unit outcomes: 1.1, 1.2)

GO! Activity 19

Exam style questions

'The Labour government met the needs of the people 'from the cradle to the grave'.'
How valid is this view?   **(22)**

(Higher British unit outcomes: 2.1, 2.2, 2.3)

Summary

In this topic you have learned:

- Why Britain became more democratic
- How democratic Britain was by 1928
- Why women had won greater political equality by 1928
- Why the Liberal reforms were introduced
- How effective the Liberal reforms were
- How effective Labour's welfare reforms were.

You should have developed your skills and be able to:

- construct an essay that describes and explains an issue in detail
- analyse an historical issue in a structured essay
- interpret and make use of a source or historiography.

Learning checklist

Now that you have finished **Britain, 1851–1951**, complete a self-evaluation of your knowledge and skills to assess what you have understood. Use traffic lights to help you make up a revision plan to help you improve in the areas you identified as red or amber.

- Describe the main factors explaining why Britain became more democratic.
- Evaluate which factors were most important in Britain becoming a democracy.
- Describe the ways in which Britain did and did not become more democratic by 1928.
- Evaluate how democratic Britain was by 1928.
- Describe the main factors explaining why women gained more political equality by 1928.
- Evaluate which factors were most important in women gaining the vote in 1928.
- Describe the main factors explaining why the Liberals introduced social welfare reforms, 1906–14.
- Evaluate which factors were most important in the Liberals introducing their social welfare reforms.
- Describe the reforms put in place by the Liberals, 1906–14.
- Evaluate the success of the Liberal reforms.
- Describe the welfare reforms put in place by the Labour government, 1945–51.
- Evaluate the success of the Labour welfare reforms.

In studying this topic you will learn about the modern history of Germany and how and why, by 1871, it came to be a united country, developed from a series of smaller, individually ruled states. You will study the democracy that was installed in Germany after the First World War and the difficulties the new Weimar Republic faced. Finally, you will learn how the Nazis took advantage of the new democracy in crisis to elevate themselves to power and how they maintained their totalitarian state from 1933 to 1939.

This topic is split into six sections:

❖ An evaluation of the reasons for the growth of nationalism in Germany, 1815–50.

❖ An assessment of the degree of growth of nationalism in Germany, up to 1850.

❖ An evaluation of the obstacles to German unification, 1815–50.

❖ An evaluation of the reasons why unification was achieved in Germany, by 1871.

❖ An evaluation of the reasons why the Nazis achieved power in 1933.

❖ An evaluation of the reasons why the Nazis were able to stay in power, 1933–39.

Activities and Outcomes

Outcome	Activity												
	1	2	3	4	5	6	7	8	9	10	11	12	13
1.1	✓	✓	✓	✓	✓	✓	✓	✓	✓	✓	✓	✓	✓
1.2			✓		✓	✓	✓	✓	✓	✓	✓	✓	✓
1.3			✓		✓	✓	✓		✓	✓	✓	✓	✓
2.1			✓		✓	✓	✓	✓	✓	✓	✓	✓	✓
2.2		✓	✓	✓	✓	✓	✓	✓	✓	✓	✓	✓	✓
2.3		✓	✓	✓	✓	✓	✓	✓	✓	✓	✓	✓	✓

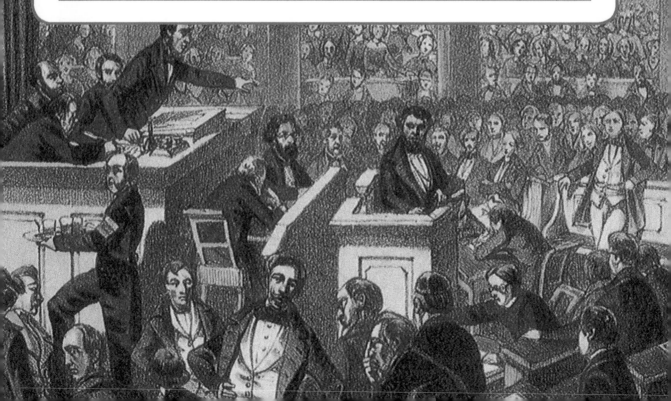

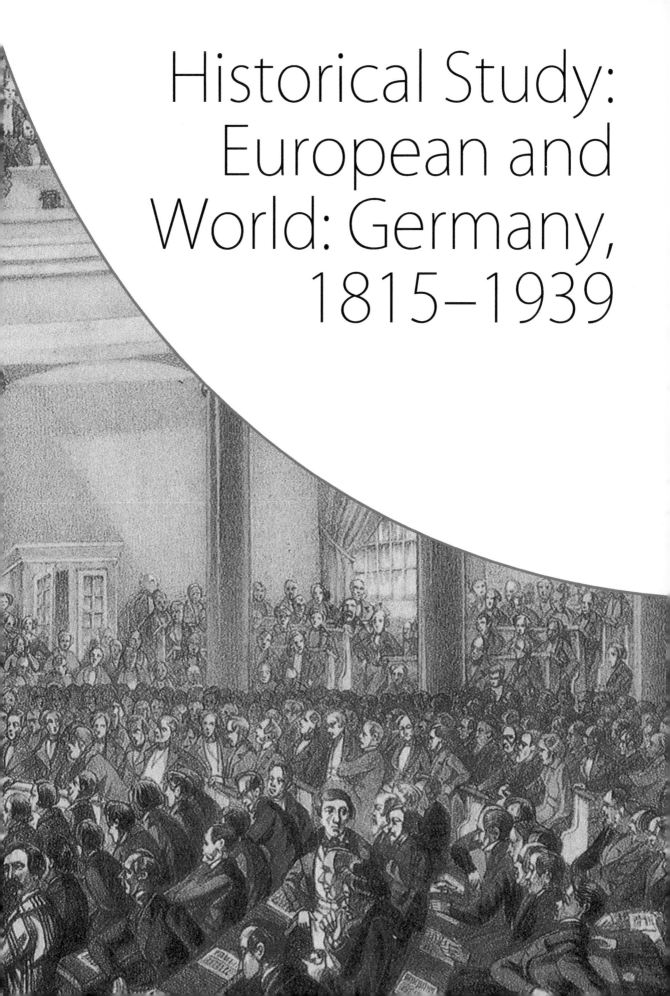

Historical Study: European and World: Germany, 1815–1939

Background

Figure 1: *The Brandenburg Gate is a symbol of peace but also of German nationalism.*

📖 Historiography

'The history of the Germans is the history of extremes. It contains everything except moderation, and in the course of a thousand years the Germans have experienced everything except normality'.

A.J.P. Taylor, The Course of German History

This quote from historian A.J.P. Taylor was written in 1945 when feelings were running high after the end of the Second World War. He points out that, from the growth of German nationalism throughout the nineteenth century to the period Germany was controlled by the fascist politics of the Nazi Party, it would be a fair assessment that Germany experienced an extreme amount of change in a relatively short period of time.

Before 1815 Germany did not exist. At the start of the nineteenth century, what became Germany in 1871 actually comprised about 400 small states, the rulers of which had no intention of uniting them as one country. Before unification the states were ruled under the Holy Roman Empire.

🔍 Hint

The French writer Voltaire famously said that 'the Holy Roman Empire was neither Holy, nor Roman, nor an Empire'. Instead, it was essentially a system of government whereby the aristocracy ruled areas of land and controlled the peasants on that land. Austria-Hungary traditionally had overlordship of the German states.

 Make the Link

If you studied the Wars of Independence, you will have learned about the effect of England's overlordship of Scotland in the late thirteenth and early fourteenth centuries.

The French Revolution was the key starting point for the rise of nationalism in Germany, with events in France in 1789 highlighting the power of the peasants in rebelling against the oppression of the ruling classes.

When Napoleon took over the individual states in 1806 he radically reduced the state numbers and established the Confederation of the Rhine. (It should be noted, however, that the state of Prussia, which would be a key player in the movement towards German unification, did not join the Confederation.) The states were forced to operate under one system, the Code Napoleon, which demonstrated some of the benefits of unifying under law. Nevertheless, the rulers of the individual states had no desire to see unification and so the states would remain separate until 1871, when a number of different social, economic and political factors drew them together.

Otto von Bismarck is often credited as being the man who finally drew the German states together in unification although there is debate over whether he alone can be credited for the creation of Germany. Bismarck's role of Chancellor and the leadership of Kaiser Wilhelm I boosted Germany's economic and political status in Europe. However, when Wilhelm I was replaced with his son, Wilhelm II, Germany became more imperial in its outlook and nations like France and Britain began to worry that Germany wanted to start a European war.

Germany's role in the First World War and treatment thereafter is well documented. They were forced to sign the Treaty of Versailles which sought to punish them severely for starting the war. The reparations clause had an overall detrimental effect on the German economy and plunged Germany not once, but twice, into a state of economic turmoil that may have given Adolf Hitler the platform he needed to rise to the top.

Economic reasons, along with social and political reasons such as the weaknesses of the new democratic system installed after the First World War, allowed for the rise of the Nazis. Once in power, Hitler set about changing the course of German history, and indeed world history, forever. He sought to revise the Treaty of Versailles, modernise Germany and create a totalitarian state. This meant he had to get rid of opposition and control people's lives with fear. The Nazi Party were a party of extremes who were willing to put people to death should they rebel against the system. They created a web of fear and lies that, along with their effective propaganda and threat of concentration camps, allowed them to maintain power in Germany for so long. It is estimated that, in total, somewhere between 65 and 85 million people died as a result of the Second World War, including the six million Jews murdered as part of the Nazis' ethnic cleansing programme during the Holocaust.

Hint

The French Revolution was when the peasants in France rebelled because the monarchy requested them to pay more tax when the economy and their livelihoods were already in crisis.

GO! Activity 1

1. Get into groups of about four or five people.
2. Take a piece of A3 poster paper and write 'German history is a history of extremes' in the middle.
3. Take 15 minutes and take points from the passage above that you think will be important to you during your study of German history. Do you agree with AJP Taylor that the 'history of the Germans is the History of extremes?' Can you think of any other nations who have experienced extreme events within their history?
4. Number the points in order of significance.
5. Share with the rest of the class your top three points. Did you all highlight the same points? Which point is deemed the most important for a discussion about German history?

(Higher European and World unit outcomes: 1.1)

1

An evaluation of the reasons for the growth of nationalism in Germany, 1815–50

In this section you will learn about:

- The effects of the French Revolution and Napoleonic Wars.
- Military weaknesses.
- The role of the Liberals.
- Cultural factors.
- Economic factors.

In 1789 the German states, which numbered around 400, were ruled by an ancient system where peasants were tied to the land and the ruler of that land controlled what they did. Rulers controlled smaller areas of land not always connected to each other and enjoyed being the aristocrats or princes of these individual states. Nationalism, even if it existed as a concept, was ignored by the princes and was certainly not in the consciousness of the peasants. It would take the actions of another country, France, before nationalism was on the agenda in the German states.

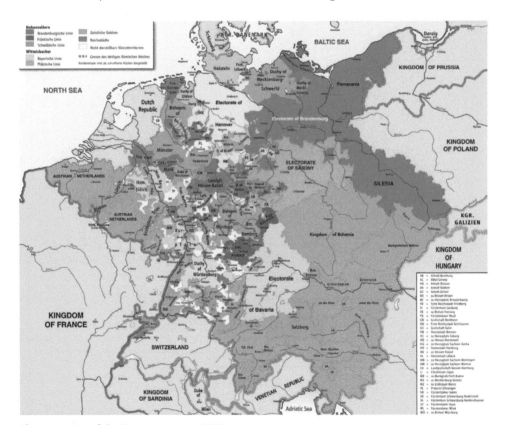

Figure 2: *Map of the German states in 1789.*

The effects of the French Revolution and Napoleonic Wars

Figure 3: *'Liberty Leading the People' by Eugene Delacroix, 1830 – a popular image depicting the ideas behind the French Revolution.*

In 1789 the French Revolution broke out. The people of France rose up and attempted to claim their social and political freedom. There was greater desire for democracy. In 1792 the French king, Louis XVI, was beheaded by the guillotine and a republic declared. Napoleon Bonaparte emerged as the leader of France and, seeking to expand his French 'Empire' to the east, looked towards the German states. This was alarming to those in the old order for many reasons. With the abolition of the monarchy in the French Revolution the autocrats of the German states panicked about their own positions. They worried about the German peasants – they too could revolt against their leaders. When Napoleon invaded the German states he caused a rise in feelings of German nationalism. The states may not have been united physically but they were united in one thing – they were not French.

In 1806 Napoleon decreased the number of states to 38 and established the Confederation of the Rhine. This made the states easier to govern and also showed their inhabitants the benefits of being more united. Napoleon introduced the Code Napoleon to his 'Empire', which replaced the old feudal laws of the Holy Roman Empire and unified the states in the way that they were governed and legislated. Even after Napoleon's defeat in 1815 at the Battle of Waterloo the Code Napoleon was influential in shaping the way the states would be governed.

📖 Historiography

'The [French] Revolution … highlighted the startling contrast between the breathtaking modernity of France … and Germany still mired in the swamplands of feudal absolutism.'

Rebecca Comay

Historian Hagen Schulze states that 'the real father of the German nation was more probably Napoleon'.

Military weaknesses

Figure 4: *This map shows the details of the new distribution of national boundaries in Europe after the Napoleonic Wars in 1815.*

While the occupation by Napoleon undeniably drew the states closer together, the invasion also highlighted how weak they were militarily. For example, the Prussian army suffered great defeats at the hands of the French in 1806 at Jena and Auerstedt. Individually, the states did not have the strength to fight the power of France and their military weaknesses forced them to unite their fighting forces.

Hagen Schulze refers to the defeat of the Prussian army in 1806: 'This catastrophe was the first spark which set German nationalism alight'.

The states, however, lacked professional soldiers. Most of the soldiers who fought against the French occupation were volunteers and it was from these volunteer soldiers that the idea of defending the 'fatherland' arose. There were many songs and poems written and recited by members of the volunteer army which demonstrated the idea that they were fighting for the common cause of German liberty. There was also a growing awareness of their shared common culture, heritage and language, which promoted feelings of German nationalism. Poet Ernst Moritz Arndt wrote in 1813:

Is it Prussia? Is it Swabia?

Is it along the Rhine where the vine resides?

Is it along the belt where the seagull glides?

O no! No! No!

His Fatherland must be greater still.

After Napoleon's defeat in the east in 1813, the Confederation of the Rhine collapsed and the German states again joined forces to fight against France. However, it still took the might of Britain, Russia, Prussia, and Austria to defeat France in 1815. This showed that, even working together, the states would always be reliant on foreign help should their status be threatened by foreign countries. This fuelled the growth of nationalism in Germany as it was felt that if they fought as one united country, they would be stronger.

📖 Historiography

Leighton James points out that many of the states were actually able to take advantage of the war and profit from selling food and supplies to soldiers. He also writes that the people of the states were excited by the mobilisation of state troops against the French and supported each other in the 'German' fight for liberation.

The role of the Liberals

The Enlightenment had swept through Europe in the late eighteenth century bringing with it ideas of rational thought, liberalism and democracy. Some thinkers tried to advance ideas of democracy and liberalism throughout Germany. Universities were steeped in ideas of nationalism and Johann Fichte put forward the idea in 1807 in his 'Addresses to the German Nation' that the German states were united by a common heritage and language and that, as such, Germany should exist as one united and distinct country and conduct its own government and affairs. In the 1830s, the symbol of

Figure 5: *Drawing of Johann Fichte, prominent Liberal thinker and German nationalist.*

German liberalism became the black, red and gold colours, later to be used in the German flag. In short, nationalist fervour was certainly present among the middle classes and university students of Germany before 1850.

📖 Historiography

'Thinkers had started to talk of a "Germany" towards the end of the eighteenth century. When the settlement of 1815 made few concessions to liberal and nationalist demands, these demands intensified.

Cameron, Henderson and Robertson

Cultural factors

Make the Link

You may have played music by Beethoven if you have studied Music, or play an instrument.

University thinkers helped to tap into a 'cultural nationalism' in Germany: the idea of *Volkstum* – that Germans were united by a common heritage and history. Writers such as Schiller and Goethe recognised the common characteristics of Germans at the turn of the nineteenth century and the Brothers Grimm highlighted German heritage with their fairy tales first published in 1812. Music also boosted the growth of nationalism with German composers like Ludwig Van Beethoven dedicating elements of his music to German pride. In the last movement of Beethoven's 6th symphony, first performed in 1808, the music symbolises peasants gathering crops during harvest. Although a subtle comment, Beethoven is acknowledging the peasant class and possibly their potential for political power in a united Germany.

📖 Historiography

'German identity was first and foremost wholly one of language and culture ... the enormous wave of new books and new editions ... all created a new sort of critical enquiring public.'

Hagen Schulze

🔍 Hint

'Deutschland über alles' was a popular song written in 1841 and highlights the nationalistic fervour of the time. It became the official national anthem of Germany in 1922.

Deutschland, Deutschland über alles über alles in der Welt

Germany, Germany above all, above everything in the World

Economic factors

Economic factors were a driving force behind the growth of German nationalism. The German states experienced rapid industrialisation during the latter half of the eighteenth and early nineteenth century. Between 1815 and 1855 the German population grew by over 50%. There were plenty of natural resources that could be exploited, like coal and iron, but the lack of unity between the states made this difficult to do. Nevertheless, coal production increased and by 1850 the Ruhr region in Germany was producing 2 million tons of coal a year. Prussia controlled the western Rhineland states in Germany and it may have been the geographical distance between Prussia in the east and their control of industrialisation in the west that encouraged feelings of nationalism and unity – it would surely be easier for Germany to industrialise more quickly if production could be organised on a larger, more unified scale. German economist Friedrich List commented that he could not look at 'the astonishing effects of railways in England and North America without wishing that my German fatherland would partake of the same benefits ... The German nation cannot be complete as long as it does not extend over the whole coast.' To help with the transportation of goods, Prussia laid many new roads to link Berlin with the west. Five thousand kilometres of railway had been laid by 1850 which, as the historian William Carr points out (below), united Germany economically but also politically.

📖 Historiography

'Railways were of great political significance. They helped to break down provincial barriers, brought town and country nearer together and underlined the need for national unification.'
William Carr

The importance of the railways cannot be exaggerated when discussing the growth of nationalism. Railways meant that people could travel and communicate with people in neighbouring towns or cities. Communities were no longer insular and were connected by a commonality of language and heritage.

Another economic factor to be considered is the creation, in 1819, of Prussia's own customs union, known as the Zollverein. Prior to this, when Prussia wished to trade with another state it would have to pay a tariff (tax) to do so. As there were many different states ruled by many different leaders, trading new industrial goods could be very expensive. To reduce costs, especially because it controlled land in the west, Prussia founded the Zollverein. Internal tariffs were eliminated and import duties were significantly reduced. For the 25 out of the 39 states that joined the Zollverein, the economic benefits were obvious – they would keep more of the profit from sale of goods. The Zollverein was not the only customs union – there was another in the mid-German states and one in the south-German states. These states had started their own because they did not like Prussian control of the Zollverein. However, both were unsuccessful and the states eventually joined the Zollverein anyway. Austria made a point of staying out of the Zollverein and, despite its wish to maintain control over the German states, found itself both economically and politically isolated when it did not join the union. The Zollverein established Prussia as the dominant economic leader in Germany. In addition, it also meant that Prussia gained a significant amount of political power.

The benefits they felt from an economic union, for example from the elimination of tariffs, encouraged greater feelings of nationalism throughout the German states.

Make the Link

If you study Britain, 1851–1951, you will learn about the political impact of the industrial revolution in this country.

Make the Link

If you study Business Management or Economics you may learn more about trade and taxes.

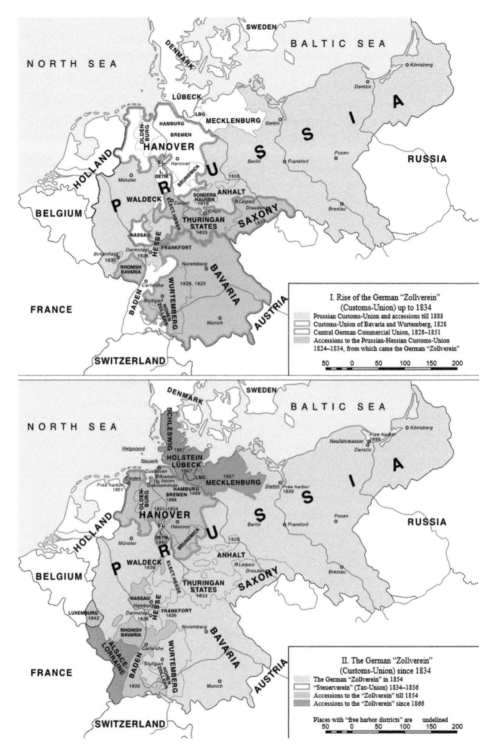

Figure 6: *The maps above show the development of the Zollverein up to 1834 and then from 1834–1866. Note the increase in Prussian control.*

📖 Historiography
_____

Historian William Carr debates the idea of whether Prussia set out to change the political status of the German states through its economic change. 'Certainly Prussia was not thinking in terms of political unification when she founded the Customs Union. Nor had the states joined it out of love for Prussia but simply and solely to escape from the financial and economic difficulties which beset them.'

Nevertheless, he still states that the Zollverein could be considered 'the mighty lever of unification', showing the importance of the customs union in advancing feelings of nationalism in Germany.

Historian Andrina Stiles disagrees with Carr to an extent and states that the success of the Zollverein meant that the other German states looked to Prussia as their political as well as economic leader. She says 'The Zollverein was a force for union in the 1840s and therefore a focal point for nationalist sentiments. As a result Prussia … came to be regarded by many as the natural leader of a united Germany'.

GO! **Activity 2**

Get into groups of five. Each person should take a factor from the following table. On a piece of A3 paper, mind map the key points for your factor, evaluate the arguments for the growth of nationalism and provide at least one piece of historiography. You could do further research online or in the school library. Once you have completed your mind map, your group will have created a comprehensive picture of the reasons for the growth of nationalism.

Factor	Key points	Evaluate the arguments FOR the growth of nationalism	Historiography
French Revolution and Napoleonic Wars			
Military weaknesses			
Role of the Liberals			
Cultural factors			
Economic factors	• The Zollverein was a customs union which meant participating states could trade with each other without high tariffs.	• This showed that the states would benefit economically from working together, increasing feelings of German nationalism.	• Stiles says the Zollverein was a focal point for nationalist sentiments.

(Higher European and World unit outcomes: 1.1, 2.2, 2.3)

GO! Activity 3

Exam style questions

Choose one of the following essay questions:

Evaluate the reasons for the growth of nationalism in Germany between 1815 and 1850. (22)

Or

'Economic factors were the most significant reason for the growth of nationalism in Germany between 1815 and 1850.' How valid is this view? (22)

For your chosen question, you must write a well-structured essay.

a) Write a practice introduction following the success criteria below:

1. Address the question.
2. Outline the key factors and arguments which you will address in the development section of your essay.
3. Give a line of enquiry (an overall 'thought' or 'argument' to drive your essay).

(Higher European and World unit outcomes: 1.1)

b) Write up the paragraphs to the main section of your essay. Use your completed table from Activity 2 to help you – the sections/headings of the table should correspond to the sections of your essay.

(Higher European and World unit outcomes: 1.1, 2.1, 2.2, 2.3)

c) Write a practice conclusion. You should effectively summarise the key ARGUMENTS you discussed in the main section of your essay to help you come to a justified conclusion – answer the question!

(Higher European and World unit outcomes: 1.2, 1.3)

d) Now practise writing your essay under timed conditions. You have 45 minutes to write up your essay!

> ### 🔎 Hint
>
> If you are completing the 'Economic factors' essay you MUST address economic factors first as this is the ISOLATED FACTOR in the question.
>
> You should also focus on ANALYSING the issue – did these factors help the growth of nationalism? Is there any HISTORIOGRAPHY you could include to support your own thoughts or show a different school of thought?

2 An assessment of the degree of growth of nationalism in Germany, up to 1850

In this section you will learn about:

- Supporters of nationalism: the Liberals and the educated middle class.
- Opponents of nationalism.
- Political turmoil in the 1840s.
- The Frankfurt Parliament.
- The collapse of revolution in Germany, 1848–49.

Supporters of nationalism: the Liberals and the educated middle class

Figure 7: *A photograph of Leipzig University in the late nineteenth century, where Johann Fichte debated nationalist ideas.*

As we have seen, there were many influential thinkers around in the early nineteenth century who advocated a united Germany and highlighted the common characteristics of the German states such as language, culture and heritage. However, those who attended the universities were from the new middle classes. Teachings about nationalism only met a selected audience and protests about nationalism would largely rely on the middle-class population. The upper classes had no real interest in nationalism – they wanted to conserve the individual powers they had over their individual states. The music of

157

Make the Link

In Modern Studies you may learn about the effect of class on political engagement in Britain today.

the Romantic Movement and the writings of authors like Hegel, Schiller and Goethe would also have only reached a limited audience – only certain people would be able to read and write or attend musical recitals. Therefore, nationalist sentiment was certainly present among the middle classes but a sense of national awareness probably less so among the peasant class of the German states.

📖 Historiography

Historian Hagen Schulze states that the rise of Liberalism was not unique to Germany but was in fact a pan-European phenomenon that had begun to filter throughout the social classes and was no longer a reserve of the educated elite.

Figure 8: *A painting of German peasants farming the land from the sixteenth century. Not much had changed for peasants in terms of status and job opportunities by the nineteenth century.*

Make the Link

In Geography you will learn about the lives of farmers in developing countries around the world today.

Another group to be considered as a supporter, to a certain extent, of nationalism is the peasants in the German states. Peasants made up the bulk of the population in Germany. They led traditional lives and lived in farming communities. In the eastern states they were still bound by the laws of the Holy Roman Empire and had the status of serfs – they were bound to the land and indebted to the landowners. Few peasants could read or write and most had very little formal education.

📖 Historiography

German historian Golo Mann wrote that the peasants 'seldom looked up from the plough'.

Peasants had little opportunity to become involved in the debate about German nationalism and are unlikely to have been involved in the cultural movements surrounding it. Therefore, historians agree that their contribution to the rise of nationalism in Germany is minimal. However, it is also acknowledged that the peasants were a body of untapped 'potential' and they could be a powerful force for change if their national consciousness could be awakened.

However, as the nineteenth century progressed, peasants left the land in increasing numbers to find jobs in the new industrial towns. Technological changes in agriculture meant there was not such a reliance on human labour. Land distribution also changed – many peasants were pressured into combining their lands into larger farms to allow the landowners to make more money by farming on a larger scale. Many peasants disliked their rulers for these changes. An increased demand for food in the towns also put pressure on the ruling classes. The peasants began to realise they had power in numbers and could instigate political unrest.

> **🔍 Hint**
>
> The changes on the land were similar to the issues that had driven the French Revolution. State leaders were well aware of the potential power of the peasants.

Opponents of nationalism

At the Congress of Vienna in 1815 Britain, Russia, Austria and Prussia, the powers who had defeated Napoleon, reorganised Europe and Germany. Plans were put into effect to reorganise Germany to establish a balance of power whereby no individual could gain too much power. The re-established network of 39 states was given a new name, 'The German Confederation', known as the Bund. Many of the old rulers Napoleon had replaced with his own people were returned to power. The Austrian leader, Metternich, who was instrumental in the reorganisation of Europe, was strongly opposed to German nationalism and made sure that the old autocratic leaders of the states returned to govern.

📖 Historiography

'Metternich was the chief architect of the German Confederation. His sole intention was to maintain Austria's domination.'
Michael Gorman

Instead of furthering nationalism, as Ian Mitchell demonstrates, 'The Bund was a means to perpetuate the division of Germany'.

To try to quash any ideas of nationalism among the states, Metternich introduced the Carlsbad decrees. These were introduced in 1819 after a conference held in Carlsbad. They banned nationalist groups (the Burschenschaften) and gave power to remove university professors who promoted nationalism, as well as increasing press censorship.

Figure 9: *A cartoon from the time making fun of the Carlsbad decrees. The sign behind the table says: 'Important question to be considered in today's meeting: "How long will we be allowed to think?"'*

Political turmoil in the 1840s

The industrial and agricultural revolution in Germany brought about many economic, social and political changes. As the work in the towns and cities was often done in poor conditions for low pay there was a call for change among the people of the German states. Working conditions in the countryside also worsened. Landowners had increased rents and those who previously worked in a skilled trade, for example cloth makers, found themselves out of jobs as the new steam-powered machinery could create more goods much more cheaply than the craft and guildsmen ever could. This led to an awakened sense of political power among the peasants and working classes. Further, bad harvests in 1846 and 1847 and the spread of the potato blight meant that there was a lack of food to feed a growing population.

📖 Historiography

Historian Hajo Holborn recognises that there was a significant increase in unrest during what he terms the 'hungry years' in Germany in the late 1840s.

Historians debate whether protests were linked to nationalism or, rather, were aimed at better working and living conditions. However, even if the peasants and workers did not consciously campaign on a wave of nationalism, they may have felt that more unity between the states and the people in them would give them a stronger and more united political voice.

📖 Historiography

John Kerr and James McGonigle point out that at this time 'There was no call for democracy, liberalism or nationalism. The workers and peasants simply wanted to be able to survive from day to day and they would support any government that might improve their conditions.'

It is likely that the peasants did not realise their potential for advancing political change in Germany at this time and only campaigned to make their immediate working and living conditions better.

The middle classes wanted to have more power and influence in the governing of the German states. They looked to countries like Britain, where change had already happened with the extension of the franchise in the 1832 Great Reform Act, to give the middle classes more of a political voice.

By the late 1840s, then, there was a hotbed of unrest in Germany, even if the different groups were not united in their aims. The unrest in Germany happened at the same time as other events of political unrest in Europe. There was a general dissatisfaction with the old feudal systems and an increased desire for democracy and participation, particularly from the lower classes. What was happening in Germany was not necessarily unique; ideas of revolution and nationalism rode on a wave of political unrest throughout mainland Europe.

Make the Link

You will learn about the political changes in Britain if you study Britain, 1851–1951 in the British History unit of Higher History.

AN ASSESSMENT OF THE DEGREE OF GROWTH OF NATIONALISM IN GERMANY, UP TO 1850 ●

The Frankfurt Parliament

Proposals for a German Parliament had come about in the February of 1848 as a direct response to the economic and political turmoil – it was an answer to the cry for democracy.

The peasants, after the bad harvests of 1846 and 1847, were looking to their leaders to change their social situation and improve living and working conditions. The middle classes wanted constitutional change, the right to vote and a united parliament. It was said that the rebellion in France against King Louis-Philippe had inspired those in the German states to protest.

The Frankfurt Parliament tried to bring a level of democratic governance to the German states that had not been seen before. After six states, including Prussia, called for a 'German Parliament', 574 delegates from most of the German states met in Frankfurt to try to establish a National Assembly for the whole of Germany. The National Assembly would then work together to write a constitution for governing Germany as one unified state. Representatives were elected to the Frankfurt Parliament and numbered 596 in total. However, most came from academic backgrounds and were well trained in the skill of debate. Anything that was debated in the Parliament took far too long – for instance, it took nine months to come up with a list of fundamental rights for German citizens. The aims of the Frankfurt Parliament were noble and the idea of nationalism was furthered by the aim of drawing up a constitution to rule the German states as one. However, the Frankfurt Parliament could never agree and collapsed because of this indecision.

Figure 10: *This painting by Philipp Veit depicts 'Germania'. It hung in the Frankfurt Parliament and displays the nationalist colours of black, red and gold.*

📖 Historiography

Historian Edgar Feuchtwanger writes of the problems the Liberals had trying to make Germany more democratic: 'The moderate liberals who dominated the Frankfurt parliament had to rely on the existing governments of kings and princes to achieve their dual objective, to unify Germany and to turn it into a constitutional state.'

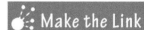 **Make the Link**

In Modern Studies you will learn how new laws pass through the Scottish Parliament.

Figure 11: *This image depicts a meeting of the Frankfurt Parliament in May 1848.*

The collapse of revolution in Germany, 1848–49

As we have seen, the Frankfurt Parliament was created in response to growing social and political unrest in the German states.

Figure 12: *The image above depicts a street battle in Alexanderplatz, Berlin, March 1848.*

However, it has been criticised for not tackling the social problems but, rather, focusing on how to effectively unite the German states. There were two schools of thought on the issue, Grossdeutschland and Kleindeutschland.

Grossdeutschland would involve uniting the German states including Austria. The south German states preferred this option as they saw Austria as their protector. However, Austria was not quite so keen – it had enjoyed having a certain element of power over the states when they operated on a more individual basis, especially as Austria controlled the Bund. If Germany was to unite as one, Austria worried that its power would not last.

Kleindeutschland would involve the uniting of the states without Austria. This was favoured by the northern states and especially Prussia. Prussia had already gained a certain amount of power and economic control with the Zollverein. Austria and the south German states were concerned about growing Prussian dominance.

The Frankfurt Parliament decided on the Kleindeutschland option and to offer the Crown to King Frederick William IV of Prussia. Frederick William had initially offered his support to the Parliament but when the delegates offered him the Crown, he changed his mind. He believed in the divine right of kings and that an elected body should have no say in choosing the monarch of Germany – only God could decide that. He did not wish to have his position as Emperor devalued.

The Frankfurt Parliament also lacked any kind of real power as it did not have an army to enforce any laws it passed. It relied heavily on the army of Prussia but Frederick William largely ignored what the Frankfurt Parliament wanted it to do.

Ultimately, the revolutions of 1848–49 in Germany failed. The protesters could not decide on a united aim – the peasants largely wanted social change and the nationalists wanted constitutional change and a united Germany. Any revolutionary behaviour that did take place was easily quashed – in fact most protests were quite peaceful. Continued arguments over whether Germany was to be Grossdeutschland or Kleindeutschland also made it difficult to move forward and the Parliament lacked a strong leader. The lack of cooperation from leaders including Frederick William of Prussia meant the Parliament could not really move forward without support for a united Germany.

🔍 Hint

The Prussian army had begun to invest a lot of money into modernising in the 1840s.

📖 Historiography

Erich Eyck wrote 'the German revolution of 1848 had failed in practice. Nevertheless it had not been in vain. It was a step forward which could not be undone completely … Although the first parliament of the whole German people had failed, the organisation of Germany without a German parliament was henceforth out of the question.'

To a certain extent, William Carr agrees: '… the Revolution in Germany had positive as well as negative aspects. It marked the entry of the German people in to the political life of the nation … The Revolution also helped to clarify political attitudes and encouraged the formation of political associations, the forerunners of modern political parties.'

As we shall see in the next section, Austria reasserted its control and in 1850 the Bund was re-established. German nationalism, again, had one of its greatest obstacles placed firmly back in its way.

GO! Activity 4

In pairs, take a piece of A3 paper. On one side, create a mind map with the following heading at the centre:

Degree of the growth of nationalism by 1850: KNOWLEDGE AND UNDERSTANDING

Following the headings in this section, construct a mind map making sure you have the relevant key knowledge and understanding points written under each heading.

HEADINGS:

1. Supporters of nationalism.
2. Opponents of nationalism.
3. Political turmoil in the 1840s.
4. The Frankfurt Parliament.
5. The collapse of revolution in Germany, 1848–49.

Now swap your work with another pair. Add in any extra information the other pair may have missed and then return their sheet to them.

(Higher European and World unit outcomes: 1.1, 2.2)

Now, turn over your piece of paper. In pairs again, create another mind map with the following heading in the centre:

Degree of the growth of nationalism by 1850: ANALYSIS AND HISTORIOGRAPHY

Under each of the headings listed above, analyse arguments for/against the growth of nationalism. Remember, you can offer more than one opinion.

Use a different coloured pen to add some historiography to support your analysis. Again, if you can find more than one point of view this will add to the quality of debate in your work.

(Higher European and World unit outcomes: 2.2, 2.3)

GO! Activity 5

Exam style questions

'By 1850 political nationalism had made little progress in Germany.' How valid is this view?   **(22)**

(Higher European and World unit outcomes: 1.1, 1.2, 1.3, 2.1, 2.2, 2.3)

3 An evaluation of the obstacles to German unification, 1815–50

In this section you will learn about:

- Divisions among the nationalists and the German princes.
- Austrian strength.
- Religious differences.
- Economic differences.
- Indifference of the masses.

Divisions among the nationalists and the German princes

The barriers to German unification were numerous, largely because the individual states had their own particular rules and customs. Even the nationalists could not decide on the best way to unite Germany. The extreme left favoured unity with Austria, thinking that the Austrians would offer the German states better military protection than if they went it alone. The centre groups did not want Austria included in unification, concerned that the Austrians would dominate the German states with their own agenda.

Each state was sovereign in its own right, although sometimes princes ruled more than one state, quite often at a significant geographical distance from each other. The leaders of the German states obstructed unification; they wished to maintain the status quo.

In the western states, the peasants had moved to the towns and participated in the industrial revolution. In the east the peasants were treated more like serfs, being tied to the land and indebted to their prince. The German princes liked their autonomy and did not want the states to unify as they would lose both their land and their authority. They supported the Bund and its policy of crushing nationalist activity. Until the old order could be changed, then, it would be difficult to unite the German states.

🔍 Hint

Sovereign rule means 'authority rule'. Each prince ruled their land how they wanted which meant that the laws governing the states differed from state to state.

⁙ Make the Link

In the USA each state has different laws. You may learn more about this in Modern Studies.

📖 Historiography

Frank B. Tipton argues that the princes enjoyed having power over their subjects and even enjoyed playing the larger and more powerful states, like Prussia and Austria, off against each other. Until the individual states could work together, there would be no unity.

Resentment towards Prussia was undeniably a barrier to unification. Austria and the Bund were the most concerned about Prussian dominance especially after 1840 when the Zollverein was such a success.

📖 Historiography

'The Zollverein drew the German states together and stimulated their economic growth, at the same time firmly establishing Prussia as the economic leader in Germany … by 1840 they [Prussia] could see its potential and exploited it fully.'

Cameron, Henderson and Robertson

Figure 13: Portrait of Frederick William IV, King of Prussia from 1840 to 1861.

Resentment towards Prussia was not confined to some of the German states and Austria. France, for example, was concerned with the growing strength of Prussia because of Prussian control of the Rhineland, which had been under French control until 1815. Not only was the Rhineland rich in natural resources that could be exploited by Prussia, but also Prussian presence halted any future French expansion into the German states.

Austrian strength

One of the main barriers to unification from 1815 to 1850 was the strength of Austria. The states within Germany had traditionally been ruled by the Austrian Empire under the Holy Roman Empire.

📖 Historiography

Finlay McKichan points out that Austria 'could not afford to encourage nationalism by permitting the unification of Germany'.

When the Bund was established after the Congress of Vienna, the chairmanship had been given to Austria on a permanent basis. Metternich, the Chancellor of Austria, had used the Bund and the Carlsbad decrees specifically to quash any ideas of nationalism and liberalism. Worried that talk of nationalism might lead to revolution, Metternich used force to keep the nationalists in check and created a network of spies and informers to inform him of any nationalist activity. The press was censored to stop nationalist ideas from being put in print. The aim was to preserve the Austrian Empire at all costs.

However, historians debate as to how effective Metternich's 'police state' actually was. For one thing, the Austrian Empire, including the German states, was vast and hard to police. Although arrests were made, it would seem that nationalists were still able to operate without much trouble from Metternich's men. Ironically, Metternich's implementation of repressive policies actually helped create the very situation that he was trying to prevent and was one of the causes of the

Figure 14: Metternich, Chancellor of Austria.

1848 revolution. The failure of the Frankfurt Parliament re-established Austrian strength. There were two more attempts after Frankfurt (Erfurt and Olmutz) to try to unify Germany but they only served to boost Austrian strength further.

The Erfurt Union

After the Frankfurt Parliament collapsed Prussia again proposed a union of the states under their leadership (the Erfurt Union). Frederick William IV had a constitution drawn up and elections were held. The Parliament met at Erfurt but Frederick William soon seemed to lose confidence and distanced himself from supporting it. Austria, ever concerned about Prussian dominance of the other states, did not actively take part in the Erfurt Parliament. They also had their own worries over threats of revolution in Austria at the time. However, once this threat subsided, Austria took control of the Erfurt Parliament by proposing that the Bund be re-established. In May 1850 the Bund met in Frankfurt without Prussia and her supporting states.

The meeting at Olmutz

Figure 15: *The meeting at Olmutz in November 1850.*

Prussia was further isolated with the 'humiliation of Olmutz'. This was prompted by the Parliament of the German state of Hesse-Cassel refusing to collect taxes for its monarch. As the Bund were happy to halt this rebellion, the Parliament looked to Prussia for help. Prussia faced a difficult situation – it did not want Hesse-Cassel to be put down by the Bund but neither could it fight, as its army was not strong enough. Prussian and Austrian officials met at Olmutz in November 1850. It was agreed that the Bund would re-establish itself as it had been before 1848, with Prussia being included, and be allowed to sort out the problems with Hesse-Cassel. The Erfurt Union was disbanded, any ideas of Prussian dominance well and truly thwarted and German nationalism halted in its tracks.

📖 Historiography

'With the Confederation [the Bund] restored, the heavy hand of autocracy descended on Germany once more.'

William Carr

Religious differences

Religious differences among the German states formed another barrier to German unification. The northern states had reformed to Protestantism but the southern states largely remained Catholic. This meant that the northern German states looked to Protestant Prussia as their natural leader and the southern states looked to Catholic Austria. These religious differences also perpetuated the Gross/Kleindeutschland argument. Since no one could decide on what was meant by 'Germany', it made unification difficult.

📖 Historiography

'Central Europe was divided by deep confessional gulfs, since the conflict between Reformation and Counter Reformation had not been resolved in Germany, unlike most of the other European states.'

Hagen Schulze

Figure 16: *The teachings of Martin Luther led to the Reformation, after which most of the northern German states were Protestant.*

⚗ Make the Link

You will learn about the different denominations of Christianity if you take RMPS.

Economic differences

Some of the German states, for example Prussia, industrialised rapidly. This led to an imbalance of economic power among the states. Prussia also controlled the Rhineland, an area rich in natural resources. This meant it had goods to trade and access to materials such as coal and iron. Austria, on the other hand, did not have access to such rich resources. It was clear that, with its economic power and control of the Zollverein, Prussia was emerging as the economic leader of the German states.

📖 Historiography

Ian Mitchell points out that 'the Zollverein had the inadvertent effect of greatly hastening Prussia's economic development, and of increasing still further the power of Prussia against Austria in Germany'.

However, it must be remembered that, although 25 states joined the Zollverein, 14 did not. Not every state was happy with the economic dominance of Prussia, and especially not Austria. Austria was not allowed to join the Zollverein and was concerned about Prussian influence over those states that had joined. This would have been a good reason why Austria was so determined to maintain the Bund – to keep Prussian power firmly under control.

Indifference of the masses

Historians debate how much consideration the mass of the population would have given to German unification. The peasants and the working classes were certainly large in number in Germany and would have had the numerical clout to make a difference. However, they themselves acted as a barrier towards unification because of their indifference. Any protests they took part in, like those of 1848, were more about social justice than about moving Germany towards unification. Most peasants and workers would have had little or no access to education, meaning that the ideas of the nationalists and the works of the writers and the poets simply would not have reached the largest audience in the German states. Thus, one of the greatest barriers to unification was that it did not have popular support – not because the arguments for unification were disliked but because they were unknown.

GO! Activity 6

1. Summarise the key points from each of the headings in this section, making sure you DESCRIBE the reasons why there were barriers to unification and EXPLAIN why the reasons were important.

   (Higher European and World unit outcomes: 1.1, 2.1)

2. With a partner, you now need to analyse how important the reasons you have written down are. Try to show connections between the relevant factors and debate different interpretations of the different factors (use historiography here!).

   (Higher European and World unit outcomes: 2.2, 2.3)

3. With your class, discuss why you think there were barriers to German unification. Write up your ideas and display them where everyone can see them. Can everyone give a suitable justification for their reason?

   Using the reasons you have debated, write a short answer to the following question:

   Do you agree that Austria posed the main barrier to German unification?

   (Higher European and World unit outcomes: 1.2, 1.3)

   Now try the question in Activity 7 under timed conditions.

GO! Activity 7

Exam style questions

'Austrian strength was the greatest obstacle to German nationalism between 1815 and 1850.'
How valid is this view?   (22)

(Higher European and World unit outcomes: 1.1, 1.2, 1.3, 2.1, 2.2, 2.3)

4 An evaluation of the reasons why unification was achieved in Germany by 1871

In this section you will learn about:

- The role of Bismarck.
- The decline of Austria.
- The role of other countries.
- Prussian military strength.
- Prussian economic strength.

The role of Bismarck

Otto von Bismarck is a hugely important figure in the history of German unification – indeed, it is often debated whether Germany could have unified without him. Bismarck was from Prussia and had been born to a Junker family.

He had a good understanding of the way politics and sovereignty worked in the German states and remained very loyal to the state of Prussia. Despite being labelled as the 'architect of German unification', it is debateable whether he actually set out to achieve unification or if he wanted instead to further Prussian dominance over the other states. Either way, he was one of the instrumental factors in explaining why German unification was achieved by 1871.

📖 Historiography

'Bismarck did not fashion German unity alone. He exploited powerful forces that already existed; the industrial revolution in Germany, the growth of liberalism and German nationalism.'

D.G. Williamson

Figure 17: *Otto von Bismarck.*

🔍 Hint

Junker families were part of the land-owning classes of Germany. They tended to be quite conservative in their political outlook and upheld the traditional system of monarchy.

Bismarck was a conservative. He had been Prussia's representative in the Bund and had opposed the Frankfurt Parliament and 1848 revolutions, in support of Frederick William IV. He wanted to secure Prussian power at the expense of Austria but also saw the need to wait until opportunities arose:

> Prussia must gather and consolidate her strength in readiness for the favourable moment, which has already been missed several times. Prussia's boundaries … are not favourable to a healthy political life: not by means of speeches and majority verdicts will the great decisions of the time be made – that was the great mistake of 1848 and 1849 – but by iron and blood. (Bismarck)

In this speech, Bismarck is saying that he feels the revolutions of 1848 and 1849 would never have been able to change things by protest alone and that there must be more 'action' taken to expand Prussian dominance over the other territories in Germany. Only then would the political situation in Germany also change for the better.

Between 1861 and 1871 Bismarck was to unite Germany on his own terms by exploiting favourable opportunities and isolating opponents like Austria.

Historiography

Historians have often said that Bismarck was a supreme realist and exploiter of events.

Bismarck first rose to prominence in 1862 when he was made Minister-President of Prussia. He was drafted in because of an internal conflict between King William I and the Liberals in the Prussian Parliament. William had introduced proposals for the reform of the Prussian army in 1861, having been concerned about recurring issues related to Prussia's military weakness, their inability to fight at Olmutz in 1850 against Austria being a prime example. As we have seen, this had resulted in Prussia accepting Austrian rule and its re-establishment as the head of the Bund. William's proposals included raising taxes, modernising the army and abolishing the Landwehr (part-time soldiers who were Liberal supporters). The majority Liberal Parliament were against this and the Prussian Constitution of 1848 did not allow the king to spend taxes without the approval of the Parliament. Bismarck was brought in to break the deadlock between the Liberals and the king. Bismarck proposed that, because the Parliament was refusing to pass the budget, the king would have to rule by himself. The deadlock was broken because the Liberals realised they could not defy the monarchy and the army reforms were passed.

Historiography

'Bismarck succeeded in taming parliament.'

Theodore Hamerow

Bismarck's methods became known as Realpolitik. This meant that he would do what was necessary to achieve his aims, even if it was not necessarily morally correct. An example of this would be seen in Bismarck's first opportunity to secure Prussian power over the other German states in the Schleswig-Holstein crisis.

Schleswig and Holstein were two duchies that lay south of Denmark and north of Prussia. There had been a long-standing argument whether the duchies were Danish or German. In fact, by the 1852 Treaty of London they were both autonomous.

However, in 1863 Christian IX of Denmark tried to incorporate Schleswig into Denmark. The Duke of Augustenburg, the ruler of Schleswig-Holstein, appealed to Prussia for help. Bismarck saw an ideal opportunity not only to claim both the duchies for Prussia but also to isolate Austria at a later date. However, he would have to employ Realpolitik and dupe Austria into helping him in the short term. He persuaded Austria to help him fight against Denmark and a joint Austro-Prussian invasion of the duchies took place. The Danes lost but rather than allow Schleswig-Holstein to maintain their autonomy, Bismarck took Schleswig under Prussian rule and awarded Holstein to Austria by the Convention of Gastein in 1865. However, Bismarck had no intention of allowing Austria to maintain control over Holstein. It was part of his grander plan to weaken Austria.

The decline of Austria

In 1866 Bismark negotiated an alliance with Italy to wage war against Austria. In return Italy would gain control of the state of Venetia. Bismarck was confident that neither France nor Russia would come to the aid of Austria if Austria and Prussia were to engage in a war. It was a risky move but, if successful, one that would isolate Austria, enabling further Prussian expansion. Bismarck accused Austria of not administering Holstein properly. Geographically, Holstein was far away from Austria and it was a valid claim to make. It had the desired effect. Austria mobilised its troops against Prussia. Prussia took this as an act of aggression and in June 1866 Prussian forces occupied Holstein and attacked Austria and most of the other German states. The Austrian army were defeated at Sadowa in July 1866.

> ### 🔍 Hint
>
> Autonomous means they had the right to self-rule. Many of the German states were autonomous and this was one of the reasons unification took so long – no leader wanted to give up their right to rule.

Figure 18: *Christian IX of Denmark gave Bismarck his first opportunity to exert Prussian control over two northern states.*

Figure 19: *A painting of a battle scene during the Austro-Prussian War.*

Historiography

Debate continues over whether Bismarck engineered a war with Austria or just took advantage of favourable conditions.

David Thomson writes 'There was no doubt that Bismarck wanted and planned a war against Austria'.

The defeat of Austria changed the momentum of German unification. By the Treaty of Prague, which was signed in August 1866, the Bund was ended and Prussia annexed Schleswig-Holstein, Hanover, Hesse-Cassel, Nassau and Frankfurt along with other states north of the river Main to create the North German Confederation. Bismarck had achieved his aim – isolation of Austria and Prussian control over the north German states.

Historiography

'In the North, Prussia had not unified Germany as much as conquered German territories.'

J.A.S. Grenville

The Gross/Kleindeutschland question had been answered – the Austrian Empire had well and truly been excluded from Germany.

Historiography

Historian Theodore Hamerow points out that although Bismarck may have taken advantage of favourable opportunities, he also felt that some form of German unification was inevitable and it 'ought to be kleindeutsch *in form to the exclusion of Austrian influence'.*

The role of other countries

Defeat of Austria in the Austro-Prussian war sent a shockwave through the southern states who looked to Austria as their protector. Moreover, France was very concerned about the expansion of this new Prussian 'Empire'. Napoleon III demanded compensation for Prussian expansion as he feared a shift in the balance of power in Europe with the growth of a united Germany. Initially, Napoleon demanded control of the southern German states but Bismarck said no – they were to remain independent. He then tried to claim control of Belgium but again Bismarck said no. Napoleon was losing face so tried to purchase the Grand Duchy of Luxemburg from the King of the Netherlands. Bismarck again stepped in and guaranteed Luxemburg's neutrality and so stopped French expansionism. The south German states became concerned about French expansion and looked towards the North German Confederation for protection.

The southern states had started their own Zollverein but this collapsed in 1867 so Bismarck allowed them to join the Zollverein of the North German Confederation. Some people in the south German states were worried that an economic union with Prussia would ultimately lead to a political union so protested this level of Prussian control. Bismarck cleverly gave money to those who supported and promoted unity with the northern states so that by the time war came about with France, he had pretty much secured the support of the south German states.

Historiography

'A war with France breaking out under the right circumstances might well be the catalyst for bringing the South German states to the side of Prussia.'

Edgar Feuchtwanger

Figure 20: *Portrait of Napoleon III.*

Bismarck stated that he 'did not doubt that a Franco-German war must take place before the construction of a united Germany could be realised.' It is debated among historians to what extent this is true. Nevertheless, when another opportunity arose for Bismarck to precipitate a war with France he took full advantage of it.

In 1869 Spain found itself with no heir to the throne. Spain asked Leopold of Hohenzollern to take up the candidature. Hohenzollern was one of the German states and Leopold was a relative of the Prussian Hohenzollern family. Bismarck pushed for Leopold to take the position – he knew it would isolate France as they would have a strong Germany to the east and now a German candidate for the Spanish throne to the south. Perhaps Bismarck hoped it would end up in a conflict in which he could secure the support of the south German states and achieve unification with them.

France was furious when they found out about the Hohenzollern candidate. The French ambassador, Benedetti, visited the King of Prussia, William, to ask him to withdraw the Hohenzollern candidate or face war. William felt extremely threatened and followed the French request. However, when Benedetti again approached William for a guarantee that never again would the Hohenzollern candidate make a claim to the Spanish throne, Bismarck took advantage. He released an edited version of the telegram he had been sent informing him of the situation, making it seem as if the Prussians were insulting the French. This telegram became known as the infamous Ems telegram.

Make the Link

If you studied the Wars of Independence you will have learned about Scotland's own succession problems in the late thirteenth century.

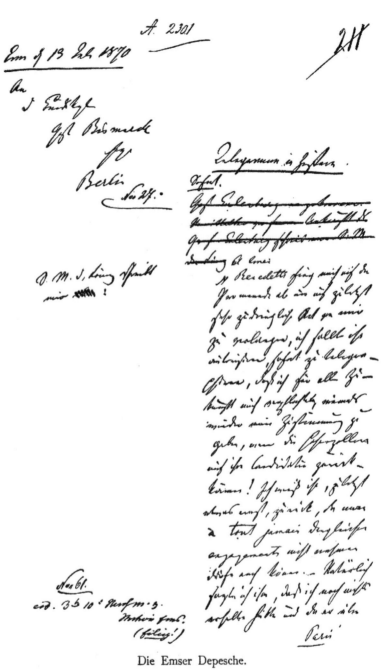

Die Emser Depesche.
1. Das Abekensche Original.

Figure 21: *The Ems telegram.*

Bismarck released the telegram to the press hoping that, in his own words, 'The Ems Telegram should have the desired effect of waving a red cape in front of the face of the Gallic [French] Bull.' He hoped that it would provoke the French into declaring war so that Prussia would not look like the aggressor. Bismarck got his wish. The French declared war and the south German states approached the north German states for protection.

Figure 22: *The Battle of Spicheren, fought during the Franco-Prussian War.*

The Prussians decisively defeated the French army, Napoleon III was overthrown and a new French Republic was established. The new Parliament realised that France could not beat the military might of the Prussian army and the peace treaty was signed in May 1871 in Frankfurt. The French states of Alsace-Lorraine were to be incorporated into Germany. France was to pay an indemnity of £200 million within four years and the Germans were to march through Paris in triumph. The seeds of resentment towards Germany had certainly been sowed among the French.

King William took up his position as German Emperor or Kaiser. Germany had been successfully united.

Prussian military strength

It would be unfair to hand all the credit to Bismarck for uniting Germany. If it had not been for the Prussian army then he would not have been able to win the wars of unification. The head of the army, General Helmuth von Moltke was known as an 'organisational genius'. Without his careful planning and understanding of battle tactics, Bismarck would not have succeeded in the wars against Denmark, Austria and France. However, Bismarck was instrumental in solving the constitutional crisis of 1862 and kept the budget for improving the army quite high. Von Moltke had realised the importance of keeping up to date with changes in modern warfare and it was the German use of guns on the battlefield that gave them such an advantage between 1865 and 1871.

"AU REVOIR!"

GERMANY: "Farewell, Madame, and if——"
FRANCE: "Ha! We shall meet again!"

Figure 23: *Punch cartoon from 1871. The prophetic captions below the cartoon read:*

'AU REVOIR!'

Germany: 'FAREWELL MADAME, AND IF – '

France: 'HA! WE SHALL MEET AGAIN!'

Figure 24: *General von Moltke.*

⚡ Make the Link

If you studied The Great War you will have learned about how warfare developed over the next 50 years.

📖 Historiography

Jonathan Steinberg describes von Moltke as the general Bismarck could not outmanoeuvre. They therefore worked together with mutual respect. He further wrote that throughout the wars 'The Prussian Generals had absolute confidence in their General Staff and in its chief, Helmuth von Moltke'.

Prussian economic strength

The Prussian economy is extremely important when considering the reasons for Bismarck's success in uniting Germany. Prussia had already emerged as the natural leader of the German states through the creation and administration of the Zollverein. Up until 1850, the German economy had been growing but not to the extent that it did between 1850 and 1870.

📖 Historiography

'Bismarck's military victories would have been much less likely without the economic growth of 1850–70.'

Ian Mitchell

The Prussian army were able to take great advantage of the new railways, often arriving in enemy territory before the opposition had even mobilised. This railway boom further created jobs and tax revenue that allowed Bismarck to allocate money to be spent on the army. Steel and coal production increased significantly and beat France's production by about 30%. Germany invested money in weapon production so as to be fully prepared for any wars and able to defeat any opposition with superior weapons.

📖 Historiography

The economist J.M. Keynes famously noted that 'The German Empire was not founded on blood and iron, but on coal and iron'.

GO! Activity 8

1. Get into groups of four. Come up with five different questions asking another group to describe the background to German unification. Swap papers and answer the other group's questions as best you can – you can include details you have studied in previous sections such as the growth of nationalism and attempts made towards unification up until 1850. Now swap back your papers and mark each other's work.

   Have the other group managed to describe the background to unification effectively?

   (Higher European and World unit outcomes: 2.1)

2. With a partner, work through the section to explain two reasons you think Germany was able to unify in 1871. You must put the factors into their historical context.

   Now share your ideas with the rest of the class. Have you come up with similar or very different arguments?

   (Higher European and World unit outcomes: 1.1)

3. With your partner, research the following factors:
   • The role of Bismarck
   • The decline of Austria
   • The role of other countries
   • Prussian military strength
   • Prussian economic strength

   For each factor, write a short paragraph analysing the reasons that were important to German unification in 1871. You should show the connections between relevant factors, giving detail, examples and evidence. You could use historiography from the section to help prove the points you have made.

   (Higher European and World unit outcomes: 2.2, 2.3)

4. Below is Bismarck's edited version of the Ems telegram.

   Source A

   > After the news of the renunciation of the Prince of Hohenzollern had been officially communicated by the Spanish Government to the French Government, the French Ambassador in Ems nevertheless demanded that his Majesty should authorise him to telegraph to Paris, that his majesty pledged himself for all future time never again to give his consent to the Hohenzollern resuming the candidature. His majesty has therefore declined to receive the Ambassador again and has informed him through the adjutant that he has nothing further to communicate to the Ambassador.

   Use at least four pieces of information from Source A and at least two points from your own knowledge to explain how Bismarck exploited events to help unify Germany.

   (Higher European and World unit outcomes: 1.1, 1.2, 2.2)

GO! Activity 9

Exam style questions

To what extent was Prussian economic strength the main reason that German Unification had been achieved by 1871?   (22)

(Higher European and World unit outcomes: 1.1, 1.2, 1.3, 2.1, 2.2, 2.3)

5 An evaluation of the reasons why the Nazis achieved power in 1933

In this section you will learn about:

- Weaknesses of the Weimar Republic.
- Resentment towards the Treaty of Versailles.
- Economic difficulties.
- The appeal of Hitler and the Nazis after 1928.
- Weaknesses and mistakes of opponents.

 Hint

The armistice was declared on 11 November 1918. The armistice was an agreement on both sides to cease fire. In the words of George V of Britain, the First World War 'achieved little except loss'.

Make the Link

If you studied The Great War you will have learned about the First World War in detail.

Make the Link

In Modern Studies you learn about the features of a democracy and the advantages and disadvantages of different types of electoral systems.

Weaknesses of the Weimar Republic

Following the armistice at the end of the First World War, Germany faced some significant problems. Kaiser Wilhelm II had been forced to abdicate shortly before the armistice was signed, leaving Germany with no leader. Democratic reforms had been brought in just before the armistice was signed in November 1918. In September 1918, the German commanders knew that the German war front was collapsing. To achieve peace, Germany had to prove to the Allies that it was prepared to change its political system and remove the Kaiser – many viewed him as the main instigator of the war. To have a reasonable chance at peace, Germany had to change its entire political structure. Germany was also in real economic difficulty and continuing the war would have received little support. There had been mutinies at Kiel when the German High Command had asked the sailors to continue to fight. Spanish flu was killing people in thousands and people were starving in the streets. It seemed that Germany had little choice but to surrender and install a democracy.

 **Historiography**

Finlay McKichan claims that the new democratic Weimar Republic was 'a Republic nobody wanted' and right from the outset it faced difficulties that it would never be able to resolve, allowing the Nazis to take power in 1933.

Prince Max of Baden was appointed Chancellor at the start of October 1918 and was given the task of negotiating the armistice with the allies. He further accepted the responsibility of helping to set up the new democracy in its early stages. The army was brought under control of the government and a new democratic voting system introduced. Every man and woman over the age of 20 was given the vote.

The Weimar Constitution set out to create the most democratic system in the world – as well as equal voting rights, a system of proportional representation was introduced whereby parties gained a percentage of seats in the Reichstag (German Parliament) equal to the percentage they achieved at the polls. This meant that there was seldom a majority government in power and coalitions were formed to rule instead. This caused problems as it meant the parties were always doing deals and no one seemed able to rule with true conviction. Further, if a coalition could not decide on the best way to govern then the government would be dissolved and an election called.

The Chancellor was responsible for the day-to-day running of the government and the head of state was President. The Chancellor needed the support of 50% of the Reichstag to change laws. The President had the power to appoint the Chancellor and call elections. Article 48 of the Constitution allowed the President to rule by decree in times of an emergency. He did not need the support of the Reichstag to pass temporary laws.

The Social Democrats (SPD) with Friedrich Ebert as Chancellor led the Provisional Government. Immediately, some problems came to the fore. Earlier, the Social Democrats had split in two, with the breakaway group forming the Independent Socialists (USPD) in 1917. Some historians point out that the lack of unity between the largest political groups in Germany was possibly one reason why the Nazis were able to get into power.

📖 Historiography

'The Social Democrats seemed less concerned to keep on good terms with the Independent Socialists who were members of the same government.'

Finlay McKichan

'German socialists were neither fully prepared for revolution nor united.'

John Hiden, The Weimar Republic

The Social Democrats faced direct opposition from both left- and right-wing political groups early on.

In January of 1919 the Weimar Republic faced its first major challenge, an attempted communist revolution. As in Russia, this period saw many Soviets and workers' councils emerge all over Germany.

The Spartacist uprising

The communist ideals of the Russian Revolution were gaining popular support in Germany. In late December 1918 the Communist Party of Germany (KPD) was formed by members of the Spartacist League. In January, a rebellion was organised by the KPD and the Spartacists, which became known as the Spartacist uprising. Although it was initially a peaceful protest, Chancellor Ebert was very worried about how the march of over 100 000 Communists would develop – by their own slogan they

Figure 25: *Friedrich Ebert, the first leader of the new Provisional Government.*

> **Make the Link**
>
> If you study Britain, 1851–1951 you will know that this made Germany more democratic, in terms of the franchise, than Britain in 1920.

> **Hint**
>
> Soviets and workers' councils were elected councils that sought to make decisions for their localities.

> **Make the Link**
>
> In Modern Studies you may study communist countries such as China.

🔍 Hint

The Freikorps disliked democracy and the new government only dealt with the Freikorps because they wanted their armed service in combating communism. Neither side actually supported each other.

wanted to 'Abolish all parliaments and transfer all power to the workers' and soldiers' councils!' What had been a peaceful protest turned violent as Ebert sent in the Freikorps, a group of battle-hardened ex-soldiers who were kept in government pay to crush any threat of a communist revolution. The Freikorps were successful, the Spartacists were crushed and the leaders, Karl Liebknecht and Rosa Luxemburg were executed. Ebert has been criticised for his harsh treatment of the Spartacists in part because it led to a distrust of the Social Democrats by the Communists. Some historians have pointed out that it was this rift that stopped the Social Democrats and the Communists ever uniting against the Nazi Party.

The Kapp Putsch

The Weimar Republic faced another rebellion in March 1920. Led by Wolfgang Kapp, 5000 Freikorps organised a march on Berlin with plans of overthrowing the government. Even though the Freikorps had helped the SPD put down the Spartacists the previous year, they did so to stop a communist takeover, not to save democracy. The Freikorps desired the Kaiser back in power. In the end, the government was saved by the people of Berlin – they went on general strike so the rebels had no food, water supplies or fuel and their rebellion was cut short. Kapp was killed while he awaited trial.

In a short space of time the Weimar Republic had faced two major threats from the left and right and it survived them both. In the case of the Kapp Putsch, it was the people that saved the democratic government – there is an argument that this proves the new democracy was not entirely unpopular.

Figure 26: *Fighting in the streets of Berlin, January 1919.*

Figure 27: *The picture above depicts demonstrators protesting against the Kapp Putsch. The caption reads: 'A quarter million participants'.*

🔍 Hint

Putsch means a violent overthrow of government.

The stab in the back

Another problem the Weimar Republic faced immediately was the legend of the 'stab in the back' or 'Dolchstosslegende'. Although it had been the German generals who had instigated the armistice and set the country on the pathway to democracy, it was Ebert's government who took the blame for ending the war. Many in the army, including men like Adolf Hitler, felt they had been 'stabbed in the back' and that

Germany had surrendered despite never having been beaten in the field. This was a myth used by Hitler to spin anti-democratic rhetoric later on. He perpetuated the idea that Germany had been betrayed by the 'November criminals': 'The name November criminals will cling to these folk throughout the centuries' (Adolf Hitler).

From its very beginning, it would appear that the Weimar Republic was built on very shaky foundations.

 Historiography

Historian Gordon Craig calls the troubles from the left- and right-wing experienced by the new Republic 'aborted revolutions'. In a time where revolutionary fever was running high, perhaps the Weimar Republic and the citizens of Germany deserve credit for persevering to maintain democracy in post-war Germany.

> ### Hint
> It was because of all the fighting and conflict in Berlin that the government had been moved to the quiet town of Weimar – hence the name, Weimar Republic.

Resentment towards the Treaty of Versailles

The Treaty of Versailles was signed in the Hall of Mirrors at Versailles Palace on 28 June 1919. Because Germany was forced to accept the terms of the Treaty, it became known as a 'diktat' (dictated treaty) by the German people. The terms of the Treaty included the following:

- Territorial losses included all overseas colonies and the return of Alsace-Lorraine to France. The Saarland was to be controlled by France for 15 years.
- The army was to be reduced to 100 000 men. There was to be no heavy artillery or military aircraft and U-boats were forbidden. The German navy was only to have merchant ships.
- The Rhineland (bordering France) was to be a demilitarised zone.
- Anschluss (union) with Austria was forbidden.
- The war guilt clause stated that Germany had to accept all blame for starting the war.
- The reparations clause stated that £6600 million had to be repaid in compensation to the Allies.

The Treaty was purposely harsh – the British politician Geddes famously said they should 'squeeze the German lemon until the pips squeak'. France, who had a leading role in creating the terms of the Treaty, wanted Germany not only to be punished but also to be prevented from ever being aggressive towards France again.

There was great resentment in Germany. The major losses of land including Alsace-Lorraine and the Saar meant that Germany lost areas rich in natural resources. Paying back the reparations would be even more difficult because Germany's means of creating wealth had been taken away. Further, Germany felt humiliated at having their means of defence stripped away and, most of all, because of the war guilt clause.

📖 Historiography

'The Versailles Treaty did not doom the Republic from birth, but it did create particularly troublesome dimensions to existing internal conflicts.'

John Hiden, Republican and Fascist Germany

Historian A. Ritschl writes that 'Keynes, an advisor to the delegation, resigned from his role citing the potential causes for Germany, both domestic and foreign, as gravely concerning.'

Economic difficulties

One of the most significant crises that faced the Weimar Republic was hyperinflation. By 1923 Germany had fallen behind with her reparation payments. To compensate for their loss, France and Belgium invaded the Ruhr region of Germany, which was rich in natural resources. The German government called on German workers in the region to stop working and passively resist the French. The French brought in strike breakers, there was some violence and 132 people were killed. To solve the crisis, the German government began to print money. They could pay the reparation demands and also pay their workers. However, this damaged the economy because low production meant the real value of German currency rapidly eroded and its purchasing power collapsed. For example, a loaf of bread in 1918 cost 0·63 marks. In January 1923 it was 25 marks. By June it was 3465 marks and by September 1·5 million marks. By November 1923, when hyperinflation reached its peak, a loaf of bread cost 2000 million marks.

Unemployment grew significantly and many Germans lost their life savings – any money in the bank was devalued so much that it was worth next to nothing. Some businessmen were clever enough to manipulate credit to enable them to buy businesses. Property owners also did well out of the crisis.

This crisis of extremes meant that many lost faith in the Weimar Republic. It was at this point that Adolf Hitler and the Nazi Party really came into public consciousness.

📖 Historiography

'… millions of Germans, who had passively accepted the transition from Empire to Republic suffered deprivations that shattered their faith in the democratic process and left them cynical and alienated.'

Gordon Craig

✦ Make the Link

If you study Economics you will look at problems like hyperinflation in detail.

Figure 28: *German children use money as building blocks, 1923. The crisis was so extreme that workers had to collect their wages in wheelbarrows.*

Adolf Hitler, the Nazi Party and the Munich Putsch

Hitler was born in Braunau in Austria on 20 April 1889. He had desires of becoming an artist and went to study in Vienna, but was rejected by the art school. He had little money and many historians think it was because of these experiences he developed a hatred of the Jews – it was a Jew who had turned his application to art school down and when he fell on hard times it seemed as if the Jewish population were prosperous and affluent. He served in the First World War and was a loyal soldier – he was made Lance-Corporal and gained the Iron Cross twice, the second award being the Iron Cross First Class. He was recovering from the effects of a gas attack when he heard of Germany's defeat. He felt Germany had been 'stabbed in the back' by those new politicians who had signed the armistice. He became involved in politics by joining the German Workers' Party led by Anton Drexler. He soon became leader of the party, thanks to his excellent oratory skills, and changed the name of the party to the Nationalist Socialist German Workers' Party or NSDAP for short.

Figure 29: *Adolf Hitler in 1923.*

Hint

The term 'Nazis' came from the pronunciation of NSDAP and was at first a joke at the party's expense. Hitler was furious but learned to run with the term when he realised how popular it was. Hitler was an effective politician in this sense – he watched and learned from public reactions.

From here the NSDAP started to gain popularity, especially in the time of hyperinflation as the people of Germany turned to more extreme parties who offered solutions to the crisis. But perhaps Hitler became over-confident because on 8–9 November 1923 he tried to overthrow the Bavarian government in what became known as the Munich Putsch.

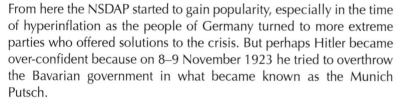
Make the Link

If you study Migration and Empire, 1830–1939 you will learn about attitudes towards Jewish people who emigrated to Scotland around this time.

In a beer cellar in Munich, Hitler held the Bavarian politican von Kahr, the army officer von Lossow and the head of the state police von Seisser at gunpoint to force them to accept his National Socialist revolution. However, when Hitler left the beer cellar to prepare for the rebellion, von Lossow organised the army against the Nazis. Hitler and his men could not match the power of the Bavarian army and their attempt at a coup was thwarted – the following day 16 Nazis lost their lives.

Hitler was put on trial for high treason. He refused to have a lawyer and instead represented himself, entertaining the court with his speeches and German patriotism. Hitler was sentenced to five years in Landsberg prison, but he only served nine months. During this time he wrote *Mein Kampf*, his autobiography, which also set out his plans for Germany – these included revising the Treaty of Versailles, obtaining Lebensraum (living space) and putting into effect his theories of the master race. The Munich Putsch gave Hitler and the Nazis publicity and placed them in the public consciousness. However, once the economic crisis of 1923 was resolved, they faded into the background. Hitler had to rethink his plans and realised power could not be taken by force. He would have to 'hold his nose and enter the Reichstag' – he would have to be voted into power legitimately. It would take another crisis in 1929 to give the Nazis their much needed opportunity to take power.

Figure 30: *Gustav Stresemann, Chancellor 1923.*

1925–9, a golden age for Weimar?

For a short time, between 1925 and 1929, the social and economic divisions within Germany seemed to disappear. Hyperinflation was resolved largely due to the expertise of Gustav Stresemann. He negotiated the Dawes plan with America, which gave Germany a loan to regenerate the economy and pull itself out of hyperinflation. He also negotiated fairer repayment terms with the Allies regarding reparations. The German government recalled all the useless banknotes and issued a new currency, the Rentenmark. Stresemann then agreed a non-aggression pact, the Treaty of Locarno, with France, as well as gaining entry to the League of Nations. What followed was a term of peace and prosperity in which Germany did well economically, and became a hub of cultural activity.

Nevertheless, not everyone benefited. Peasant farmers did not do well during this era and small businesses were adversely affected by the dominance of big businesses, many of them Jewish owned. Scratching beneath the surface of Weimar's Golden Age it was apparent that a social and economic divide continued. Although during this time the extremist parties became less popular, there were still many who disliked democracy. There were traditionalists who longed for the 'good old days' of the Kaiser and the extremist parties like the Communists and the Nazis were always lurking in the background.

Make the Link

In Modern Studies you may learn about the political spectrum, from the extreme Right to the extreme Left.

📖 Historiography

'Stresemann and his times denied the Nazi fire the oxygen of misery and it was all but extinguished.'

Cameron, Henderson and Robertson

Written into the Dawes plan was a recall clause, which meant that should America need the money, especially in a crisis, it could recall the loan. On 24 October 1929, the American stock market crashed. America recalled the loan from Germany, which plunged it back into economic crisis. Unemployment rose significantly and Germany, like many other countries, felt the economic hardships of the Great Depression.

📖 Historiography

Richard Evans argues the Depression helped to make the Nazis, a catch-all party of social protest, appealing to a greater or lesser degree to virtually every social group in the land. The Nazis, succeeded in transcending social boundaries and uniting highly disparate groups on the basis of a common ideology, as no other party in Germany had managed to do before.

'The Great Depression put the wind in Hitler's sails.'

A.J.P. Taylor, The Origins of the Second World War

The appeal of Hitler and the Nazis after 1928

The Nazis began to campaign on the idea of strong government and promised to sort out the economic crisis. By 1932, unemployment was at around 6 million – 30% of the population – and people feared a return to hyperinflation. However, by the time the Nazis got into power in January of 1933, the unemployment rate was actually falling so it could not just have been because of this that the Nazis took power.

The Nazis appealed to many sections of the population. They promised that they would rip up the Treaty of Versailles, rearm Germany and stop paying reparations (although these had been cancelled in 1932 when the Allies realised there was no hope of getting paid). They won favour with rural farmers as they promised to pay good prices for their produce. Hitler appealed to the middle classes and businessmen because he promised to protect their wealth from the Communists. For the unemployed, he promised 'work and bread'.

Figure 31: *A Nazi election poster from 1932. After 1928 Hitler tried to broaden his appeal to as many sectors of society as possible. The poster reads 'Hitler Our last hope'.*

Nevertheless, even at their most popular, the Nazis never polled a majority, with 37·3% being their highest figure – it even dropped to 33·1% in the election before Hitler was made Chancellor. There is a theory put forward by historians called 'negative cohesion' – that many people only voted for the Nazis because they were disillusioned with democracy or worried about the Communists, rather than being genuine supporters.

That is not to say that the Nazis did not have a great deal of popular support. The Sturmabteilung (SA), Hitler's Brownshirts, were a popular group especially among working-class men. Joining the Nazi Party gave them a sense of purpose and many people liked the fact that they dressed and acted in a military fashion – it gave a sense of order in a time of chaos. Of course, in reality the SA were no more than hired thugs. Hitler used them to instigate fights in the streets with Communists – and then promised to resolve the increase in street violence. They also came in useful for intimidating people at elections.

📖 Historiography

While Hitler basically appealed to negative feelings – anger, resentment, hatred – there was also a 'positive' element in the proposed remedy to the proclaimed ills. Historian Kershaw puts forward the argument that Hitler was at the helm of a party which had broad appeal and that he was able to tap into the 'national mood' of the time very effectively.

Hitler's speeches and rallies always attracted many followers: even if they were not Nazi supporters, his popular appeal was such that people would pay to hear him speak. The Nazis invested a lot of time and money in propaganda. Joseph Goebbels, Minister for Propaganda and Enlightenment, stated 'If you tell a lie, tell a big lie and tell it often, people will believe you'.

Weaknesses and mistakes of opponents

The weaknesses and mistakes of opponents certainly helped Hitler into power. Between the years of 1930 and 1932 Germany had three different Chancellors – an indication to many that democracy was not working. In 1930, Heinrich Bruning, leader of the Catholic Party, was made Chancellor. He was unpopular because he cut back on Germany's public spending so significantly that those who had been able to claim benefits started to break the law to get into prison just to get fed. He was replaced by Franz von Papen in 1932, and then von Papen was replaced by Kurt von Schleicher. By this time, the Nazis were gaining nearly 40% of the votes so Hitler was offered the position of Vice Chancellor. He refused because he did not want to accept anything but the position of Chancellor. Since no government could be formed, elections had to be called again. Although Nazi votes fell slightly in the November election they were still the biggest party and von Papen persuaded Hindenburg, the President, to make Hitler Chancellor. They thought it would be easy to control Hitler when he was in power – when von Papen was asked if there might be danger ahead he replied 'No danger at all. We've hired him for our act'. (As cited in Alan Bullock.) Thus, Hitler was sworn in as Chancellor of Germany on 30 January 1933.

If there had been an effective coalition against the Nazis then Hitler may not have been able to take power. However, previous arguments and continued ill-feeling led to the inability of the Social Democrats and the Independent Socialists to work together. Further, neither of these parties could work with the Communists, which meant that Hitler did not face an effective challenge to his claim of being the biggest party in the Reichstag. In addition, it seems as if the Nazis and Hitler were grossly underestimated by their political opponents, von Papen and President Hindenburg in particular.

Still, without the economic crisis of 1929 it is safe to say the Nazis would have found it quite difficult to gain popularity. Overall, they were able to capitalise on the weaknesses of their opponents. It certainly seemed that the Chancellors throughout the early 1930s were unable to lead Germany effectively and provide solutions to any of its problems.

📖 Historiography

'The Nazis' growing electoral support in the elections of 1930 and 1932 was directly related to the growth of mass unemployment and the growth of political instability in this period.'

Mary Fulbrook

Activity 10

1. Take notes under the following headings:
   - Weaknesses of the Weimar Republic
   - Resentment towards the Treaty of Versailles
   - Economic difficulties
   - The appeal of Hitler and the Nazis after 1928
   - Weaknesses and mistakes of opponents.

   Make sure you take down at least four key points for each section demonstrating the weaknesses of the Weimar Republic, or evidence to counter this point.

   (Higher European and World unit outcomes: 2.1, 2.3)

2. Read Source B, from Nazi Albert Speer writing in 1931 and Source C, from an eyewitness describing unemployed vagrants in 1932.

   Source B

   > My mother saw a storm trooper parade in the streets of Heidelberg. The sight of discipline in a time of chaos, the impression of energy in an atmosphere of universal hopelessness seems to have won her over.

   Source C

   > No one knew how many there were of them. They completely filled the streets. They stood or lay about in the streets as if they had taken root there. They sat or lay on the pavements or in the roadway and gravely shared out scraps of newspapers among themselves.

   Use at least four pieces of information from Sources B and C and at least two points from your own knowledge to explain how Hitler and the Nazis got into power in 1933.

   (Higher European and World unit outcomes: 1.1, 1.2, 2.2)

3. Now analyse the importance of the reasons you have written down in questions 1 and 2. Try to show connections between the relevant factors and debate different interpretations of the different factors (use historiography here!).

   (Higher European and World unit outcomes: 2.2, 2.3)

4. Now conclude why you think Hitler and the Nazis were able to gain power. Give a justified reason!

5. Using the reasons you have written, write a short answer to the following question:

   Do you agree that the Great Depression allowed the Nazis to take power?

   (Higher European and World unit outcomes: 1.2, 1.3)

Activity 11

Exam style questions

To what extent was the Nazi rise to power between 1919 and 1933 caused by resentment towards the Treaty of Versailles? **(22)**

(Higher European and World unit outcomes: 1.1, 1.2, 1.3, 2.1, 2.2, 2.3)

6 An evaluation of the reasons why the Nazis were able to stay in power, 1933–39

In this section you will learn about:

- The establishment of a totalitarian state.
- Fear and state terrorism.
- Social controls.
- Propaganda.
- Economic policies.
- Social policies.

The establishment of a totalitarian state

When Hitler became Chancellor, he did so holding only 33·1% of the seats in the Reichstag. Hitler wanted to form a majority government so he called another election to be held in March 1933. However, just before the elections were to take place the Reichstag building went on fire.

Figure 32: *The Reichstag on fire, 27 February 1933.*

This was either a complete stroke of good luck for the Nazis or had been engineered by the Nazis in the first place, as it allowed them to blame the Communists for starting the fire and to proclaim them 'anti-democratic'. A Dutch Communist called Marinus van der Lubbe was caught inside the building with firelighters and fuel and gave the Nazis the scapegoat they needed.

Hitler claimed there was a Communist conspiracy against Germany and asked Hindenburg for the emergency powers detailed in Article 48. Hitler issued the 'Reichstag Fire Law' which gave him the power to arrest enemies of the state, suspend free speech and assembly, and censor newspapers. He could now do this without the support of the Reichstag. Communists were rounded up and sent to concentration camps and van der Lubbe was executed for treason the following year.

Hint

Article 48 has been given the nickname, 'the suicide clause'.

The elections took place on 5 March. Hitler probably expected an overall majority since the Communists had been removed from opposition. However, the Nazis only achieved 43·9% of votes in their last public election. Historians are mindful of this figure when analysing how popular the Nazis actually were.

Hitler then decided to try to extend the powers afforded to him by the Reichstag Fire Law. He asked Hindenburg for 'four more years' and asked to pass the Enabling Act. He needed the support of three quarters of the Reichstag to allow him to pass this Act and the Catholic Centre Party obliged with the extra support. The passing of the Enabling Act on 23 March 1933 marked the death of the Weimar Republic and the birth of Hitler's period as Führer of Germany. The Weimar Republic had effectively voted itself out of existence.

Hitler's next move was to get rid of anyone or any group he perceived to be a threat.

Historiography

Michael Burleigh states: 'The Enabling Law permitted the government to pass budgets and promulgate laws, including those altering the constitution, for four years without parliamentary approval ... There was no need to promulgate a new Nazi constitution ... for the substantive parts of the Weimar constitution had been nullified.'

He first banned the Communist Party, then the Social Democrats. This was followed by a law that made it illegal to form a new political party. Then trade unions were banned which made it difficult for workers to have any kind of political voice.

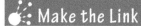

Make the Link

You may learn about trade unions in Modern Studies and Business Management.

The Night of the Long Knives

On 30 June 1934 Hitler murdered 400 of the SA and their leader, Ernst Röhm, the very men who had helped him into power. He did this with the help of the Schutzstaffel (or the SS), who were Hitler's 'protection squad'. Hitler had been worried about Röhm's popularity among the Brownshirts (another name for the SA) and, after rumours that Röhm was going to merge the regular army with the Brownshirts, thus having the support of three million men, Hitler acted to eliminate the SA leadership.

Other people were also killed that evening, the Night of the Long Knives, including von Schleicher, who had been Chancellor in 1932. Hitler was purging Germany of people he viewed to be a threat or who had opposed him in the past.

 Historiography

'In a rapid series of moves, Hitler consolidated his own position, extended the authority of the Reich government over the individual German states and crushed all potential sources of opposition.'

William Simpson

Fear and state terrorism

Hitler set out to create a totalitarian state. As well as banning political parties and other opposition groups, he set up concentration camps to 're-educate' those who did not toe the Nazi line. The first was set up in Dachau in 1933 and was primarily to house political offenders like Communists. As time went on, the list of those the Nazis objected to got longer and longer and eventually the list extended to any 'undesirables' like the Jews. Concentration camps became widespread as the Nazis expanded into Eastern Europe and many evolved into the death camps of the Holocaust, such as Auschwitz.

Figure 33: *The first arrivals in Dachau, 1933.*

The rights set out by the Weimar constitution were taken away by the Nazis. There was no freedom of speech, no right to privacy and newspapers were censored. The SS maintained control with brute violence.

📖 Historiography

'The force that prevented the regime from dissolving into chaos was terror and its instrument was the SS.'

Gordon Craig

Hitler's maintenance of power was only possible because the 'opposition was crushed, broken, cowed and neutralised through unprecedented and unmitigated levels of repression by the Nazi state'.

Ian Kershaw

Hitler himself said 'Nothing drives people harder than the fear of sudden death.' The Nazis set up the Gestapo, the secret police, to spy on people. The Gestapo were difficult to spot because they operated in plain clothes. To begin with there were around 45 000 in the Gestapo and about another 160 000 employed as informants. People did not know who they could trust and rarely did anyone speak out against the Nazis. Even a joke at Hitler's expense could end up with the joke teller being put in a concentration camp. The Nazis created a web of fear that became impossible to break free from because the ultimate penalty was death.

Propaganda

The propaganda machine in Nazi Germany was fundamental to the running of the state. In order to keep the population effectively brainwashed, the Nazis used speeches, posters and rallies – a million people attended one of the Nuremberg rallies. Hitler provided the people of Germany with cheap radios for their homes but, as they could only be tuned into a selected number of stations, all that could be heard was more Nazi propaganda.

Historians have debated the effectiveness of Nazi propaganda. Many think that most people just came to ignore the plethora of posters on the streets and were well aware that news stories were selective in their use of facts. Nevertheless, it would be fair to say that the whole Nazi regime was a superb propaganda exercise. People in Germany had to eat, sleep and breathe National Socialism, and the SS and Gestapo ensured no one deviated from total conformity.

Figure 34: *Nazi propaganda poster. The caption reads, 'One Country, One People, One Leader!'*

> ### Make the Link
> You may learn about persuasive images and speech in Graphic Communications and English.

📖 Historiography

Propaganda in Nazi Germany is described by Murphy, Morris and Fulbrook as a cohesive agent, along with the Gestapo, in ensuring the maintenance of power. They cite that for the Nazis to maintain power, solving the economic crisis was more important.

Economic policies

The Nazis did have some real economic achievements. They promised work and bread and they delivered on their promise. They set about revitalising Germany, building autobahns (motorways) and modernising farming. They also appeared to solve the problem of unemployment, although it must be remembered that by the time the Nazis came into power the economy was recovering. Nevertheless, unemployment figures were reduced to zero by 1939. However, Jews were not included in the figures and the army accounted for many of the jobs done by young men. Other work schemes were also set up. The German Labour Service employed men aged 19–25 on a compulsory basis. They wore military uniforms and were not paid for their work but were given accommodation and food. There were no trade unions so no one could protest. In the German Labour Front, there were incentives of holidays but working hours were long and wages were low. One incentive scheme, to give participants a new Volkswagen if they paid 5 marks a week into a payment scheme, came to nothing as the Nazis used the money for weapons production.

Figure 35: *Hitler gets into a Volkswagen – a 'people's car'.*

The Nazis were able to regenerate the economy by following a policy of protectionism, which meant that no wealth travelled outside Germany. It had short-term success but could not be sustained. Wages were kept low or, for those in programmes like the German Labour Service, non-existent! In fact, the Nazi economy was not in good health as war drew near in 1939 but the prospect of a European war helped distract people from the economic issues at home. However, it is difficult to assess what ordinary Germans felt about the economic situation in Germany at the time.

📖 Historiography

P. Adam says that 'it was hard to understand how he was able to convince anyone with his ideas, and yet his success was overwhelming. Hitler was a man who could deal in simple images. The platitudes were uttered with a rare energy and charisma. It was not reasoning but passion that made him so convincing.'

'Even Goebbel's full bag of tricks could not turn black into white.'

Ian Kershaw

Social policies

The Nazis tried to control every part of everyday life. They controlled who was in government, appointed Nazis as civil servants and got rid of anti-Nazi teachers, doctors and lawyers. No one could complain to the police because the Nazis were the police. They set up their own religion, the German Christian Church, to alter people's faith to worship Hitler instead of God. One of Hitler's most effective social controls was on the youth of Nazi Germany. The Hitler Youth provided extra-curricular activities including hiking, marching and weekend camping. Young Germans loved the activities and the uniforms; it gave them a sense of importance. In 1936 the Hitler Youth Law made membership compulsory and parents could be imprisoned in concentration camps if they did not follow orders and send their children to the Hitler Youth, or the League of German Maidens.

Figure 36: *A Hitler Youth rally. Hitler said 'who owns the youth, gains the future!'*

There were some groups that challenged the Nazis. The Edelweiss Pirates and Swing Kids were just two of the youth groups that refused to follow the orders of the Nazis and conform to their ideals. The White Rose also handed out anti-Nazi leaflets and actively protested against them. However, opposition was difficult because of the reign of terror conducted by the Gestapo and SS. It is estimated that 800 000 people actively resisted the Nazis during their time in power, but 500 000 lost their lives.

📖 **Historiography**

'The German opposition to Hitler was not only numerically broader than has often been conceded, but was much more widespread than could have been expected in conditions of terror.'

Hans Rothfels

Most historians agree that the majority of people in Germany acquiesced – they went along with the Nazis to avoid extreme punishment.

📖 **Historiography**

'Although the regime deployed a formidable apparatus of terror, it is clear that it was also based on a large measure of consent from broad sections of the population.'

Noakes and Pridham

Another of the key social policies of the Nazi regime that must be assessed was their policy of racial superiority – they were the 'master race' and any undesirables, notably the Jews, were regarded as 'Untermenschen' (sub-humans). Hitler wanted what he saw as the perfect Aryan race, free from Jews. Under the Nuremberg Laws the Jews lost their citizenship and thus were not protected by law. These policies, such as banning Jews from using public facilities and holding jobs such as civil servants and doctors, came to a head in Germany in November 1938 when the Nazis enacted a pogrom – Kristallnacht (Night of Broken Glass). Under the pretext of a Jew killing a Nazi official in Paris, Jewish shops, businesses and synagogues were destroyed, around 400 Jews were killed and thousands of others put in concentration camps.

In short, Hitler was able to use the Jews as scapegoats and blame them for Germany's economic problems and the Treaty of Versailles while making Germans feel racially superior through propaganda. This harnessed people's anger against the Jews and made Nazi activity against them seem legitimate.

Overall, the Nazis effectively controlled Germans with a totalitarian regime based on fear and mistrust. How much genuine support they had continues to be debated.

🔵 GO! Activity 12

You are going to present a group presentation on the Nazi state focusing on the following question:

To what extent did the Nazi regime depend on the use of force and terror to remain in power, 1933–39?

Your presentation must contain the following:

Introduction

A detailed description of the Nazi state.

(Higher European and World unit outcomes: 2.1)

An explanation of two reasons why you think the Nazis were able to maintain power between 1933 and 1939.

(Higher European and World unit outcomes: 1.1)

Main presentation – can be done on PowerPoint, poster – you choose!

An analysis of the main factors that enabled the Nazis to stay in power between 1933 and 1939. You should show the connections between relevant factors, giving detail, examples and evidence. You could use historiography from the section to help prove the points you have made.

Include information from the following headings:

- Establishment of a totalitarian state
- Fear and state terrorism
- Propaganda
- Economic policies
- Social policies.

(Higher European and World unit outcomes: 1.1, 2.2, 2.3)

Conclusion

Summarise the key factors to the audience and make a judgement on the issue. Provide two developed points to support your overall judgement.

(Higher European and World unit outcomes: 1.2, 1.3)

🔵 GO! Activity 13

Exam style questions

To what extent did the Nazi regime depend on the use of force and terror to remain in power, 1933–39?   (22)

(Higher European and World unit outcomes: 1.1, 1.2, 1.3, 2.1, 2.2, 2.3)

Summary

In this topic you have learned:

- How and why nationalism grew in Germany between 1815 and 1850
- The obstacles to German unification, 1815–50
- The reasons why unification was achieved in Germany by 1871
- The reasons why the Nazis achieved power in 1933
- The reasons why the Nazis were able to stay in power between 1933 and 1939.

You should have developed your skills and be able to:

- construct an essay that describes and explains an issue in detail
- analyse an historical issue in a structured essay
- interpret and make use of historiography.

Learning checklist

Now that you have finished **Germany, 1815–1939**, complete a self-evaluation of your knowledge and skills to assess what you have understood. Use traffic lights to help you make up a revision plan to help you improve in the areas you identified as red or amber.

- Describe the effects of the French Revolution and Napoleonic Wars.

- Explain the military weaknesses of the German states.

- Explain the role of the liberals in the rise of nationalism.

- Describe and analyse the cultural factors in the rise of nationalism.

- Describe and analyse the economic factors in the rise of nationalism.

- Explain the role of the Zollverein.

- Describe the supporters of nationalism.

- Describe the opponents of nationalism.

- Explain the political turmoil of the 1840s.

- Describe the role of the Frankfurt Parliament and analyse the importance of its failure.

- Explain and analyse the importance of the collapse of the revolution in Germany, 1848–49.

- Describe the divisions among the nationalists and the German princes as a barrier to German unification.

- Explain the strength of Austria as a barrier to German unification.

- Describe the religious differences among the German states.

- Analyse the indifference of the masses.

- Analyse the resentment towards Prussia as a barrier to unification.

- Describe and explain the role of Bismarck.

- Describe and explain the decline of Austria.

- Explain the attitude of the other states towards Bismarck and unification.

- Describe the role of other countries.

- Describe and analyse the importance of Prussian military strength.

- Describe and analyse the importance of Prussian economic strength.

- Describe the weaknesses of the Weimar Republic following the First World War.

- Explain the resentment towards the Treaty of Versailles.

- Explain the economic difficulties experienced by Germany.

- Explain and analyse the appeal of the Nazis after 1928 and the role of Hitler.

- Describe and analyse the weaknesses and mistakes of opponents.

- Describe the establishment of a totalitarian state.

- Describe fear and state terrorism.

- Explain the use of social controls.

- Analyse the use of propaganda.

- Analyse the importance of economic policies in helping the Nazis maintain power.

- Analyse the importance of social policies in helping the Nazis maintain power.

Studying this topic will provide you with an understanding of how and why opposition to autocracy in Russia developed, eventually causing the collapse of the Tsarist regime in February 1917. Further, it will allow you to understand how and why the Bolsheviks were able to seize power in October 1917 and then consolidate their hold over Russia up until 1921. By the end of the topic you will have developed a detailed understanding of a fascinating and important period in Russian history that not only shaped Russia's twentieth century, but also had a significant impact on European and world politics.

This topic is split into six sections:

❖ An assessment of the security of the Tsarist state before 1905.

❖ An evaluation of the causes of the 1905 Revolution.

❖ An assessment of the attempts to strengthen Tsarism, 1905–14.

❖ An evaluation of the reasons for the February Revolution, 1917.

❖ An evaluation of the reasons for the success of the October Revolution, 1917.

❖ An evaluation of the reasons for the victory of the Reds in the Civil War.

Activities and Outcomes

Outcome		1	2	3	4	5	6	7	8	9	10	11	12	13	14	15	16	17	18	19
	Activity																			
	1.1				✓	✓		✓	✓	✓	✓		✓	✓	✓	✓	✓		✓	✓
	1.2				✓	✓		✓	✓	✓	✓		✓	✓	✓	✓	✓		✓	✓
	1.3				✓	✓		✓	✓	✓	✓		✓	✓	✓	✓	✓		✓	✓
	2.1					✓	✓		✓		✓		✓		✓	✓	✓	✓		✓
	2.2					✓	✓		✓		✓		✓		✓	✓	✓	✓		✓
	2.3					✓	✓		✓		✓		✓		✓	✓	✓	✓		✓

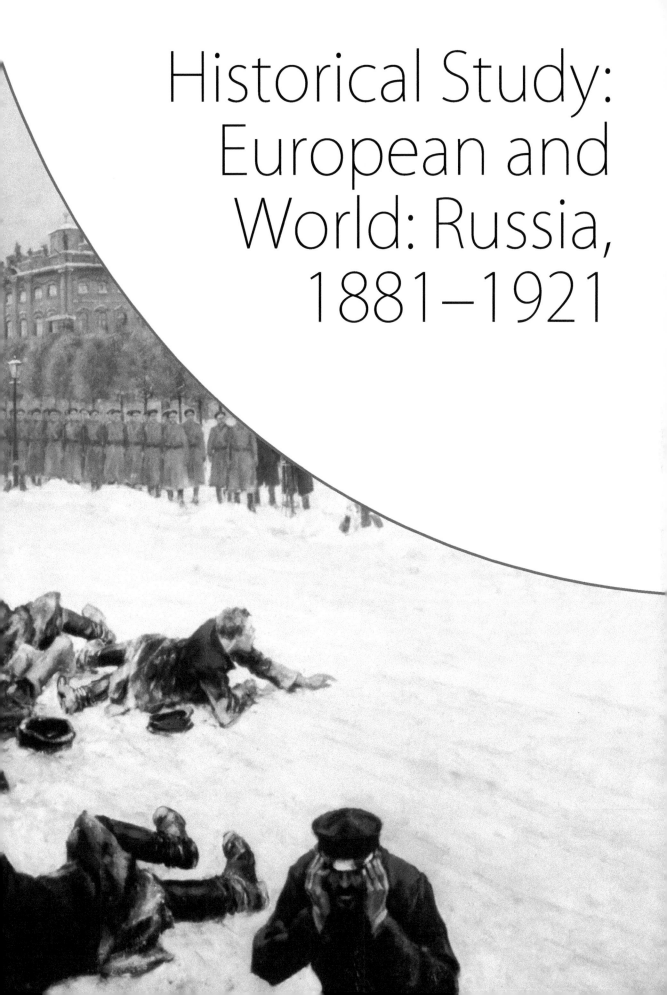

Historical Study: European and World: Russia, 1881–1921

Background

In 1881 the Russian Empire was ruled by Tsar Alexander III. The Tsar was the emperor and an autocrat, meaning that he had complete control over the Empire and his word on any issue was final. His government existed purely to advise him and there was no parliament or popular vote. His family, the Romanovs, had ruled Russia since 1613, and in 1881 this vast, populous Empire appeared to be very powerful. In reality, however, the size of Russia actually made it difficult for the Tsar to maintain control and there were many other problems, economic and political. The Tsar's power may have been absolute, but he also faced many challenges.

Figure 1: *The Russian Empire was vast, stretching from modern-day Poland in the west to the borders of China and Japan in the east.*

Figure 2: *Tsar Alexander III is seated centre, with his son and heir Nicholas directly behind him.*

Alexander III and his advisors were well aware that Russia was falling behind other modernising, industrial economies. Keen to keep pace, the Tsar recognised the need for economic change in Russia. At the same time, however, Alexander and then, after him, Nicholas II, did not want to relinquish any political power by reforming the autocratic system. Relying on repression, censorship and blind faith to rule, both Tsars remained devoted to the outdated autocracy; this ultimately led to the downfall of the Romanov dynasty in 1917.

Following the abdication of Tsar Nicholas II in March 1917, there was a vacuum of power in Russia. Into this stepped the Provisional Government who, as their name suggests, were only in charge of the country temporarily until elections could take place. As the Great War claimed more casualties and Russia struggled to cope economically, so the Provisional Government became increasingly unpopular. The revolutionary Bolshevik Party, led by Vladimir Lenin, exploited the unique circumstances to seize power. Over the next four years, Lenin's Bolsheviks would consolidate their power and emerge victorious from a brutal civil war, establishing a Communist state in the process. In 40 years Russia had gone from autocracy to Communism, and it is this journey that this topic seeks to investigate and make sense of.

GO! Activity 1

Create either a poster, presentation or a comic strip that summarises the above paragraphs. Note the following:
- You can only use a maximum of 30 words.
- Use a dictionary to clarify any words or terms you are unsure of.
- Be prepared to explain your piece of work to others once it is finished.

1 An assessment of the security of the Tsarist state before 1905

In this section you will learn about:

- The structure of society.
- Difficulties in governing the Tsarist state.
- Tsarist methods of control:
  1. The Okhrana.
  2. The army.
  3. Censorship.
  4. The Orthodox Church.
  5. Russification.
  6. The nobility.

In 1881 Tsar Alexander II was assassinated by political revolutionaries. His son assumed power, becoming Tsar Alexander III. He reacted swiftly and firmly to his father's death, clamping down on any opposition to the Tsarist state. For Alexander III, and then Nicholas after him, it was of paramount importance that the security of the autocracy should be maintained and both men used all the power and resources at their disposal to ensure this. The effectiveness of these methods, however, is open to debate.

The structure of society

Make the Link

In Modern Studies and Geography you study the causes and effects of inequality within different societies.

Hint

As you read through this information, refer to the cartoon in Figure 3. See if you can find the group in the cartoon that the text refers to.

In 1881, there was a clear hierarchy in Russian society, with wealth, power and influence concentrated among a relatively small number of people at the top; at the bottom there was a much larger number who survived on very little and had no political or economic power. Over time, the massive gulf between the rich and poor created anger and resentment.

The Tsar was at the head of Russian society. The Fundamental Laws of 1832 clearly stated that the Tsar, as 'Emperor of all the Russians, is an autocratic and unlimited monarch'. Although he could do as he wished, he did rely on certain groups to enforce his rule.

The Tsar relied upon the relatively large upper class and nobility to govern Russia, as well as the Orthodox Church and army. None of these groups wanted to see any real changes in Russia because they benefited from the status quo. As we shall see later, they all helped to reinforce Tsarist power in a variety of ways.

The middle classes comprised the liberal intelligentsia and the small commercial class. They were fairly wealthy, generally in favour of some kind of political reform and could be critical of the conservative Tsarist regime.

Figure 3: *This cartoon from 1900 is a socialist interpretation of the Russian social structure.*

The industrial workers were a relatively small group in industrially underdeveloped Russia. They were poor and lived and worked in terrible conditions in overcrowded towns and cities.

The peasants made up the largest group of people in Russia, at around 82% of the population, and lived in poverty. The upper classes often referred to them as the 'dark masses' because they were largely illiterate, deeply conservative and resistant to change.

🔍 Hint

In the nineteenth century, countries that industrialised quickly saw the commercial and industrial working classes grow significantly.

📖 Historiography

'… the Russian Empire was deeply fissured between the government and the tsar's subjects.'

Robert Service

Difficulties in governing the Tsarist state

Figure 4: *The Winter Palace, St Petersburg. This was the Tsar's residence in the capital.*

In 1881, the Russian Empire was massive, covering one sixth of the world's surface. With underdeveloped and inefficient transport and communication networks, it was therefore difficult to know exactly what was happening in the far reaches of the Empire and then get troops there quickly to deal with any problems. This made it difficult to govern the Tsarist state effectively.

With such a vast area and population to govern, the Tsarist regime required an effective bureaucracy to deal with the day-to-day running of the country. Unfortunately, the bureaucracy in Russia was corrupt, ineffective and inefficient, hampering the Tsarist government's ability to rule the whole Empire effectively from St Petersburg.

Russia was poor. Its economy was weak and backward, relying mainly on agriculture and with an underdeveloped industry. As a result, the vast majority of the population lived and worked in terrible conditions and were very unhappy.

The peasants had been freed from serfdom in 1861 meaning they could now own their own land. However, it was very expensive so few could afford it. In essence, the peasantry resented their lack of control over the land they worked and lived on. As a result they were always a potential problem for the Tsar, with any protests brutally suppressed by the army.

There were over 20 different nationalities in the Russian Empire, each with its own language, culture and religion. These national minorities increasingly resented Tsarist rule, with many calling for independence from the Russian Empire.

In the late nineteenth century various opposition groups emerged in Russia. Many took their inspiration from the writings of Karl Marx, styling themselves as revolutionary socialists. The most important of these groups were the Social Democrats (SDs) and Social Revolutionaries (SRs).

The SDs were supported by industrial workers and wanted a workers' revolution. The SRs were supported by peasants and wanted a peasant-led revolution that would bring land reform. These groups, however, were not powerful enough to cause significant harm to the Tsar because, firstly, political parties were illegal in Russia, meaning groups had to meet in secret and being a member was dangerous. This obviously discouraged people from joining them. Secondly, their illegal status made communication and coordination between groups difficult. Also, the leaders of these groups were often in exile or had been arrested. Lastly, these groups were often divided and disorganised. For example, in 1903 the SDs split into two separate parties: the Bolsheviks and the Mensheviks.

Another group who opposed the Tsar was the liberal middle classes. They did not want a revolution; instead, they wanted a Duma, a British-style parliament. However, they were not organised and suffered similar problems to the revolutionary groups.

While opposition groups could not hope to overthrow the Tsar, their presence showed that the Tsar could not take his security for granted.

🔍 Hint

Throughout history empires have always found it difficult to control vast areas and govern different nations.

🔍 Hint

Serfdom existed in many countries in medieval times but had largely died out in the rest of Europe by the nineteenth century.

🔍 Hint

Karl Marx's *The Communist Manifesto* was published in 1848. In it he called for workers to rise up and seize power from the ruling classes.

⁘ Make the Link

In Modern Studies you may learn about different political ideologies.

🔍 Hint

Throughout this topic, the Social Democrats are referred to as SDs and the Social Revolutionaries, SRs.

Tsarist methods of control

1. The Okhrana

The Okhrana was formally established in 1881, following the assassination of Tsar Alexander II. It was a secret police force, tasked with ensuring that all enemies of Tsarism were rooted out and dealt with accordingly.

Although the Okhrana started off as a small organisation, it grew steadily in the 1890s as the number of revolutionary groups increased. By 1911 there were more than 60 Okhrana stations scattered throughout Russia. The Okhrana used methods such as covert surveillance, informers, espionage, torture and, where necessary, execution. It is thought that by 1917 the Okhrana may have been responsible for executing 26 000 suspected opponents of the Tsar. Others were often sent into internal exile to labour camps in remote areas of Russia such as Siberia. Conditions in these camps were terrible.

Figure 5: *A page from an Okhrana file on the revolutionary, Joseph Stalin.*

 Historiography

Orlando Figes stresses the power of the Okhrana: 'No subject of the tsar, regardless of his rank or class, could sleep securely in his bed in the knowledge that his house would to be subject to a search, or he himself to arrest'.

Clearly, the existence of the Okhrana was an important method of control for the Tsar. It struck fear into the hearts of potential revolutionaries and dealt ruthlessly with the existing ones. However, the Okhrana's brutal methods served to reinforce resentment of the repressive Tsarist regime.

2. The army

Throughout the nineteenth century Russia maintained a massive standing army of around one and a half million troops. The Tsar and his government believed that, with such a large Empire to police and govern, a large and loyal army was needed to quickly quell rebellions and protests. Indeed, between 1883 and 1903 troops were called out to deal with unrest nearly 1500 times, showing how vital the army was to restoring order and maintaining the Tsar's hold on power.

Heading the army were members of the nobility, who were utterly loyal to the Tsar. These men usually gained their positions because of their connections to the Romanovs or through bribes, not because of their abilities as officers. This undermined the organisation and effectiveness of the army in the long term. These officers in turn insisted on the complete loyalty of troops to the Tsar, using extreme discipline to ensure this.

Perhaps the most notorious and brutal of the Tsar's soldiers were the Cossacks. Cossacks were elite troops who rode horses expertly and were often used by Tsarist authorities to put down riots and rebellions.

The large, loyal army was clearly vital to the security of the Tsarist state before 1905. However, the fact that the army had been trained to respond to any real or imagined threat with a disproportionate level of violence meant many Russians hated it.

Figure 6: *Cossacks were the elite cavalry unit in the Russian army. They were often used to suppress revolts in the countryside.*

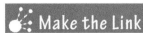

Make the Link

In Modern Studies you may learn about the important role the military plays in many countries today.

📖 Historiography

'*Nothing was closer to the Romanov court or more important to it than the military.*'

Orlando Figes

3. Censorship

Following his father's assassination in 1881, Tsar Alexander III passed the Statute of State Security. This increased the power of the Tsarist government in various ways, including extending censorship.

The Tsar was keen to ensure that information was controlled so that anti-Tsarist opinions could not be read or distributed. Any material that the government felt was dangerous was banned, and any person who was found to be circulating any revolutionary pamphlets or banned books would be dealt with by the Okhrana.

In 1887 the Tsar passed the University Statute of 1887 which meant that his government had control over what was taught in universities. Anything considered revolutionary or in any way anti-Tsarist was banned. This angered students and led to protests in St Petersburg and Moscow in 1899 and 1900 that were dealt with by the army.

Censorship may have allowed the government to control information in a variety of ways, but it created much resentment among students, the increasingly literate working class and the liberal intelligentsia.

4. The Orthodox Church

To ensure the long-term security of the Tsarist state, it was crucial that the Russian people were loyal to their leader and the Orthodox Church was right at the heart of this. Extremely conservative, it had for many years opposed political change while supporting the autocratic Tsarist state.

Figure 7: *The Orthodox Church played a key role in maintaining the Tsarist state. This is a photo of one of the most famous churches in St Petersburg.*

Orthodox Church priests were highly respected in Russian society. In the Russian villages in which they preached, peasants were largely illiterate and extremely devout, and these priests therefore wielded much power. They taught the Russian people that the Tsar had been chosen by God to rule Russia, and that they must therefore be completely loyal to him as they were to God. The Church denounced any opposition to the Tsar and called on Russians to inform the police of any people who held anti-Tsarist opinions. Also, the fact that the Church ran 41 000 parish schools meant that their message of obedience and loyalty to the Tsar began early in a Russian's life. The vast majority of Russians therefore grew up with an acceptance of the social order and a respect and love for their 'little father', the Tsar. Clearly, the Church was a powerful tool in maintaining the security of the Tsarist state before 1905, effectively ensuring the obedience of the vast majority of Russian citizens.

📖 Historiography

Orlando Figes argues that 'the Church was an essential propaganda weapon and a means of social control'.

5. Russification

The census of 1897 showed that only 44% of the Russian Empire's population was Russian. That meant that the majority of people living in the Empire were of a different nationality, sometimes not of the Orthodox religion. For the Tsarist government this posed a threat to the unity and security of the Empire and, under Tsar Alexander III, the policy of Russification was pursued to restrict the influence of national minorities.

Russification saw the Tsarist government try to 'Russify' everyone in the Empire. In practice, this meant making Russian the official language of the Empire, banning the language of national minorities from those nations' schools, courts, public offices, literature and even street signs. For example, in Poland, high school students could be expelled for speaking Polish in their dormitories. Obviously, this whole policy created a huge amount of resentment towards the Tsar and pushed many people in these countries towards revolutionary groups. Indeed, in 1892 the Polish Socialist Party was formed. Similar groups emerged in Lithuania, Finland and Ukraine in the years before 1905.

Another aspect of Russification was the persecution of non-Orthodox religions. The main victims of this were the Jews, who were used as scapegoats for the problems in Russia. After 1881 there were an increasing number of fierce attacks on Jews, known as pogroms. A group of ultra-nationalists, called the 'Black Hundreds', became notorious for these pogroms. Also, 600 new measures were introduced by the government to restrict the Jewish population, socially, politically and economically. Such persecution saw the large movement of many Jews abroad. For those who chose to stay, it solidified their hatred of the Tsarist regime and pushed them to form opposition groups. In 1897, the Jewish Bund was formed, essentially a revolutionary union with a clear opposition to Russification.

🔆 Make the Link

In RMPS you will learn about different religions around the world including branches of Christianity like the Orthodox Church.

🔍 Hint

The author of *The Communist Manifesto*, Karl Marx, called religion 'the opiate of the people'. Can you think what he meant by this?

🔆 Make the Link

In the Higher Scottish topic Migration and Empire, 1830–1939 you will learn about Jews and Lithuanians who came to Scotland having fled from persecution in Tsarist Russia.

It is quite clear that Russification did not increase the security of the Tsarist state, arguably doing exactly the opposite. It created enemies for the Tsar at a time when he needed all the friends he could get, and served to further divide an already fractured Empire.

Figure 8: *These marchers, carrying Russian flags and a picture of the Tsar, are supporting the Black Hundreds in 1905.*

📖 Historiography

Michael Lynch calls Russification 'peculiarly ill-judged'.

Orlando Figes argues that 'The effect of the Russification campaign was to drive the non-Russians into the new anti-tsarist parties'.

6. The nobility

The nobility were completely loyal to the Tsar and for that reason the Tsar surrounded himself with them, appointing them to lofty positions in the military and government. The Tsar ensured their loyalty by granting them land and titles. However, the fact that many members of the nobility were only concerned with bettering their own positions in life meant that the Tsar was rarely questioned on important issues, with most advisors serving as 'yes men'. This had the effect of stifling necessary political and economic reform and the modernisation of the military in Russia.

GO! Activity 2

Create your own drawing/diagram/cartoon of the social structure in Russia, clearly labelled with facts about each group.

GO! Activity 3

Create a storyboard or visual presentation that explains why governing the Tsarist state was difficult. Use your imagination to make it as interesting as possible.

Activity 4

How secure was the Tsarist state before 1905?

Take two columns in your jotter:

Ways it was secure	Ways it wasn't secure
Orthodox Church made the Tsarist state secure because ...	

Your challenge is to put as much evidence in each column as possible, adding facts, figures, dates and historiography to reinforce your point. Remember that you can have the same issues/factors on both sides. You should use information from the whole section.

Once you have two full columns, compare them with the person sitting next to you and be prepared to justify your points to them and to the class.

Finally, write a concluding paragraph that clearly addresses the question above in a balanced manner, all the while using evidence to back up your argument.

(Higher European and World unit outcomes: 1.1, 1.2, 1.3)

 Activity 5

Exam style questions

How secure was the Tsar's hold on power in the years before 1905? (22)

(Higher European and World unit outcomes: 1.1, 1.2, 1.3, 2.1, 2.2, 2.3)

2 An evaluation of the causes of the 1905 Revolution

In this section you will learn about:

- Long-term causes:
  1. Working-class discontent.
  2. Discontent among the peasantry.
  3. Political problems – discontent with repressive government and its policies.
  4. Economic problems.

- Short-term causes:
  1. Military defeat in the war against Japan.
  2. Bloody Sunday.

Figure 9: *Sergei Witte was the architect of rapid industrialisation in Russia.*

Hint

Trade unions exist to protect the rights of workers. They were illegal in Russia before 1905.

Make the Link

In Modern Studies you learn about the power of trade unions today.

In 1905, Russia descended into chaos and the Tsar's reign was seriously threatened. Peasants seized land in the countryside, workers went on strike in the cities and many national minorities claimed independence from the Russian Empire. There has been much historical debate as to why the 1905 Revolution occurred, with historians focusing on a variety of long- and short-term factors.

Long-term causes

1. Working-class discontent

In the 1890s, Russia underwent rapid industrialisation. The idea of Sergei Witte, one the Tsar's closest advisors, it was hoped that industrialising quickly would allow Russia to compete with the other great powers. Soon factories were springing up in Russia's cities and peasants were migrating there in the hope of work. Unfortunately, the cities were not equipped to cope with the influx of people and quickly became overcrowded. Living conditions deteriorated and in the workplace low pay, long hours and dangerous conditions were the norm. As strikes were illegal, workers felt powerless to improve their lives. The situation became worse in 1900 when a recession resulted in many workers losing their jobs. With the government doing nothing to help them, they became increasingly angry and began to join illegal trade unions and revolutionary groups like the SDs.

These discontented workers were ripe for the anti-Tsarist rhetoric of revolutionaries, and in 1902 and 1903 there was a series of mass strikes. The warning bells had sounded and following the events of Bloody Sunday in January 1905 (which we will look at later) there was a further wave of strikes that saw nearly half a million people down tools. The revolution had begun and, as it gathered pace, workers began to barricade streets, attack factory owners and openly protest and demonstrate against

Tsarist rule. By October 1905 around two and a half million workers had gone on strike and industry was at a standstill. Moreover, by this point the workers had shown an ability to organise themselves, electing representatives to workers' councils known as Soviets.

Figure 10: *In 1905 workers went on strike, crippling Russian industry and the economy. This is a photo of a train that has been overturned by striking workers at a railway depot.*

The St Petersburg Soviet was dominated by revolutionaries, and had as its Chairman the Social Democrat Leon Trotsky. Trotsky and the other Soviet delegates had the clear long-term aim of deposing the Tsar, showing just how dangerous working-class discontent had become to the Tsarist state.

Clearly, long-term working-class discontent played a significant role in causing the 1905 Revolution. It was the workers who moved quickly to show their discontent with the Tsar and go on strike. It is worth considering, however, that behind working-class discontent lay fundamental economic reasons as to why this discontent came about. These will be considered later in the section.

📖 Historiography

Alan Wood argues that the working and living conditions of workers 'created a situation that was obviously conducive to the spread of mass discontent [which saw workers develop an] increasing receptivity to the agitation and propaganda of revolutionary activists'.

2. Discontent among the peasantry

By 1905 the peasantry had many reasons to be unhappy with the Tsar. They lived in simple conditions, worked long hours and had few rights. Bad harvests and out-dated agricultural techniques often led to famines, which, again, the government and landowners did little to alleviate. Many were also burdened with redemption payments.

Having been freed from serfdom in 1861, peasants were given the right to buy their land. However, they could only afford to do so by taking out long-term loans from the government. These loans were paid back, with interest, through redemption payments. These redemption payments had to be paid back over generations, meaning families inherited the debt of those who had taken out loans. What is more, taxes were high for those who owned land, the best land was held back for the landowners and, as the population increased in Russia, prices for land went up. Peasants also had little control over their own affairs.

Figure 11: *The peasantry had many reasons to be unhappy with Tsarist rule, not least the lack of control they had over the land on which they lived and worked. What do you think is happening in this painting?*

The Zemstva Act of 1890 was created by Tsar Alexander III to afford him more direct control over local government. Zemstva were a Russian form of local government and prior to 1890 the peasantry had exercised some control over their own affairs through the Zemstva. However, Alexander III wanted the nobility to have the decision-making powers in rural Zemstva. The Zemstva Act did just this by creating 'land captains', essentially nobles whose job it was to administer and run local government. This angered the peasants greatly. Any protests were dealt with violently by the army.

All these factors meant that by the turn of the century the peasantry were extremely unhappy and when bad harvests resulted in famine in 1902 and 1903 there was a wave of unrest that gradually increased until 1905. By the late summer of 1905 there was widespread disorder in the countryside that took the form of timber cutting, seizing land belonging to the aristocracy, labour strikes and rent strikes, and attacks on landlords' grain stocks. Peasant discontent clearly had an important role in causing the revolution of 1905.

📖 Historiography

Robert Service notes that, 'The peasantry had not been much slower to move against the authorities than the workers'.

3. Political problems – discontent with repressive government and its policies

By the turn of the century the Tsarist regime still relied on repression and violence to govern the Empire. As a result many groups had emerged who called for political change.

Many middle-class liberal Russians were unhappy with their lack of political power and disliked the regressive and repressive policies of the Tsarist government. They wanted the legalisation of political parties and the creation of a Duma so that they could effect real change in Russia. Indeed, by 1905 many liberals had signalled their dissatisfaction by combining with other opposition groups and trade unions to create a Union of Unions, which called for significant political and economic reform in Russia. This, like previous calls for reform, was largely ignored, and led many liberals to join the revolution.

National minorities, as we have seen, had a particularly difficult time in Tsarist Russia and greatly resented the policy of Russification. The Tsar had continually ignored their desire for more independence and throughout the revolution many nations, such as Georgia, took the opportunity to show their discontent by asserting their independence from the Empire. This made the revolution truly Empire-wide.

Revolutionary groups, like the Mensheviks, Bolsheviks and SRs, did not play a significant role in starting the revolution, mainly because it was a fairly spontaneous event with little planning or direction from the beginning. However, they did play a part in it. For example, the Mensheviks, led by Trotsky, were influential in the growth of Soviets in the cities and the Bolsheviks played an important role in the unsuccessful Moscow Uprising in December 1905 when workers took up arms against the government.

Overall, the Tsarist government's repressive policies and lack of political reform played a significant part in causing the revolution of 1905. Had the Tsar been open to political reform, then it would not be too bold to say that the revolution of 1905 may have been avoided.

📖 Historiography

Orlando Figes argues that 'Time and time again, the obstinate refusal of the tsarist regime to concede reforms turned what should have been a political problem into a revolutionary crisis'.

4. Economic problems

As we have seen, economic problems, and the way that the Tsarist government failed to deal with them, were significant in causing working-class discontent. Rapid industrialisation in the 1890s had led to overcrowded cities with terrible living and working conditions and the recession had worsened the situation. The result was widespread anger followed by strikes. Similarly, economic problems were at the heart of peasant dissatisfaction. The government did little to help the peasantry when famine struck in 1897, 1898 and 1901, heaping misery on top of the already dire land situation and terrible conditions in which peasants lived and worked. Therefore, it could be argued that long- and short-term economic problems, and the inadequate way the Tsarist government dealt with them, were a root cause of the 1905 Revolution.

📖 Historiography

Michael Lynch argues that 'the strikes and demonstrations in the pre-1905 period had been the result of economic rather than political factors. It was the tsarist regime's ill-judged policies that turned the disturbances into a direct challenge to its own authority.'

Short-term causes

1. Military defeat in the war against Japan

In 1904 Russia went to war with Japan. The official reason was to protect Russia's interests in the far east of the Empire. The real reason was simply to distract the Russian population from the many problems at home with, as Plehve, the Minister of the Interior said, 'a short, victorious war.' In both senses, the war was a failure.

Figure 12: *This Japanese print from 1904 shows Russian battleships being sunk by the Japanese. The Russo-Japanese war was a failure for the Tsar and his military.*

Initially, the nation got behind the Tsar in a wave of patriotism. However, as news of significant defeats at the hands of the Japanese military surfaced, public opinion turned against the war and, as a consequence, the Tsar. The Russian people had been led to believe that their mighty army and navy would have no problem crushing tiny Japan yet it soon became clear that the exact opposite was happening. In February 1905 the Russian army was defeated at Mukden and three months later the navy suffered a resounding defeat in the battle of Tsushima. Defeat was followed by a mutiny on the Battleship Potemkim and rebellions by troops in the east. The military, it quickly became apparent, had not been well led or well equipped, despite the government pouring so much money into it. To ordinary Russians the war was a humiliating farce that simply highlighted the incompetence of the Tsar and the military commanders he had appointed. Far from providing a distraction from problems at home, the war actually served to highlight them and stimulate further unrest.

📖 Historiography

Michael Lynch argues that 'the incompetence of the government, which the war glaringly revealed, excited the social unrest which it had been specifically designed to dampen'.

2. Bloody Sunday

Figure 13: *An artist's interpretation of Bloody Sunday, 1905.*

On Sunday 22 January 1905 Father Gapon, an Orthodox priest, led a peaceful march of around 100 000 workers and their families to the Winter Palace. He was delivering a petition that over 150 000 people had signed, asking the Tsar to improve the living and working conditions of the workers. The Tsar was not staying in the Winter Palace at the time but the petition could have been received on his behalf. Instead, the peaceful marchers were fired upon by troops and then charged down by mounted Cossacks. As always with the Tsar's army, violence was the answer when faced with a protest of any kind, no matter how peaceful. Estimates vary, but it is thought that around 200 people were killed and 800 wounded. The event became known as Bloody Sunday.

Bloody Sunday caused a wave of revulsion to spread across Russia and immediately there were strikes and marches in protest. The image of the Tsar as the 'little father' of the Russian people was shattered, with people of all classes openly expressing their anger at the Tsarist regime. The Tsar did little until his own uncle, Grand Duke Sergei, was assassinated in February, at which point he announced that there would be political reforms. In many respects, Bloody Sunday was the spark that ignited the revolution of 1905 and set the people firmly against the Tsar.

📖 Historiography

'Bloody Sunday was an overwhelming display of tsarist incompetence.'

Richard Pipes

Regarding Bloody Sunday, Orlando Figes writes: 'In that one vital moment the popular myth of a Good Tsar which had sustained the regime through the centuries was suddenly destroyed'.

🔵 GO! Activity 6

What were the main reasons there was a revolution in 1905?

In pairs, you are going to prepare a lesson designed to answer the question above. You must produce the following:

- An information sheet that describes why the different groups were so unhappy by 1905 and summarises the short-term factors.
- A keynote or PowerPoint presentation that explains the issue. You must say how important each factor is and why.
- An activity for your 'pupils' to complete. You could have them complete a card sort you've made, design a comic strip or simply answer questions on a worksheet.

Your teacher will give you an appropriate amount of time to complete this.

(Higher European and World unit outcomes: 2.1, 2.2, 2.3)

🔵 GO! Activity 7

Forming an argument and reinforcing it with historiography

Discuss in your pairs which factors you believe were most important in causing the revolution. Your challenge is to produce a diagram/picture or simply write a paragraph explaining your reasoning, making sure that you back up your point with clear evidence. Use historiography to reinforce the points you make.

(Higher European and World unit outcomes: 1.1, 1.2, 1.3)

🔵 GO! Activity 8

Exam style questions

How important was working-class discontent in causing the 1905 Revolution in Russia? **(22)**

(Higher European and World unit outcomes: 1.1, 1.2, 1.3, 2.1, 2.2, 2.3)

3 An assessment of the attempts to strengthen Tsarism, 1905–14

In this section you will learn about:

- Measures used by the Tsar:
  1. The October Manifesto and the Fundamental Laws.
  2. Cancellation of redemption payments.
  3. Repression.
  4. Accommodation with the army.
  5. Russification.
- Relations with the Dumas.
- Stolypin: repression, land reforms and industrial reforms.

The 1905 Revolution did not topple the Tsar from power but it did force him to make changes in the way he ruled his empire. From 1905 until the outbreak of the Great War in 1914, various reforms and measures were put into place by the Tsarist government, their aim being to strengthen the Tsarist state following the tumultuous events of 1905. There remains, however, considerable debate as to how successful these reforms were in strengthening Tsarism in this period.

Measures used by the Tsar

1. The October Manifesto and the Fundamental Laws

In October 1905, with the revolution at its height, the Tsar issued the October Manifesto, on the advice of Sergei Witte. This Manifesto promised the creation of an elected Duma that would participate in the passing of laws, and the implementation of a national constitution. It also promised improvements to civil liberties, such as individual rights and freedom of the press. These had been the very reforms that the liberal middle classes and many moderate socialists had long called for, and upon its announcement many of the opposition forces began to disband. Indeed, this was the purpose of the October Manifesto: to placate the liberal middle classes and moderate socialists, thereby splitting them off from the more revolutionary forces.

Figure 14: *A painting showing Russians celebrating the granting of the October Manifesto.*

📖 Historiography

David Welch notes that the October Manifesto was successful in splitting the opposition forces.

The October Manifesto promised many reforms, but the Tsar never intended for it to curb his powers. Indeed, in April 1906, just before the first Duma was due to meet, the Tsar issued the Fundamental Laws.

The Fundamental Laws confirmed and laid out in detail the promises of the October Manifesto. However, they also restated, in no uncertain terms, the authority of the Tsar. They stated, for example, that the Tsar was still 'the supreme autocratic power', that 'no law can come into force without his approval' and that the Tsar could dismiss the Duma when he chose to. Having appeared to give some of his power away with the October Manifesto, the Tsar was firmly taking it back again with the Fundamental Laws. It was a show of strength from the Tsar who, by April 1906, was confident he had now regained control of his empire.

📖 Historiography

Graham Darby notes that the Fundamental Laws was a 'strikingly conservative document … a far cry from the aspirations of liberal society'.

2. Cancellation of redemption payments

Having used the October Manifesto to win over the liberals and some moderate socialists, by November 1905 the Tsar was still faced with a peasantry who were in full revolt in the countryside. Clearly, if the revolution was to be quelled then the peasants would need to be dealt with and the army was still not reliable enough to deal with them all. Again acting on the advice of Witte, the Tsar issued an announcement that redemption payments would be progressively reduced and then eventually abolished in January 1907. This was enough for many peasants, and there was an immediate decline in land seizures and lawlessness in the countryside. Loyal army units dealt with those peasants who continued to rebel. As with the liberals, the policy here had been one of concession, of placation, and it certainly worked in the short term. However, it should be noted that in 1906–07 there were disturbances in the countryside showing that some peasants felt that their position had not really improved.

3. Repression

With two groups placated, the Tsar now had to deal with the workers. Because of their revolutionary ideology, they posed the most immediate threat to his reign. Perhaps because of this, the Tsarist government chose to deal with them quite differently from the other groups. From October onwards, loyal army units were deployed, arresting the leading revolutionaries such as Leon Trotsky, and closing down the Soviets in St Petersburg and Moscow. Violence was at the heart of much of this, illustrated most clearly in the suppression of the Moscow Uprising in December 1905 when rifle fire and artillery bombardment of workers' homes and factories resulted in the deaths of over 1000 people. By the New Year, the workers had been violently and effectively suppressed and the cities again came under the command of Tsarist authorities.

Figure 15: *The army were brought in to violently suppress the workers in the cities.*

📖 Historiography

With regard to the workers, Michael Lynch argues that, 'Here the policy was not one of concession but of suppression'.

4. Accommodation with the army

As we have seen, the Tsar was able to rely on loyal units in St Petersburg and Moscow to suppress the Soviets and workers but it was vital to the regime's security that the whole army could be relied upon. To ensure this, the government introduced reforms to the army, dismissing around 7000 officers who, in the wake of the disastrous Russo-Japanese War, had been found to be either too old or simply unfit for duties. This restored some confidence in the army high command. Also, the daily life of soldiers was improved with a more generous food and clothing allowance provided. In return, the army agreed to help suppress the revolutionaries. Clearly, the accommodation with the army was vital to the Tsar in regaining control of Russia.

5. Russification

Those national minorities who claimed independence amid the turmoil of the revolution were dealt with severely by the Tsarist government. Loyal troops were sent to suppress these groups and the nations were brought back under the rule of the Tsar. Moreover, the policy of Russification was intensified with the aim of re-establishing control over, and reuniting, the Russian Empire. For example, in Ukraine nationalists were dismissed from positions of power and in Poland councils were established that placed power in the hands of Russians. Also, there were violent pogroms in Odessa and Kiev in 1905 and 1906 that saw thousands of Jews killed by pro-Russian groups who blamed them for the revolution. Russification may have helped the Tsar secure power in the short term but in the long term it did not strengthen his position.

Relations with the Dumas

Figure 16: *Tsar Nicholas II formally opens the Duma at a ceremony in the Winter Palace in St Petersburg.*

The Tsar did not intend for the Duma to limit his power and its very structure ensured this. It was bicameral, meaning it had two chambers. The lower chamber was where the elected deputies met to discuss and propose new laws. The upper chamber was called the State Council and its members were appointed directly by the Tsar. The State Council had the power to veto any laws that the deputies proposed, meaning that even before the Duma had met, the Tsar held all the power.

The 1st Duma met in April 1906, with the elections having delivered a mixture of left- and right-wing deputies. These deputies proposed land reform and military funding and urged the Tsar to amend the Fundamental Laws. These ideas were far too radical for the Tsar, and using the powers he had given himself in the Fundamental Laws, he dissolved (closed) the Duma in June.

Following the dissolution of the Duma, unhappy and disillusioned liberal deputies met in Vyborg in Finland, and produced what came to be known as the Vyborg Manifesto. This openly called for civil disobedience in protest at the Tsar's actions. Most Russians ignored it, but there was some violence and disobedience around the countryside, which was dealt with by the army. The Tsar was unimpressed and had these deputies arrested and banned from future Dumas. The failure of the Vyborg Rebellion clearly shows that the Tsar's power remained intact and that he could rely on his army to do his bidding.

Following nationwide elections, the 2nd Duma convened. It once again saw relations between the Tsar and the deputies strained. The two groups disagreed on the issues put forward for discussion and in June 1907 it too was dissolved. (It had only begun in February.) For the new Prime Minister, Peter Stolypin, it was clear that changes had to be made to ensure that the Tsar could work effectively with the Duma. After all, Stolypin argued, the Duma must be made to work if the

Tsarist state was to survive. With that in mind, before the elections for the 3rd Duma, Stolypin violated the Fundamental Laws and restricted the franchise so only the richest Russians could vote. This meant that only 1 in 6 men could now vote, but succeeded in creating a 3rd Duma dominated by conservative, pro-Tsar deputies. As a result, the 3rd Duma would be the most successful.

With Stolypin guiding it, the 3rd Duma worked well with the Tsar. It proposed and carried through reforms to primary education, agriculture and the armed services, as well as improving conditions for industrial workers. The 3rd Duma lasted its full term of five years, ending in 1912, and its success shows us that the Tsarist regime was not completely closed to change. However, these changes only occurred because the franchise had been manipulated to create a pro-Tsar Duma that Nicholas could work with. Arguably, the 3rd Duma increased the power of the Tsar as it demonstrated to some cynics that reforms could be made, but importantly reaffirmed that these changes would only go ahead on the Tsar's terms.

The 4th Duma was less successful than its predecessor, mainly because Peter Stolypin was not there to lead it. In 1911 Stolypin had been assassinated by the leftist revolutionary Dimitri Bogrov and those men who succeeded Stolypin as Prime Minister were incompetent and lacked imagination. Under these men the Duma ceased to be effective at all.

📖 Historiography

With regards to Stolypin's successors, Michael Lynch notes: 'Since they lacked political imagination, their only course was further repression'.

By the time the Great War began in 1914 you could argue that the Dumas had in some ways made the Tsarist state stronger, providing the illusion of reform that so many liberals craved. However, in the long term, the lack of real reform once again built up anger towards the rigid, repressive Tsarist regime.

Stolypin: repression, land reforms and industrial reforms

Peter Stolypin firmly believed that for the Tsarist state to survive, reform was essential. Before reforms could be put in place, however, existing opponents of the Tsar in the cities and countryside had to be dealt with.

Stolypin was unafraid of using violence to deal with revolutionaries. He used the police, army and Okhrana to locate opposition groups. Once arrested, he used courts martial throughout the countryside and in the cities to arrest, try and execute anyone suspected of revolutionary activity. Between 1906 and 1909 Stolypin had around 3000 revolutionaries hanged. As a result, the hangman's noose came to be called 'Stolypin's necktie'. This brutal way of dealing with opposition

Figure 17: *As Prime Minister, Peter Stolypin attempted to save Tsarism by reforming it.*

221

groups resulted in a reduction in the number of protests and rebellions in Russia throughout Stolypin's time as Prime Minister.

📖 Historiography

Robert Service notes that 'Stolypin's necktie ... reduced the countryside to quiescence'.

Stolypin believed that the best way to ensure the long-term security of the Tsarist state was to win over the peasantry. He believed that if he could help make peasants wealthier then they would be more likely to support the Tsar. The first part of this, as we have seen, was the abolition of redemption payments. Further land reforms were introduced that allowed peasants to leave the village commune and own their own property. To help them do this, Stolypin created a land bank to allow peasants to borrow money from the government. While some peasants bought into Stolypin's land reforms, most peasants were resistant to change and did not. Stolypin said it would take 20 years for his land reforms to be successful but, as it was, his assassination in 1911 meant they would only be given five. Because of that, it is hard to say for sure whether or not the land reforms strengthened the Tsar's position, but the Tsar's lack of support for them perhaps meant they were destined to fail in the long run anyway.

📖 Historiography

Orlando Figes argues that by 1914 'Stolpyin's land reforms had ground to a halt'. He also argues that it would have taken a century for these reforms to create a wealthy peasantry who supported the Tsarist regime.

Stolypin also reformed industry. He helped to introduce laws designed to improve working conditions and created a scheme of national insurance for workers. Although living conditions in the cities remained terrible, by 1911 there were some signs of a more content workforce and a growing economy. On the other hand, in 1912 the Bolsheviks returned six deputies to the 4th Duma and the number of industrial strikes rose from 24 in 1911 to 2401 in 1914. Clearly, Stolypin's industrial reforms had not brought long-term peace to the cities or quelled the revolutionary nature of the workers.

📖 Historiography

'The relative calm which had existed during the Stolypin years was coincidental, and was not a positive response from factory workers.'

Martin McColgan

Overall, Stolypin's actions strengthened Tsarism in the short term but failed to fully address the fundamental problems that had caused the 1905 Revolution. The Tsar remained an autocrat and continued to rule Russia in much the same repressive manner as before. When the Great War broke out in August 1914, the Tsar's hold over his empire may have appeared strong, but in reality it was anything but.

 Historiography

Robert Service argues that after 1905 Nicholas II 'had recovered his position, but the basic tensions in state and society had not been alleviated'.

 Activity 9

How well did the Tsar re-establish his control over Russia?

Imagine you are a Russian worker who lived through the 1905 Revolution. Write a diary entry/create a storyboard that describes how the Tsar dealt with the revolution and whether his measures made his position stronger.

(Higher European and World unit outcomes: 1.1, 1.2, 1.3)

Activity 10

Was the Tsarist state stronger in 1914 than in 1905?

Get into groups of three or four and write the following headings on a piece of A3 paper. As you all read through the information in the section, fill in the columns if and when you come across relevant information. Once you have all finished reading and adding in information, go through the points to make sure you all agree on them.

Evidence suggesting it was stronger	Evidence suggesting it was weaker
The Fundamental Laws made the Tsarist state stronger because ...	

Finally, using the information you've gathered, produce an individual piece of work that clearly answers the question above. You must:

- Describe the background to the policies and methods the Tsar employed.
- Explain the various ways the Tsar tried to control Russia in this period.
- Analyse and evaluate how strong the Tsar was by 1914.
- Come to a clear, balanced and evidenced conclusion.

This piece of work could be in the form of a booklet, a presentation, an illustrated mind map, a detailed comic strip or simply an essay.

(Higher European and World unit outcomes: 1.1, 1.2, 1.3, 2.1, 2.2, 2.3)

Activity 11

Summarising historiography

Your challenge is to create a simple poster that summarises each piece of historiography in as simple terms as possible, using pictures if need be. The purpose of this task is to get you thinking about what each historian means and then put it in your words. For example:

Welch: October Manifesto split opposition forces.

> ### Hint
>
> Try to use one or two piece of historiography in your essays to reinforce your points.

Activity 12

Exam style questions

To what extent was the power of the Tsarist state weakened in the years between 1905 and 1914? (22)

(Higher European and World unit outcomes: 1.1, 1.2, 1.3, 2.1, 2.2, 2.3)

4 An evaluation of the reasons for the February Revolution, 1917

In this section you will learn about:

- The role of Tsar Nicholas II.
- The role of Tsarina Alexandra.
- Political problems: discontent among all classes – middle class, working class and peasantry; the inherent weaknesses of the autocracy.
- The impact of the First World War: military defeat; economic problems.

On 2 March 1917 Tsar Nicholas II abdicated his throne. A popular revolution in February had forced him from power, bringing the Romanov dynasty to an end. Historians have long grappled with the question of why the February Revolution occurred, examining the roles of the Tsar and Tsarina and the many political problems that plagued Russia by 1917. They have also stressed the importance of the impact of the Great War, a conflict with which the Tsarist regime struggled to cope.

The role of Tsar Nicholas II

When Nicholas became Tsar in 1894 he was reported to have said 'I am not ready to be Tsar. I know nothing of the business of ruling.' This set the tone for his reign as Tsar.

Nicholas was a firm believer in autocracy and was opposed to political reform in Russia. Throughout his rule this never wavered, highlighting his inability to adjust to changing circumstances or grasp the seriousness of the events that faced him. This was especially evident in February 1917 when he was urged to return to Russia from the front to deal with the mounting problems in the capital. Nicholas was a weak leader who lacked the political intelligence required in his role as Tsar and the Great War served to highlight his failings.

> ### 🔍 Hint
> When the war broke out, the Tsar changed the name of the capital from the German sounding St Petersburg to the more Russian Petrograd.

Figure 18: *Tsar Nicholas II. Some historians believe that he was wholly unsuited to being Tsar and that he played a pivotal role in his own downfall in 1917.*

> ### 🔍 Hint
> Nicholas's son and heir, the Tsarevich Alexei, joined him at the front to boost troop morale.

Figure 19: *A photo of the Tsar with his troops in 1915. His decision to take command of the army would prove to be a mistake.*

In 1915, with Russia struggling against Germany on the eastern front, Nicholas felt it was his duty to lead and took personal control of the armed forces. This allied him to the fate of his army and as defeats mounted on the battlefield, he became personally accountable for their failures. His lack of military knowledge also quickly became clear and he lost the support of his troops and officers as a result. The decision to lead the armed forces was a significant mistake and contributed to the perception of him as a weak and incompetent ruler.

📖 Historiography

Orlando Figes argues that 'Nicholas was the source of all the problems. In a sense, Russia gained in him the worst of both worlds: a Tsar determined to rule from the throne yet quite incapable of exercising power'.

The role of Tsarina Alexandra

> ## ☄ Make the Link
>
> In Biology you may learn about genetic disorders like haemophilia.

The Tsarina Alexandra was a significant influence on her husband, acting as confidant and advisor to him. She too firmly believed in autocracy and had no time for those who urged her husband to introduce political reform. When the Tsar left Petrograd to take control of the armed forces in 1915, Alexandra was left in charge. As a German, she was not fully trusted or liked by the Russian people and her reputation and credibility, and that of the Tsarist regime, were irreparably damaged by the presence at court of a priest named Rasputin.

Gregory Rasputin was a priest and mystic who became very close to the Tsarina. She believed that Rasputin was able to alleviate her son the Tsarevich's haemophilia, a blood disorder that was potentially fatal. There were various instances where Rasputin appeared to be able to do just this and it allowed him to gain considerable influence in the Tsarina's court, meddling in key areas of government. Rumours began to spread of an affair between Alexandra and Rasputin, and Russians began to question Rasputin's influence in government affairs. Public opinion turned sharply against the Tsarina and her husband with many in the Tsar's inner circle becoming increasingly worried about the damage Rasputin was doing. Indeed, it was the Tsar's nephew, Prince Yusopov, who, in trying to bring an end to the whole scandal, murdered Rasputin in December 1916. By this point, however, the damage had been done. The scandal had undermined the credibility of the Tsarist system and highlighted the corruption at the heart of the regime.

📖 Historiography

Figure 20: *A caricature of Rasputin and the royal couple. What do you think the artist is trying to say?*

Michael Lynch argues that 'The Rasputin scandal had been a bizarre symptom of the disease affecting Russian politics rather than a cause'.

Political problems: discontent among all classes and the inherent weaknesses of the autocracy

By the time of the Great War, the Tsarist government had not dealt with the long-term political problems that had caused the 1905 Revolution. While political parties were now legal and citizens had more civil rights, the reforms that the October Manifesto and Stolypin promised had not really materialised. As a result, the bourgeoisie, the peasantry and the workers felt removed from the running of the country; these feelings only became more acute during the war.

Discontent among the bourgeoisie

When the war began the Duma voted to suspend itself so as to allow the Tsar to focus on the war. The bourgeoisie were keen to contribute to the war effort and, with the liberal Prince Lvov leading them, set up the Zemstvo Union.

The Zemstvo Union was a large organisation of town councils that essentially ran the war effort in Russia since the government seemed incapable of doing so. Supporters of the Tsar disliked it as they believed it undermined Tsarist authority but without it Russia would have struggled even more. The Zemstvo Union's success served to highlight the failures of the Tsarist government and show the Russian people that there was a working alternative to Tsarism.

By July 1915 there were major problems on the eastern and home fronts. When the Tsar allowed the Duma to reconvene in July 1915, the main liberal and nationalist parties, supported by the SRs, formed a progressive bloc in the hope of persuading the Tsar to form a national government that would win the people's support. The Tsar refused to listen, seeing it as an attempt to dilute his power. He dissolved the Duma on 2 September. From September 1915 until February 1917, the Tsarina appointed and dismissed numerous ministers in what became known as 'ministerial leapfrog'. There was no continuity at all and the work of the government ground to a halt. Liberal politicians began to make speeches denouncing the ineffective and corrupt Tsarist government and soon Duma politicians from across the political spectrum, from the liberal Prince Lvov to the SR leader Kerensky, were agreed that something needed to be done about the monarchy. The Tsar had finally lost the support of the bourgeoisie and political elite.

📖 Historiography

J.P. Nettl argues that during the war it became clear to politicians and ministers that 'nothing could be done with the obstinate and totally unperceptive autocrat'.

🔍 Hint

The term bourgeoisie is often used by Marxists to describe the affluent middle class.

Make the Link

In Modern Studies you may learn about how political or charitable groups organise themselves to address issues about which they are concerned.

Figure 21: *Soldiers quickly joined workers in the marches and strikes in Petrograd in February 1917.*

Working-class discontent

Politically, the working class supported the revolutionary Bolsheviks and Mensheviks. However, their leaders were generally in exile in Siberia or abroad. Still, these groups continued to grow in power and support as the effects of the war made the already terrible living and working conditions of the workers worse. Food shortages became acute in the cities, resulting in long queues and bread riots. Housing and sanitation fell into disrepair and cities became overcrowded with refugees fleeing German occupation in the east. On 22 February 1917 there was a strike at the huge Putilov armaments factory in Petrograd. The following day, International Women's Day, women textile labourers began a demonstration and by 24 February industry was virtually at a standstill in the capital. The streets flooded with workers who were spurred on by revolutionaries and the army units sent to put them down refused, with many joining in the demonstrations. Working-class discontent was such that the Tsar had lost control of his capital and the factories that were vital to the war effort.

📖 Historiography

Alan Wood has argued that the February Revolution 'was caused by the spontaneous upsurge of the politically radicalised masses'. However, since the fall of the Soviet Union and the opening of the Soviet archives, we are now more aware of the main actors in the revolution and that it was perhaps not quite as spontaneous as Wood argues.

Peasant discontent

Peasant discontent over the land issue did not subside during the war years. Most of the conscripts to the army were peasants, which meant fewer men to farm the land and, as horses were also requisitioned by the army, those peasants who relied on the animals to survive suffered. Most notably, however, the massive number of casualties in the Russian army was felt most among the peasantry. When order broke down in the army many peasant soldiers deserted to claim the land they worked on, prompting those in the countryside to do the same. Before long the countryside was in open revolt and the Tsar could no longer rely on the army to deal with it.

The inherent weaknesses of the autocracy

The autocratic system had only functioned in the past because Russia had remained largely unchanged for centuries. As Russia tried to modernise its economy under Nicholas II, the autocracy did not modernise with it and this created tensions that it did not deal with. Also, the corrupt and centralised nature of the autocracy was highlighted during the war as the badly led military and inefficient transport system and economy struggled to cope under the leadership of the weak Tsar. In essence, the inherent weaknesses of the autocracy, and the Tsar's inability to confront them, arguably lie right at the heart of the February Revolution. In many respects, the Tsar's blind devotion to autocracy made him the architect of his own downfall.

📖 Historiography

Christopher Hill argued that 'The fundamental cause of the Russian Revolution, then, was the incompatibility of the tsarist state with the demands of modern civilisation'.

Orlando Figes argues that '… the tsarist system proved much too rigid and unwieldy, too inflexible and set in its ways, too authoritarian and inefficient, to adapt itself to the situation as it changed'.

The impact of the First World War: military defeat

The war did not start well for Russia, with the army suffering defeats and sustaining heavy losses at Tannenberg and the Masurian Lakes in August and September 1914. The Russian army now relied heavily on their reserve troops who had barely been trained, and often did not know how to march or load a rifle. To make matters worse, the army experienced terrible shortages as the transport network struggled to deliver munitions, food, clothes and medical care to the front. By the spring of 1915 there was a real shortage of weapons with some battalions having to undergo training without rifles and others having to rely on picking up rifles from those shot in front of them. As defeats mounted casualty rates soared and morale plummeted. Before long officers were struggling to control their troops with many choosing to desert their trenches in favour of returning home. Peasant soldiers felt little loyalty to a Tsar who clearly cared little for them.

By the end of July 1915 the Russian army was in retreat and the Tsar's ill-fated decision to take control of the army in August did not deliver the boost to morale he had hoped. Instead, revolutionary propaganda spread, desertions increased and over a million men surrendered to the advancing Germans and Austrians. By early 1917, the officers and troops had completely lost faith in the Tsar and his leadership. Soldiers joined the strikes in Petrograd and it was the generals who forced the Tsar's abdication at Pskov in March 1917. The loyalty of the army, for so long the backbone of Tsarist rule, had been lost and military defeat had played a pivotal role in this.

🔍 Hint

The First World War is often called the 'Great War' or 'World War One'.

💥 Make the Link

If you study the Scottish topic, The Impact of the Great War, 1914–28, you will look at the First World War in more detail.

Figure 22: *A Russian soldier tries to stop two fellow troops deserting during the First World War.*

📖 Historiography

Graham Darby argues that '... it was the decision of the generals not to support Nicholas and not to restore order that brought him down'.

The impact of the First World War: economic problems

🔍 **Hint**

The First World War impacted the economies of every nation that took part, with some coping better than others.

The Great War put a massive strain on the already fragile Russian economy. The inefficient transport system meant trains full of food destined for the cities were pushed off the line to make way for military trains. This led, of course, to food shortages that were then made worse by the growing refugee crisis. What is more, inflation was running high in Russia: wages may have doubled by 1917, but food prices, on average, had quadrupled. In the countryside, the government ordered that grain be taken from peasant farmers to feed the cities but it was impossible to force them to do so. When the strikes in Petrograd began in late February, there were shouts of 'Down with the Tsar!' and, tellingly, 'Bread!' The economic effects of the war, therefore, were considerable. They contributed to the public's loss of support for the Tsar that was most clear in the strikes that crippled Petrograd.

📖 Historiography

S.A. Smith argues that 'When the February Revolution came, it was not as the result of military defeat, or even war weariness, but as the result of the collapse of public support in the government'.

🔵 Activity 13

Why was there a revolution in February 1917?

Get into groups of three and number yourselves 1–3.

Each person will now become an expert on their two respective sub-topics below, creating an A3 poster presentation on each that will be used to teach the other members of the group.

Your teacher will give you an appropriate amount of time to complete this activity.

Rules!

- Your poster is your teaching aid, and should contain pictures and no more than 40 words.
- Remember to include historiography where possible.
- When explaining your posters, you should not be writing anything and the other members should be taking notes.

Number 1s

Evidence that the Tsar and Tsarina caused the revolution.

Evidence that inherent weaknesses in the autocracy caused the revolution.

Number 2s

Evidence that peasant discontent caused the revolution.

Evidence that the First World War caused the revolution.

Number 3s

Evidence that bourgeoisie discontent caused the revolution.

Evidence that working-class discontent caused the revolution.

Weighing up the evidence

In your groups of three, discuss which factors you think are most important and why. Write them down in order of importance with a clear paragraph below that explains your reasoning and overall argument.

(Higher European and World unit outcomes: 1.1, 1.2, 1.3)

 Activity 14

Exam style questions

To what extent did working-class discontent cause the outbreak of the February Revolution in 1917?
(22)

(Higher European and World unit outcomes: 1.1, 1.2, 1.3, 2.1, 2.2, 2.3)

5 An evaluation of the reasons for the success of the October Revolution, 1917

In this section you will learn about:

- The inherent weaknesses of the Provisional Government: Dual Power and the role of the Petrograd Soviet.
- The decision to continue the war.
- Economic problems.
- The land issue.
- Political problems: the Kornilov Revolt.
- The appeal of the Bolsheviks: policies, propaganda and the leadership of Lenin.

When the Tsar abdicated on 2 March 1917, he also did so on behalf of his ill son and heir. The monarchy was offered to his younger brother, the Grand Duke Mikhail, who a day later gave it up. Russia was now without a monarch but in its place a Provisional Government had emerged, appointing itself to run the empire before elections could be held. However, in October 1917 there was another revolution, and the Provisional Government was ousted by Lenin's Bolsheviks. There are various reasons why the October Revolution was successful, with some historians pointing to the failures of the Provisional Government to command popular support, and others highlighting the success of the Bolsheviks in capitalising on the fragile and uncertain political situation of the time. For good reason, it remains one of the most discussed and debated issues in Russian and modern European history.

The inherent weaknesses of the Provisional Government: Dual Power and the role of the Petrograd Soviet

The Provisional Government was led by Prince Lvov but lacked legitimacy from the start as it had not been elected. When the names of the government were being read out, someone in the crowd shouted 'Who appointed you?' summing up many Russians' feelings at the time. The Provisional Government stressed that it was only in charge until a Constituent assembly could be elected in November, but in the meantime that meant it relied on the goodwill of the people to rule. Clearly, its lack of legitimacy meant it lacked authority. The government was also faced with the fact that there existed a rival power structure in the form of the Petrograd Soviet.

📖 Historiography

Orlando Figes argues that the Provisional Government should have organised elections quicker, and by not doing so, 'it enabled the Bolsheviks to sow serious doubts in the people's minds about its intentions to hold them at all'.

The Petrograd Soviet had first assembled during the 1905 Revolution and in late February 1917, as revolution swept the Tsar from power, it did so again. It was led by Mensheviks and SRs and contained representatives of workers, sailors and soldiers who saw the Soviet as the only legitimate authority in the land. As a result the Soviet wielded much power from the beginning, essentially being in control of the city's industry and military. Indeed, by passing Soviet Order No. 1, it meant that the military orders of the government were only to be obeyed if the Petrograd Soviet had approved them. This obviously undermined the power of the government. Politically, it meant a period of Dual Power in Russia, where the Provisional Government had to compromise with the Soviet as it ran Russia.

🔍 Hint

In February 1917 the Bolsheviks were not as popular as the Mensheviks or SRs.

📖 Historiography

'It is a commonplace of history that any government that cannot control its army cannot wield real power.'

Michael Lynch

Figure 23: *The Petrograd Soviet had considerable power following the abdication of the Tsar.*

To begin with, relations between the two were fairly positive. The Soviet supported the new civil, religious and political freedoms that the government had introduced. The fact that some members of the government, such as the SR leader Kerensky, were also members of the Soviet helped the Dual Power function. However, as problems in Russia mounted in the coming months, each group developed very different ideas as to how they should be dealt with. The government became more right wing in its outlook and the Soviet more left wing, especially as the more radical Bolsheviks gained influence. Cooperation became very difficult and the government struggled to run Russia as part of the Dual Power.

The decision to continue the war

The Great War was not popular in Russia and had almost bankrupted the country. Despite this, the Provisional Government decided to continue with it. This was an almost impossible decision for the government because its ministers recognised that if Russia pulled out of the war, they would have to pay back the loans the Tsarist government had taken out and no more loans from foreign bankers or countries would come in. The economy would collapse in such circumstances. The other side of the coin was that by staying in the war the government made itself very unpopular. The decision to stay in the war, therefore, was not an easy one and while it allowed the economy to stay afloat, it also meant the Bolsheviks were able to gain support from those who saw them as the only party that would remove Russia from the war.

📖 Historiography

Michael Lynch argues that the government was in '… an impossible and paradoxical situation: in order to survive it had to keep Russia in the war, but in keeping Russia in the war it ruined its chances of survival'.

In June, Kerensky, the Minister of War, launched an offensive against the Germans in an attempt to rally the people behind the government. SRs and Mensheviks who had joined the government supported him but the offensive did not go to plan. 60 000 soldiers were killed and the operation collapsed amid large-scale desertions and a total breakdown in the army's power structure. The failure of the June offensive had worsened troop morale and made the government even more unpopular. This obviously played into the hands of the anti-war Bolsheviks.

📖 Historiography

Alan Wood argues that, 'The "collaboration" of Menshevik and SR ministers with the bourgeois, pro-war government meant that the Bolsheviks were now the only political faction which pursued an unswervingly anti-war policy'.

Economic problems

The Provisional Government was faced with a dire economic situation due to the continuing war. 476 million roubles were printed in April, one billion in July. Inflation reached 1000%. Wages couldn't keep up with inflation and there were large bread queues in the cities. At the same time taxes rose and power cuts were still common. Many Russians were poor, hungry and unhappy, and the lack of help from the Provisional Government pushed them evermore towards the revolutionary Bolsheviks.

Make the Link

If you take Business Management you may learn about why inflation occurs.

 Historiography

Edward Acton notes that 'the Government failed to cater for the needs of the people and paid the political price'.

The land issue

The peasantry had hoped that the Provisional Government would give them the land they lived and worked on. However, this did not happen as the government claimed it was too large an administrative task to complete before the elections in November and that it really should be left for a democratically elected government to decide upon. Both points can be seen as fair but to the peasantry they were little more than excuses from a government full of landowners. From April onwards, urged on by Lenin's Bolsheviks, peasants took matters into their own hands and the number of land and property seizures by peasants increased markedly. In March there had been only 49 risings; this leapt to 378 in April, 678 in May and in October there were 1169. The failure of the government to address the land issue resulted in revolution in the countryside and pushed many peasants into the grateful arms of the Bolsheviks who supported the peasants' actions.

📖 Historiography

Graham Darby points out that the Provisional Government's land policy resulted in peasants losing faith with the administration.

Political problems: the Kornilov Revolt

In July 1917 the Bolsheviks attempted to take over Petrograd but were suppressed by troops loyal to the Provisional Government. As a result of this attempted coup, some Bolshevik leaders were arrested and Lenin fled to the countryside. However, a month later General Kornilov attempted a military coup and the Provisional Government did not have the men to stop him. The new Prime Minister, Kerensky, was desperate, freeing and then arming the Bolsheviks to help suppress Kornilov. As it turned out, force was not required to stop the revolt because railway workers loyal to the Soviets refused to operate the trains bringing Kornilov and his troops to Petrograd. In the end the revolt was significant because it showed how weak the Provisional Government had become and it resulted in the Bolsheviks gaining weapons and confidence. In acting to save itself, the Provisional Government had handed the initiative to those who sought to destroy it.

> 🔍 **Hint**
>
> A coup is when a group tries to seize power suddenly, usually through force.

Figure 24: *General Kornilov tried unsuccessfully to seize power in August 1917. In the end, the Kornilov Revolt actually helped the Bolsheviks.*

Hint

A German officer likened Lenin's return to a 'virus in a test-tube' being delivered to its host. What do you think he meant?

Hint

A thesis is a set of ideas (plural: theses).

The appeal of the Bolsheviks: policies, propaganda and the leadership of Lenin

Led by Vladimir Lenin the Bolsheviks were a Marxist party who sought the immediate overthrow of the existing order through a workers' revolution. Lenin envisaged himself leading this revolution but, when the Tsar fell from power, he was in exile in Switzerland. Seeking help from the German government – who hoped his presence in Russia would further destabilise Russia – he was smuggled through Europe in a sealed train. His arrival in April changed the course of Russian history.

Bolshevik policies

Figure 25: *Lenin was the leader of the Bolsheviks. Here he is making a speech in 1920, with Trotsky looking on at the side.*

Upon Lenin's return to Russia, he published his April Theses. These called for an end to the war; the overthrow of the Provisional Government; an increase in the power of the Soviets; and for land to be given to the peasants. The April Theses provided the Bolsheviks with clear policies that were easily summed up in the slogans 'Peace, Bread, and Land' and 'All Power to the Soviets'. Lenin had quickly identified the main problems in Russia and offered simple solutions to them. Further, by adapting Marxist theory to include the peasantry as part of the revolution, Lenin brought this large group into the fold and increased the number of Bolshevik supporters. With all this in mind, it is clear that the policies of the Bolsheviks were crucial in the success of the October Revolution. When the time came to seize power these policies had helped create a broad base of support but had also, perhaps more crucially, helped to undermine the popularity and credibility of the Provisional Government.

📖 Historiography

Ronald Suny argues that the Bolsheviks came to power because their policies 'placed them at the head of a genuinely popular movement'.

Michael Lynch thinks differently to Suny, arguing that 'His [Lenin's] objective had not been to win mass support but to create a party capable of seizing power when the political circumstances permitted'.

Bolshevik propaganda

The Bolsheviks had been spreading revolutionary propaganda in the trenches throughout the war and this continued when the Provisional Government came to power. Pamphlets openly calling for the overthrow of the government and an end to the war were distributed in trenches, and Bolshevik troops did their best to undermine officers.

The Bolsheviks used their party newspaper, *Pravda*, to spread their revolutionary propaganda and party slogans. Propaganda had the dual effect of undermining the policies of the Provisional Government and highlighting what Russia could expect under Bolshevik rule.

The leadership of Lenin

Lenin was a skilful politician and leader, with a real determination to succeed. He convinced many sceptical Bolsheviks to adopt his April Theses as party policy, even though he had not been in Russia for years, and he oversaw the massive growth in party membership and support in 1917. Some estimates put Bolshevik membership at around 20 000 in February and then 340 000 in October. Also, it was Lenin who insisted that Bolshevik members attend Soviet meetings, whatever time they were on, so that votes could be won and the Soviets thus dominated. As a result, by late September 1917 the Bolsheviks controlled the urban Soviets in northern, central and south-eastern Russia, including those in Petrograd and Moscow. Crucially, in a meeting in October 1917 Lenin used all his skills as a politician and leader to convince the Bolshevik Central Committee that the time was ripe for an armed uprising, despite many doubting whether this was possible. Clearly, Lenin's leadership was vital to the success of the October Revolution.

> **Hint**
>
> Pravda means 'truth' in English.

Figure 26: *Lenin reading the Bolshevik newspaper* Pravda *in 1918. Pravda published Lenin's April Theses and was responsible for spreading Bolshevik propaganda.*

> **Hint**
>
> Any essay on the October Revolution has to recognise the role of Lenin.

📖 Historiography

Orlando Figes stresses Lenin's role in the October Revolution: 'Without his decisive personal influence, it is hard to imagine the Bolshevik seizure of power'.

Lenin was important in the actual seizure of power on the 26 October but so was Trotksy. As the Chairman of the Military Revolutionary Committee it was Trotsky who, on the night of 24 October, ensured that Bolshevik troops were in place and that key points around Petrograd were under Bolshevik control. The successful seizure of power in October therefore owes a lot to Trotsky. Others might argue, however, that it was Lenin who, as leader, had given Trotksy the job to do.

Summary

When Bolshevik troops stormed the Winter Palace on the night of 25 October they were faced with little resistance, with only a dozen or so people losing their lives. Clearly, the government had lost all support, mainly because of the problems it faced and the decisions it made, but also because the Bolsheviks capitalised on these at every turn. In the end, the Provisional Government had been faced with an impossible task; Lenin just made sure that this was the case.

📖 Historiography

Michael Lynch argues that 'In October 1917 the Bolsheviks were pushing against an already open door'.

'The October insurrection was a coup d'etat, actively supported by a small minority of the population … but it took place amidst a social revolution, which was centered on the popular realisation of Soviet power'.

Orlando Figes

GO! Activity 15

Why were the Bolsheviks able to seize power in October 1917?

You are going to collect evidence that addresses the above issue and then use the evidence to form an argument.

Firstly, collect evidence under the headings/factors given at the start of the section. Do not copy directly from the text; instead, summarise points in your own words and note down any important dates or statistics. For each factor, write a sentence at the end of your notes saying how important it was in the success of the October Revolution and why.

(Higher European and World unit outcomes: 2.1, 2.2, 2.3)

Secondly, go through your notes with the person sitting next to you, discussing your findings and your arguments for each factor. Discuss the relative importance of each factor, comparing them against each other.

Thirdly, on a piece of A4 paper, list the factors in order of importance with historiography beside or below each one to show your awareness of alternative interpretations.

(Higher European and World unit outcomes: 1.1, 1.2, 1.3)

Lastly, use all this information to answer the exam style question below, ensuring your conclusion is well evidenced.

GO! Activity 16

Exam style questions

How important was Lenin's leadership in the success of the 1917 October Revolution?   **(22)**

(Higher European and World unit outcomes: 1.1, 1.2, 1.3, 2.1, 2.2, 2.3)

6 An evaluation of the reasons for the victory of the Reds in the civil war

In this section you will learn about:

- Superior Red resources and geography.
- Unity of the Reds and disunity among the Whites.
- The leadership of Lenin.
- The role of Trotsky: the organisation of the Red Army.
- The use of terror.
- The effects of foreign intervention and propaganda.

Following the success of the October Revolution the Bolsheviks still had a lot of work to do. In reality, they had only seized the capital, were faced with opposition from Mensheviks and SRs who were angry that the Bolsheviks had chosen to act alone, and had no popular mandate to rule. Following the Constituent Assembly elections in which the Bolsheviks gained only a quarter of the votes, Lenin used his soldiers, the Red Guards, to dissolve the Assembly in January 1918. This act of violence was a sign of things to come and in the coming months opposition to Bolshevik rule grew.

By the summer of 1918 various groups had formed who wanted to rid Russia of the Bolsheviks. They became known, collectively, as the Whites, although each group and its leader had different ambitions and aims for a post-Bolshevik Russia. Between 1918 and 1921, these Whites fought the Reds – the Bolsheviks – for control of Russia, in what was to be a bloody civil war. Ultimately, the Reds emerged victorious. A number of factors contributed to this, not least the superior resources of the Reds and the leadership of Trotsky.

Superior Red resources and geography

From the outset the Reds had a significant advantage over the Whites, namely the fact they controlled the heavily populated and resource-rich central-west region of Russia. This gave them, firstly, a bigger reservoir of manpower to call on than the Whites. As a result, the Red Army was around ten times the size of the collective White forces.

Secondly, the weapons left over from the Great War, and the armament factories, were in the large cities that the Reds controlled. As a result the Reds had a far superior arsenal to the Whites throughout the civil war.

Also, the Reds controlled Moscow, the main hub of the railway network, allowing them to transport resources and troops easily. This also enabled them to establish a solid defensive line in the western-central region of

Make the Link

In Modern Studies you may study modern-day civil wars.

Hint

The Bolsheviks pulled Russia out of the Great War in March 1918.

Russia. The Whites, by contrast, were divided, meaning they could not coordinate their strategies or move resources easily between armies. Unsurprisingly, many of the bloodiest battles were fought over railway heads that would have allowed the victors control over a vast area.

Figure 27: *As the map shows, the White forces were divided. Also, the Red-controlled area contained the largest industrial areas.*

Figure 28: *A Red Army detachment fighting White forces in the civil war.*

Clearly, the Reds' control of the western-central areas in Russia was vital as it meant they controlled the resource-rich areas and could defend their position more easily. The geography of the civil war, therefore, played a major role in the Red victory.

📖 Historiography

Richard Pipes believes that the Reds had such an advantage from the beginning in terms of resources and geography, that the outcome of the civil war was a 'foregone conclusion'.

Orlando Figes stresses the importance of geography noting that 'the Whites were fragmented units separated by large distances which meant they had difficulty coordinating their operations'.

Unity of the Reds and disunity among the Whites

The Red Army was united: its leaders, officers and soldiers were driven by the shared ideological goal of establishing a Communist state in Russia. This helped keep morale high as soldiers believed in what they were fighting for. The unity of the Reds made them a stronger, more formidable, fighting force in stark contrast to the Whites.

Make the Link

In PE you may learn about the importance of unity and working together as a team towards a common goal.

The White armies were divided, not only by geography, but also by their vision for a post-civil war Russia. The only thing each White leader had in common was their desire to defeat the Reds. After this, they differed massively, with some favouring a military government, others a democracy. There were even some who wanted to restore the monarchy. Indeed, the fact that the White leaders were associated with the old Tsarist regime meant troops often distrusted their officers and commanders, affecting morale and discipline. Moreover, the White leaders, whether it was Admiral Kolchak or General Denikin, did not fully trust one another, often disagreed on strategy and tactics, and failed to coordinate attacks on the Reds. As a result, they ended up fighting their own individual wars with the Red Army, making it easy for Reds to direct resources to whichever front they were being attacked on and to pick off each army one by one.

📖 Historiography

Orlando Figes argues that the Reds' 'crucial advantage' was unity; that 'they could claim to be defending the Revolution.' The Whites, on the other hand, suffered 'a problem of image … that they were associated with the old regime'.

The leadership of Lenin

Make the Link

In Business Management you may learn about different economic models.

Following the seizure of power in October, Lenin's authority within the Bolshevik Party was unquestioned. In the civil war he had an iron grip over the area the Reds controlled and ruthlessly ensured the Red Army had all the resources necessary to win.

In the civil war, Lenin introduced War Communism. This meant that the Bolsheviks took control of industry and the economy and essentially directed all energies and resources towards the war effort. For example, peasants were forced to sell their grain to the Reds for a fixed price, even if they had little to eat themselves. This resulted in terrible famines in many areas of Russia. It did, however, ensure that Red troops were always well supplied and well fed. For ordinary Russians, Lenin's War Communism was a disaster but it helped the Reds win the war.

The role of Trotsky: the organisation of the Red Army

Leon Trotsky was a key figure in the Russian civil war. Lenin had made him Commissar for War, putting him in charge of creating and then leading the Red Army. Trotksy had no formal military training or background but he would prove to be an excellent military strategist and leader.

Figure 29: *Trotksy, second from right, inspects Red Army troops along one of the vital railways.*

Trotksy had a free hand in military affairs meaning that he alone decided on issues such as recruitment. Indeed, it was Trotsky's decision to recruit 50 000 ex-Tsarist officers so as to bolster the discipline, experience and professionalism of the Red Army. He introduced conscription, and by 1921 the Red Army as a whole had grown to around three million men.

In terms of discipline, Trotksy appointed political commissars to observe any soldiers, officers or regulars whose loyalty to the cause was questionable. He put into place firm punishments for desertions, proclaiming that 'if any unit retreats without orders, the first to be shot down will be the commissary of the unit, and next the commander.' Trotsky even sanctioned the kidnapping of soldiers' families as a punishment or deterrent. He was ruthless and single-minded in his pursuit of a disciplined, formidable Red Army.

Trotksy also recognised the importance of morale. He travelled along the front line in his armoured train, which doubled as his military headquarters, stopping to deliver inspirational speeches to troops. Throughout the course of the war Trotsky's train covered 65 000 miles, demonstrating the importance he attached to being as close to his troops as possible. His energy and determination rubbed off on his army and his presence on the front line was known to have a positive effect on morale.

Trotsky undoubtedly played a significant role in the Red victory in the civil war. His organisation, vision, determination and energy were in stark contrast to the Whites who lacked a leader of his stature and suffered accordingly.

📖 Historiography

Robert Service believes that the Reds won due to Trotsky's ruthlessness, as he rebuilt and transformed the Red Army into an effective fighting force.

Richard Pipes highlights the inadequacies of the White leaders in explaining Trotsky's success.

Use of terror

On 20 December 1917, Lenin created the Cheka. The Cheka was the Bolshevik secret police force, essentially Lenin's version of the Okhrana. In July 1918 the Cheka executed the Tsar and his family, thereby removing the possibility of a Romanov restoration. A month later, following a failed assassination attempt on his life in August 1918, Lenin instructed the Cheka to 'prepare for terror'. Throughout the civil war the Cheka brutally suppressed opposition through the use of terror.

The Cheka had almost unlimited power to eradicate opposition to the Reds. Torture was widely used and by 1922 it is thought around 140 000 people had been executed, including leaders of other political parties (Lenin had made political parties illegal). This not only removed opposition to the Reds but also created a climate of fear in Bolshevik Russia, thereby reducing potential opposition.

> 🔍 **Hint**
> Trotksy was considered a better orator than Lenin by those who heard them both speak.

> 🔍 **Hint**
> The woman who shot Lenin was a Social Revolutionary. This gave him an excuse to remove SR leaders.

Effects of foreign intervention and propaganda

When the civil war began, Russia's former wartime allies – France, Britain, Japan and the USA – came in on the side of the Whites. They were keen to install a new government in Russia that would re-open the Eastern Front against Germany.

Initially, foreign countries supplied the Whites with munitions and some troops. However, when Germany surrendered in the Great War in November 1918, the Allies' enthusiasm for involvement in Russia began to wane. By the end of 1919 most foreign troops had left Russia, having made little impact on the war.

In many respects, the intervention of foreign countries actually benefited the Reds more, as they were able to use it in their propaganda. The Reds showed the Whites as the agents of anti-Russian foreign powers who were seeking to return Russia to its pre-revolutionary state. The Reds, unsurprisingly, depicted themselves as the patriotic saviours of Russia and the revolution. Unwittingly, the Allies' intervention actually served to undermine the White cause rather than reinforce it.

The Reds also used propaganda, in the form of posters, pamphlets, cinema newsreels and speeches, to further the idea that the people were in charge of Russia now, through the Soviets, and that the Whites wanted to take this away from them. This helped to increase support for the Bolsheviks in the civil war.

📖 Historiography

Evan Mawdsley argues that 'foreign intervention was often half-hearted and militarily ineffective.'

Summary

Victory in the civil war was all but assured for the Reds in late 1920 when the last remaining White army was defeated in the Crimea. Russia was now under Bolshevik control, with a brutal army and secret police in place to suppress any opposition to the dominant ideology. In 1921, Russia was in many ways not dissimilar to how it had been 40 years earlier.

🔍 Hint

It is not unusual for foreign powers to intervene in civil wars to protect their own interests.

⁞∴ Make the Link

In Geography or Modern Studies you may learn about countries that receive foreign aid in war and peacetime.

Figure 30: *This piece of Red propaganda is designed to make the White generals appear as though they are being controlled by foreign forces.*

Activity 17

Your challenge is to create a set of A5 flashcards on all the factors explained in this section. These will help you summarise the issue and will be useful for revision.

Why were the Reds victorious in the civil war?

On one side of an A5 flashcard, write and underline the factor, e.g.: THE LEADERSHIP OF LENIN. Below that, write: EVIDENCE. On the other side write: ANALYSIS AND ARGUMENTS. Do this for each factor, so you'll have six flashcards in total. Here are some hints as to what you should write down on each side of the flashcard.

EVIDENCE: dates, statistics, facts – everything that helps you describe and explain the factor.

ANALYSIS AND ARGUMENTS: why the factor was important in the Red victory; historiography.

It is vital that you summarise what you have read and put it into your own words unless you're quoting arguments directly. You can also use pictures on your flashcards.

(Higher European and World unit outcomes: 2.1, 2.2, 2.3)

Activity 18

Working in threes, take a set of flashcards and arrange them in order of importance according to the factors they show. Negotiate with those in your group and ensure that you are all happy with the order because your teacher may call on you to justify it.

Now, write a conclusion to the question, **Why were the Reds victorious in the civil war?** using your flashcards to provide evidence and support your overall argument.

(Higher European and World unit outcomes: 1.1, 1.2, 1.3)

Activity 19

Exam style questions

How important was Trotsky in the Red victory in the civil war? (22)

(Higher European and World unit outcomes: 1.1, 1.2, 1.3, 2.1, 2.2, 2.3)

Summary

In this topic you have learned:

- How secure the Tsarist state was before 1905
- Why there was a revolution in 1905
- How successful attempts to secure Tsarism were, 1905–14
- Why there was a revolution in February 1917
- Why the October Revolution was successful in 1917
- Why the Reds won the civil war.

You should have developed your skills and be able to:

- construct an essay that describes and explains an issue in detail
- analyse an historical issue in a structured essay
- interpret and make use of historiography.

Learning checklist

Now that you have finished **Russia, 1881–1921**, complete a self-evaluation of your knowledge and skills to assess what you have understood. Use traffic lights to help you make up a revision plan to help you improve in the areas you identified as red or amber.

- Describe the main methods of Tsarist control before 1905.

- Evaluate how strong the Tsarist state was before 1905.

- Explain in detail why each main group in Russia disliked Tsarist rule.

- Evaluate which factors were most important, and why, in causing the 1905 Revolution.

- Explain how the Tsar tried to re-establish control over Russia.

- Describe Stolypin's attempts to strengthen Tsarism.

- Evaluate how successful attempts to strengthen Tsarism were, 1905–14.

- Describe the impact of the First World War on Russia.

- Explain why the credibility of the Tsarist regime had crumbled by 1917.

- Evaluate which factors were most important, and why, in causing the February Revolution in 1917.

- Describe Lenin's actions between April and October 1917.

- Explain the problems the Provisional Government faced during its time in power.

- Evaluate which factors were most important, and why, in the Bolsheviks' success in October 1917.

- Describe the weaknesses of the Whites.

- Describe the advantages the Reds had.

- Explain why Lenin and Trotsky were so important to the Reds.

- Evaluate which factors were most important, and why, in the Reds' victory in the civil war.

This topic will provide you with an understanding of the politics of the USA from 1918 to 1968. You will study the growing tensions in American society, focusing on immigration, racial divisions and economic difficulties. You will also study the growth of Federal powers after the Wall Street Crash in 1929 and then analyse the struggle for civil rights, illustrating the themes of ideology, identity and rights.

This topic is split into six sections:

❖ An evaluation of the reasons for changing attitudes towards immigration in the 1920s.

❖ An evaluation of the obstacles to the achievement of civil rights for black people up to 1941.

❖ An evaluation of the reasons for the economic crisis of 1929–33.

❖ An assessment of the effectiveness of the New Deal.

❖ An evaluation of the reasons for the development of the civil rights campaign, after 1945.

❖ An assessment of the effectiveness of the civil rights movement in meeting the needs of black Americans, up to 1968.

Activities and Outcomes

		Activity												
		1	2	3	4	5	6	7	8	9	10	11	12	13
Outcome	1.1	✓	✓	✓	✓	✓	✓	✓	✓	✓	✓	✓	✓	✓
	1.2			✓		✓	✓	✓	✓	✓	✓	✓	✓	✓
	1.3			✓		✓	✓	✓		✓	✓	✓	✓	✓
	2.1			✓		✓	✓	✓	✓	✓	✓	✓	✓	✓
	2.2		✓	✓	✓	✓	✓	✓	✓	✓	✓	✓	✓	✓
	2.3		✓	✓	✓	✓	✓	✓	✓	✓	✓	✓	✓	✓

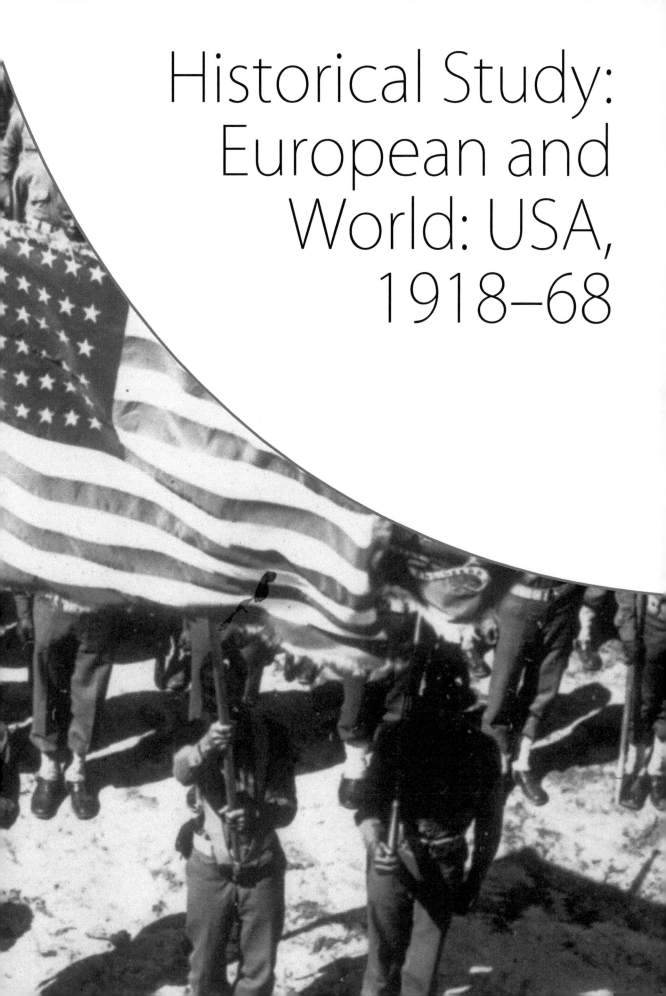

Historical Study: European and World: USA, 1918–68

Background

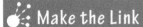 Historiography

'America was a land and later nation, imagined before it was ever conceived.'

Susan-Mary Grant

Make the Link

If you take Modern Studies you may study modern-day USA in detail.

America is a nation with a current population of about 330 million and a diverse range of ethnic backgrounds, languages and politics. In many ways its history is short, only becoming the United States of America in the late eighteenth century, once it had broken away from its role as a colony and moved to self-rule. In the nineteenth century, the population of America exploded as many people came from Europe and beyond to seek out opportunities. Many left their original homes because of poor social and economic conditions or religious persecution, hoping for a better life. It was even written down in the American Constitution that 'all men are created equal'. The Statue of Liberty bears the words of Emma Lazarus and her sonnet 'The New Colossus' – 'Give me your tired, your poor, Your huddled masses yearning to breathe free'.

Figure 1: *Immigrants approaching the Statue of Liberty.*

For some, America was a safe haven. Others came for the better life and new opportunities America offered – in pursuit of the 'American Dream'. With easier access to steam travel, and plenty of land and job opportunities once they got there, many people were encouraged to travel to America to improve their lives. However, this 'open door' policy dramatically halted in the 1920s. Resident Americans became suspicious of new immigrants, in large part fuelled by the First World War.

There was an economic boom in the 1920s which saw American prosperity excel in the global economy. However, the boom was short-lived and a gross miscalculation of how long the success could last resulted in the Great Depression, a time of grave economic darkness in the USA when it is estimated that almost 17 million people were unemployed, and many became homeless and hungry.

President Roosevelt's 'New Deal' in the 1930s saw necessary government intervention on a widespread scale to pull the USA out of the Depression. To an extent it worked, but many historians are critical that the policies did not go far enough and the government could never fully let go of its laissez-faire principles.

For a nation founded on the principles of equality it is interesting to note that much of the history of the United States in the twentieth century is notable because of its struggle with race relations. From the implementation of Jim Crow laws in the South in the late nineteenth century to the civil rights movement of the 1960s, the struggle of black people for equality is a defining feature of American history and, as such, has attracted a lot of historical comment and debate.

GO! Activity 1

1. Get into groups of about four or five people.

2. Take a piece of A3 poster paper and write 'American history has been short but eventful' in the middle.

3. Take 15 minutes and take points from the passage that you think will be important to you during your study of American history.

4. Number the points in order of significance.

5. Share with the rest of the class your top three points. Did you all highlight the same points? Which point is deemed the most important for a discussion about American history?

(Higher European and World unit outcomes: 1.1)

1

An evaluation of the reasons for changing attitudes towards immigration in the 1920s

In this section you will learn about:

- Isolationism.
- Fear of revolution.
- Prejudice and racism.
- Social fears.
- Economic fears.

Isolationism

Figure 2: *For immigrants in the nineteenth century, the Statue of Liberty on Liberty Island was a symbol of welcome. Indeed, Ellis Island, near Liberty Island, was the gateway for millions of immigrants as it was an immigration station in the nineteenth and twentieth centuries.*

🔍 Hint

Congress is the law-making body of the US Federal government.

Isolationism is the term given to the US policy of trying to stay out of foreign affairs. This policy was favoured in the nineteenth and early twentieth centuries but was especially evident after the First World War. Although it would be fair to describe the USA as a nation that was built on the back of immigrants, nevertheless increased numbers of immigrants in the latter half of the nineteenth century gave rise to a considerable level of xenophobia and a concern that rising levels of immigration from Asia and South America were destroying what had been put in place by 'good' immigrants.

Although the government had actively encouraged immigration, the increase in immigration also resulted in the growth of Nativism, a political movement that aimed to protect the interests of native-born or established inhabitants against those of immigrants. In 1882 Congress began to pass legislation limiting immigration, including the Chinese Exclusion Act of 1882 (renewed in 1892 and 1902), a 50 cent tax on each immigrant and the prohibition of people previously convicted of political offences.

Before the twentieth century, America had only been involved in three foreign wars. There had been a determination to remain neutral in the face of a conflict that was not of America's making. Thus, America's entry into and participation in the First World War was controversial. Many Americans took different sides in the war depending on their country of origin.

In 1915 a passenger ship, *Lusitania*, carrying American passengers was sunk by a German U-boat. This attack was viewed as an act of aggression and provoked outrage in America. It convinced many that if America was to enter the war, it would do so on the side of the Allies.

In 1917 President Wilson made the decision to support the Allied cause and enter the war. This was met with a mixed reception – some approved and some opposed it outright. Not only did anti-German feeling strain relationships between ethnic groups, but Irish Americans were also suspected of being anti-British.

📖 Historiography

Historian Eric Foner points out America relied heavily on the support of immigrants and 'The most common visual image in wartime propaganda was the Statue of Liberty, employed especially to rally support among immigrants. "You came here seeking Freedom," stated a caption on one Statue of Liberty poster. "You must now help preserve it."'

Figure 3: RMS Lusitania. *The sinking of this ship in 1915 was what led to America entering the First World War.*

Immigrants were encouraged to buy Liberty Bonds to support the war effort and they did so in their thousands. Thus, America was reliant on immigrants but at the same time struggled with the idea of continuing immigration.

🔍 Hint

A Liberty Bond was a way for the government to raise revenue for the war effort. It was like borrowing money from the people, which they could get back after the war was over.

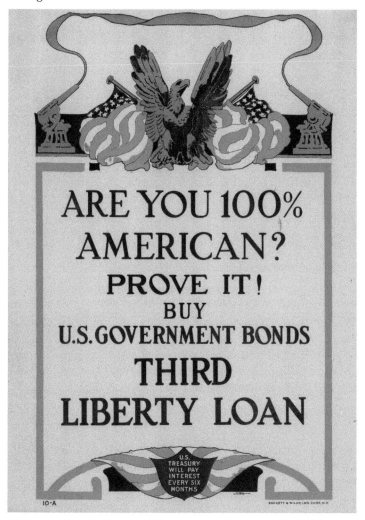

Figure 4: *A poster advertising Liberty Bonds.*

HISTORICAL STUDY: EUROPEAN AND WORLD: USA, 1918–68

> **Make the Link**
>
> If you studied the Scottish topic The Impact of the Great War, 1914–28, you will look at the First World War in more detail.

The return of American soldiers from the First World War, as we shall see, led to new social and economic frustrations that were blamed on immigration. Further, the 1920s saw a slew of anti-immigration policies put in place.

Figure 5: *American troops return from the First World War.*

Many anti-immigration laws were passed during the 1920s. The 1921 Emergency Quota Act reduced immigration from Eastern and Southern Europe drastically by regulating entry into the USA. The 1924 National Origins Act took this further by reducing the Eastern European quota to 2% of the existing population from the same background per annum. It also excluded Asian immigrants completely.

📖 Historiography

Historian Hugh Brogan points out that on the question of immigration, there was a concern over eugenics – that certain races did not carry the desirable qualities to be 'American'.

> **Make the Link**
>
> If you studied the Scottish topic Migration and Empire, 1830–1939 you will have learned that many people who immigrated to Scotland in the early twentieth century intended to continue on to America.

Brogan further argues that, even for the 'Americans' already living in the USA, there was not one single thing that could really define them as American: 'In short, not everything was melted into the pot'.

These Acts signified a policy shift towards isolationism and also perhaps highlighted institutional racism present in government policy. 'New' immigrants were targeted disproportionately by immigration legislation. American policy towards immigrants can be best summed up by Calvin Coolidge's view on the matter (Republican President, 1923–29): 'America must be kept American'.

 ## Historiography

'The adoption of a quota system … all but slammed the door on the southern and eastern Europeans who had formed the bulk of the arrivals in the prewar and immediate postwar periods.'

M.A. Jones

'From an asylum for the oppressed, America, with this single act [National Origins Act], transformed itself into a glorified gated community.'

Susan-Mary Grant

Fear of revolution

The Russian Revolution of 1917 affirmed America's desire to isolate itself further. After the First World War a fear of a Communist revolution took hold of America. This fear manifested itself through intolerance and suspicion of immigrants. The US Attorney-General, Mitchell Palmer advocated that America must purge itself of 'foreign-born subversives and agitators'.

Make the Link

You may have studied the Russian Revolution at N5.

Hint

The Russian Revolution of 1917 saw the Bolsheviks led by Lenin dispose of the old autocratic order and replace it with Communism – a society based on equality.

Figure 6: *A bomb blast on Wall Street in 1920 increased fears over immigration.*

The Palmer Raids began in January 1920. Perhaps as many as 6000 'aliens' were rounded up and put in prison or expelled from the USA. In New York, five elected members of the New York State Assembly were not allowed to take their seats. Other states followed suit, especially after an anarchist bomb was exploded on Wall Street in September 1920. The attack had been carried out by Italian anarchists and was particularly anti-capitalist. As 38 people were killed in the blast, other states began to panic and started to carry out their own purges. When put on trial, the anarchists were denied the same civil rights afforded to others at the time. Such activity increased the paranoia of the authorities in the USA and increased hostile attitudes towards immigrants.

📖 Historiography

'The country was seized with the fear that the last great wave of immigrants had brought the revolutionary spirit with them.'

Alistair Cooke

Conversely, Susan-Mary Grant argues that for many in the USA the Palmer Raids were a step too far and that, even after the bomb on Wall Street, many ordinary Americans were shocked but such events 'no longer sent them running to check for Reds under the bed'.

When discussing the fear of revolution, the different attitudes of government and civilians need to be carefully considered.

Prejudice and racism

America's previous 'open door' policy had led to an influx of immigrants from across the world, from Europe to the Far East, and immigrants' language and culture became less and less akin to that of the original settlers (white European). These immigrants also often looked different

> **Make the Link**
>
> This bombing was a terrorist act – if you take Modern Studies you may learn more about terrorism.

and new tensions were ignited between 'old' immigrants and 'new' immigrants. The old immigrants had assimilated into their new surroundings and had worked hard to make better lives for themselves and bolster the American economy. New immigrants arrived to the new urban areas in America like New York where they were met with overcrowding and unsanitary conditions. They were criticised for not integrating, preferring to stick with the people they had travelled to the USA with. They also kept up with their own cultures, for example wearing traditional dress and talking in their mother tongue. White Anglo Saxon Protestants (WASPs) who had been the original settlers from north and Western Europe greatly disliked many of the new immigrants and especially disliked Jews and Catholics.

📖 Historiography

'… it was not the increased numbers, but the changing nature of the immigrants which led to calls for tighter controls and immigration restrictions in the early 20th century'.

M.A Jones

'An upsurge of passionate nationalism … the peoples [of the USA] … clung to each other for reassurance and cemented their union with hatred, fear and contempt of foreigners.'

Hugh Brogan

🔍 Make the Link

You may learn about discrimination against different religious groups in RMPS.

Those already settled were worried about the new cultures eroding what was already established. In particular, the 1913 Alien Land Law reveals how American society was changing. This legislation applied to all 'aliens', but practical application was directed at the Japanese. It barred Japanese 'aliens' ineligible for citizenship from owning agricultural land, first in California, but this was soon adopted in 11 other states.

The Dillingham Commission added credence to the argument that immigration must be restricted and particularly among certain races. It was published in 1911 in 42 volumes and compared old European immigrants to new immigrants. It found that the 'new' immigrants were unsuited to life in the free, Protestant, European-origin American Republic.

🔍 Hint

'Alien' simply means 'foreigner'.

📖 Historiography

'In this way official support was given to the ever-more-popular farrago of racist nonsense that was then masquerading as anthropology.'

Hugh Brogan

Social fears

Many WASP Americans also believed that 'new' immigrants were responsible for increased levels of crime. One case in particular highlighted these fears.

Figure 7: *A photograph of Sacco and Vanzetti who were convicted of murder and robbery in 1920.*

In 1920 Nicola Sacco and Bartolomeo Vanzetti were put on trial for the robbery and murder of two men carrying a $15 766 payroll to a shoe factory in Massachusetts. They were found guilty and sentenced to the electric chair. It is still debated whether the two men were actually guilty of the crime but the trial became notable for the prejudice of the judge, Webster Thayer, against Sacco and Vanzetti. The two men were Italian immigrants and political activists, who had supported workers' strikes and protested against America's entry into the First World War. Because of their background, they were denied freedom of speech and the right to a fair trial. Vital evidence in their defence was ignored and they were convicted largely on circumstantial evidence.

After the case of Sacco and Vanzetti, hostility towards immigrants increased. Not only was it thought that they were responsible for increased crime levels, but the fact that many immigrants did not assimilate into society and preferred to remain in their own social groups heightened suspicion against them – many thought they were plotting revolutionary acts. As new immigrants usually lived in areas of extreme poverty, crime was rife. Many immigrants fell into the trap of organised crime gangs, such as the mafia, as it was almost impossible for those newly arrived to gain lucrative employment and pull themselves out of poverty.

📖 Historiography

'The Sacco-Vanzetti case laid bare some of the fault lines beneath the surface of American society during the 1920s ... It demonstrated how long the Red Scare extended into the 1920s and how powerfully it undermined basic American freedoms.'
Eric Foner

'Sacco and Vanzetti [became] symbols of a divided nation.'
Susan-Mary Grant

> **Make the Link**
>
> If you studied the Scottish topic Migration and Empire, 1830–1939 you will have learned about attitudes towards immigrants in Scotland at around this time.

Economic fears

The return of troops from the First World War meant that there were too many men chasing too few jobs. This resulted in a short economic recession from 1920–22. However, it was immigration that got the blame – there was a perception that immigrants were stealing all the jobs and causing economic decline. Trade unionists had campaigned for better wages and working conditions and felt they were being undermined by immigrants who would work for lower wages and in poor conditions. Employers would not negotiate with trade unionists because there was a wealth of workers who would accept the current pay and conditions. Immigrants were often used as strike-breakers – they were brought in to work if the regular workforce went on strike. This meant that the trade unionists greatly disliked immigrants, blaming them for the lack of progress in improving pay and working conditions.

Once the short recession was over, the economy recovered in spectacular fashion throughout the rest of the twenties. Nevertheless, this economic boom only allayed temporarily the fears that immigrants were driving down wages and stealing 'American' jobs.

> **Make the Link**
>
> You learn more about trade unions in Modern Studies and Business Management.

📖 Historiography

Hugh Brogan states that the government had to take control in the early 1920s again – strikes were broken and the government lost popular support. Old conflicts over race flared up again as the government prevented people from campaigning for better pay and opportunities.

It is perhaps interesting to note that between 1870 and 1913 there were no amendments to the Constitution and that increased levels of government intervention primarily focused on immigration. Traditionally, the US government has prided itself on low government intervention – increased government involvement was considered undemocratic.

Further, while many of the immigration policies in the 1920s seem xenophobic, it is noteworthy that nowadays most countries have strict immigration policies and freedom of movement is largely restricted.

> **Make the Link**
>
> If you study Modern Studies, you may learn about modern-day immigration policies that apply to the UK, Europe and the USA.

Activity 2

Get into groups of five. Each person take a factor from the table below. On a piece of A3 paper, mind map the KEY POINTS for your factor, evaluate the arguments FOR the change of policy towards immigration and provide at least ONE piece of historiography for each section. You could do further research online or at the school library. Once you have completed your mind map, your group will have created a comprehensive picture of the reasons for the change in policy towards immigration.

Factor	Key points	Evaluate the arguments for the change of policy towards immigration	Historiography
Isolationism			
Fear of revolution			
Prejudice and racism			
Social fears			
Economic fears	Too many men chasing too few jobs Many felt they were undermined by immigrants who would work for lower wages	Economic decline meant that many people used immigrants as a scapegoat despite the fact the post-war socio-economic conditions were really to blame.	Brogan states that government had to take control and lost popular support by breaking strikes.

(**Higher European and World unit outcomes: 1.1, 2.2, 2.3**)

GO! Activity 3

Exam style questions

To what extent does a fear of revolution explain the changes in American policy towards immigration in the 1920s? **(22)**

For the question, you must write a well-structured essay.

a) Write a practice introduction following the success criteria below:

1. Address the question.

2. Outline the key factors and arguments that you will address in the development section of your essay.

3. Give a line of enquiry (an overall 'thought' or 'argument' to drive your essay).

(Higher European and World unit outcomes: 1.1)

b) Write up the paragraphs to the main section of your essay. Use your completed table from Activity 2 to help you – the sections/headings of the table should correspond to the sections of your essay.

(Higher European and World unit outcomes: 1.1, 2.1, 2.2, 2.3)

c) Write a practice conclusion. You should effectively summarise the key ARGUMENTS you discussed in the main section of your essay to help you come to a justified conclusion – answer the question!

(Higher European and World unit outcomes: 1.2, 1.3)

d) Now practise writing your essay under timed conditions. You have 45 minutes to write up your essay!

🔍 Hint

You must address the fear of revolutions first as this is the ISOLATED FACTOR in the question.

You should also focus on ANALYSING the issue – did these factors change American policy towards immigration? Is there any HISTORIOGRAPHY you could include to support your own thoughts or show a different school of thought?

2 An evaluation of the obstacles to the achievement of civil rights for black people up to 1941

In this section you will learn about:

- Legal impediments.
- Activities of the Ku Klux Klan.
- Popular prejudice.
- Lack of political influence.
- Divisions in the black community.

Legal impediments

After slavery in the USA ended in 1865, black Americans who had been subjugated finally had their freedom. However, it would be an arduous struggle for them to win their civil rights. In the Southern states, black people were segregated and even in the more liberal Northern states they faced discrimination. In the South, as well as being segregated, they had to face hostility and violence from the Ku Klux Klan and they had few political rights.

Legally, black people faced many challenges. There had originally been a proposal that land would be granted to black families but once President Lincoln was assassinated this did not happen, so black people were left to sharecrop – where tenant farmers would pay their landlord in kind and live off the land. For most, this was no better than slavery. Further, black people did not find themselves in an equal society but were segregated in public services such as schools, had different taxation and limited voting rights.

The 'separate but equal' decision of the Supreme Court

In the American Constitution it was written that 'We hold these truths to be self-evident, that all men are created equal, that they are endowed by their Creator with certain unalienable Rights, that among these are Life, Liberty and the pursuit of Happiness.' However, this did not seem to apply to black people and in 1892 the US Supreme Court case *Plessy v. Fergusson* ruled it constitutional that black people in the South should be considered 'separate but equal'. In the state of Louisiana, a black man called Homer Plessy had refused to give up his

Make the Link

You may have studied the Atlantic Slave Trade at N5, or in Higher.

seat on a train and move to the back of the carriage. In court he argued that the Fourteenth Amendment had been broken – black people should have full civil liberties which included their right to freedom and should be treated by law in the same way as whites. The laws passed under this ruling are most commonly referred to as 'Jim Crow laws'.

Figure 8: *Jim Crow laws were so called because of the popular song 'Jump Jim Crow' which satirised black people as lazy and stupid.*

Although they asserted that black people were 'separate but equal', Jim Crow laws followed old legal proceedings, known as the Black Codes, that denied black Americans civil rights and equal voting rights. They were segregated from whites in every walk of life including schools, churches, buses, restaurants and hospital wards. The Federal system in the USA allowed the states to make their own Jim Crow laws. For instance, in South Carolina black and white textile workers were not even allowed to use the same doorways. Black people found it difficult to register to vote as they were subjected to ridiculous literacy tests that were impossible to pass. In 1919 when President Woodrow Wilson was challenged by black protestors that Jim Crow was unconstitutional he deemed that segregation was a 'benefit' to black people. Many historians have cited that Wilson was in fact a racist and welcomed the rise of white supremacy in the South as he felt that white Southern values had come under threat since the end of slavery. Jim Crow laws would characterise the South until the civil rights movement in the 1960s.

Make the Link

If you take Modern Studies you may learn about social inequality in Britain and around the world today.

📖 Historiography

'Black disenfranchisement persisted largely unchecked until the 1960s.'

Kervern Verney

Activities of the Ku Klux Klan

The Ku Klux Klan (KKK) was a terrorist organisation founded in the late 1860s to prevent the slaves who had been granted their freedom from attaining equal rights with other Americans. With the rise in racial tensions in both the South and the North, the Klan experienced a rise in popularity in the 1920s. Klan leader Hiram Wesley Evans said, 'The history of the world is the fight for survival of the White race. Either we win or we die. The Klan will not die.'

Figure 9: *Ku Klux Klan rally 1922.*

By 1925 it had three million members. It used violence and terror against anyone, black or white, who advocated equal rights. In the South, many policemen, politicians and judges were also Klansmen, which made it difficult to hold them to account in a court of law for their actions.

Figure 10: *Lynchings by the Klan became common in the South but even spread North during race riots. Lynchings gained popular support – this image was turned into a postcard and sent to family who lived elsewhere.*

🔍 Hint

The KKK still exists today but claims not to be a racist organisation. Research with your teacher and judge for yourself!

🔍 Hint

A lynching is the informal trial and execution by a mob. The term tends to apply to black people who were punished and murdered (normally by hanging) in the Southern US states.

Black people could be beaten, tortured or lynched by the Klan. The reasons varied – for example, if they had committed a crime against a white person or, frequently, because they had just tried to stick up for themselves when being bullied by whites. They were given no trial and allowed no defence and the lynching would often be a public event. Such treatment was permitted because of the involvement and collusion of members of law enforcement. The Federal government seemed powerless to interfere although it would seem that they continued to let the Klan do as they wished in order to keep white voters happy.

Figure 11: *The KKK would terrorise black farmers and rural dwellers by burning crosses outside their homes in the night and waiting with guns and ropes ready for lynching.*

Black people were terrified of the KKK – for many who had little formal education and were superstitious, they often believed 'white ghosts' had come to kill them. As mentioned above, the police were often involved in the Klan so offered no protection to black people being terrorised and courts would not try or convict Klan members for their actions.

📖 Historiography

David M. Chalmers writes that the Klan relied on 'local anarchic autonomy' – in other words, they could do what they wanted because no one held the Southern states to account.

The Klan further benefited from the feature film 'Birth of a Nation' directed by D.W. Griffiths in 1915. It was extremely popular across America. It benefited the Klan as it depicted the old Klan members from the 1860s as heroes.

In addition, an increase in the number of Southern Democrats in the White House meant that there were a lot of supporters of Jim Crow in central government. This made it hard for people to oppose the activities of the Klan.

📖 Historiography

Historian Frederick Lewis Allen cites that the Klan resurgence in the post First World War era was born out of the growing social and economic inequalities of the time. It was 'a movement conceived in fear and perpetuated fear and brought with it all manners of cruelties and crimes'.

Popular prejudice

📖 Historiography

'The Constitution … set out to protect rights, liberties and freedom – but only of white men.'

Vivien Saunders

🔍 **Hint**

The American Dream was the idea that America offered each person an equal opportunity to succeed, that if you worked hard then you would be rewarded with a job, money and a comfortable lifestyle. Many still subscribe to the notion of the American Dream today but the concept has come under extreme criticism from social commentators as not everyone has the same background or opportunities.

The Jim Crow laws affected everyday life for black people in the South so to escape poverty, segregation and violence many began to migrate north to chase the American Dream.

The movement of black people from the South began in 1915–16 when the war industries were desperate for workers. In the period 1910–20 the South lost 5% of its black population; by 1930 a further 8% had moved north. By 1940 the overall figure was 22%. Many black people believed the North was a land of opportunity where they could find the American Dream. Northern industrial cities saw a remarkable increase in black populations. From 1910 to 1930 the black population of Chicago rose from 44 103 to 233 903. New York went from 91 709 to 327 706. Between 1920 and 1930, 824 000 black people moved north but even in 1930 over 50% of the country's black population remained in the South. Living conditions in the North for black people were relatively poor compared to that of whites. The housing shortage in cities like New York can be attributed to the swift population growth and black people were marginalised because they had less money. They grouped in areas known as 'ghettos' where the housing conditions were poor and rents were high.

🔍 **Hint**

Ghettos still exist in America today and poverty among the black population tends to be relatively high compared to the population as a whole – about 24·8% of black people are poor compared to 11·2% of all races.

Jobs available to black people in the North remained low skilled and low paid. Black people worked in industry in the North rather than in agriculture but factory owners often preferred to employ white people over black. If black people thought that the liberal Northern states would bring freedom from the oppression of the South they were sorely mistaken. Black people had always lived in the Northern states but the Great Migration brought an influx of new black settlers that were not always appreciated by residents in the North, even among the black people already settled there.

📖 Historiography

'The influx of the new settlers after 1915 greatly increased the visibility of African American communities. Racial tensions increased and segregation spread to northern cities for the first time.'

Kervern Verney

Figure 12: *Race riots erupted in 1919 across the Southern and the Northern states.*

Once the black population started to grow exponentially, white workers resented the spread of black ghettos and competition for jobs. Black people themselves were disappointed with the levels of discrimination in the North – many black soldiers had fought for the USA in the First World War and were no longer prepared to put up with the levels of discrimination they experienced.

Race riots erupted around the USA in 1919 – some of the cities were in the South, like Charleston, South Carolina, but they spread to the North too, to cities like Chicago. The violence lasted 13 days and saw 23 blacks and 15 whites killed and 537 injured. About 1000 families, mostly black, were left homeless. At this time 70 black people were lynched and the Federal government did very little. Lynchings were ignored by the government despite the fact that they were racially motivated attacks, and excused on a basis of white superiority and 'maintaining order'. It seemed that the problems so prevalent in the South had spread to the North.

📖 Historiography

'… segregation was still firmly entrenched in the South and inequality – racial and economic – entrenched nationally.'
Susan-Mary Grant

Lack of political influence

Blacks did not have equal voting rights with whites, which made it difficult to find a voice to represent them. Black voting rights were denied with the introduction of literacy tests, as well as having to answer impossible questions like 'how many bubbles are in a bar of soap?' However, as the black population spread from the South to the North, those in the larger cities seemed to gain political leverage. Some black leaders achieved important political status and were able to apply pressure for change. Early leaders such as Booker T. Washington had advocated that to make economic progress black people should try to work with and exploit the white power structure. However, it became apparent that the white social system was so formidable that separate political movements would have to develop to campaign on the issues unique to black people.

Make the Link

In Modern Studies you learn about the voting processes in the UK and USA today.

Figure 13: *W.E.B. DuBois founded the National Association for the Advancement of Colored People in 1909.*

Figure 14: *Marcus Garvey founded the Universal Negro Improvement Association which called on black people to be proud of their race and heritage.*

In 1909 W.E.B. DuBois founded the National Association for the Advancement of Colored People (NAACP). It aimed to reduce racial segregation and white supremacy and believed the answer to achieving this lay in education. By 1919 the NAACP had 91 000 members. It was quite moderate in its tactics, preferring to challenge Jim Crow through lawsuits and protests. Its main success was the introduction of an anti-lynching bill in Congress in 1922 but, although it passed the House of Representatives, it was defeated by Southern Senators before it could become law. Nevertheless, it is estimated that lynchings fell dramatically after this bill had been debated. The NAACP has been criticised for not attracting enough support from poorer black people as it tended to concentrate on the middle-class black population. Its political influence then was somewhat thwarted by lack of support from its own people and the continued strength of the whites in American society.

If the NAACP was too moderate in its aims and did not push hard enough then it may be fair to state that the Universal Negro Improvement Association (UNIA) founded by Marcus Garvey in 1914 was too aggressive. Garvey advocated black separatism and 'black pride'. He further advocated that black people in the USA should return to their 'African homeland'. Although this might have been an extreme and ultimately unachievable goal, it certainly drew the black population together and gave black people a sense of pride of their race and history they had previously been denied. 'Black is beautiful' resonated particularly with black urban workers in unskilled, low paid jobs. By 1923 there were six million members. The UNIA helped black people to start businesses and promoted the belief that separate black enterprise was the best way forward. However, the UNIA could only achieve so much without political support.

It was probably the Great Depression – or at least the solutions that were put in place after the Depression hit – that helped to change things for the black population rather than the protest groups. The Depression hit black people the hardest as any jobs that were available went to whites – black unemployment was typically up to 60% higher than that of white.

📖 Historiography

Peter Clements references a commentator from Georgia, who said that 'Most blacks did not even know that Great Depression had come. They had always been poor and only thought the whites were catching up.'

The New Deal (policies designed to help the USA out of depression) helped black people by providing one million jobs, 50 000 houses, financial assistance and skilled occupation training for 500 000 black youths. However, times were still hard and the Federal government allowed businesses to continue to pay blacks less than whites under the National Recovery Administration. Some black people were given government jobs but this was controversial as were any policies designed to help both blacks and whites.

Divisions in the black community

The NAACP and UNIA remained highly critical of each other and were divided in their aims – the NAACP was for integration but the UNIA was for separatism. It is noteworthy that in the hard economic times of the early 1920s, UNIA was the more popular even though many black leaders remained very critical of Garvey. Garvey disappeared after being convicted of mail fraud and was imprisoned in 1925, and UNIA's 'black pride' movement all but collapsed when the Great Depression hit the USA in 1929.

It was perhaps the inability of the NAACP and UNIA to work together that stopped them from achieving their potential in terms of political influence. Nevertheless, they achieved some success. The NAACP had highlighted the horror of lynchings and their number had been greatly reduced. They had also won some court victories and the South had had its image irrevocably damaged, while Garvey had helped to promote black consciousness.

However, many black people remained uninvolved in protests and groups and there was a disparity in the treatment of black people in the Northern and the Southern states. Although far from having equal rights with whites, Northern blacks certainly had more freedoms – they could vote and there were better job opportunities, and the threat of the Ku Klux Klan was not present. Rather than join either the NAACP or the UNIA, Northern blacks concentrated on trying to improve their living standards.

Ultimately, the divisions between North and South perpetuated divisions in the black community. With increased job opportunities came divisions of class among black people. A black working class grew and with it emerged a new black middle class who experienced improvements in health care and education as well as social and economic progress. Some black people in the North, for instance, were able to run their own businesses successfully. The success of some black people in the North fostered resentment among the black working classes, which only contributed to divisions within the black community.

Make the Link

You learn more about class inequality in Modern Studies.

📖 Historiography

'… it may appear that very little had been gained, in real terms, to advance the cause of civil rights … There was, however, an increased awareness of cultural identity, particularly among the mass of African-Americans and the rights to which they were entitled. This was accompanied by a growing expression of the determination to gain improvement.'

Susan Willoughby

Activity 4

In pairs, take a piece of A3 paper. On one side, create a mind map with the following heading at the centre:

Evaluation of the obstacles to the achievement of civil rights for black people up to 1941: KNOWLEDGE AND UNDERSTANDING

Following the headings in this section, construct a mind map making sure you have the relevant key knowledge and understanding points written under each heading.

HEADINGS:

1. Legal impediments
2. Activities of the Ku Klux Klan
3. Popular prejudice
4. Lack of political influence
5. Divisions in the black community.

Now swap your work with another pair. Add in any extra information the other pair may have missed and then return their sheet to them.

(Higher European and World unit outcomes: 1.1, 2.2)

Now, turn over your piece of paper. Create another mind map with the following heading in the centre:

Evaluation of the obstacles to the achievement of civil rights for black people up to 1941: ANALYSIS AND HISTORIOGRAPHY

Under each of the headings listed above, analyse how much of an obstacle each factor was to the black community.

Remember, you can offer more than one opinion.

Use a different colour of pen to add some historiography to support your analysis. Again, if you can find more than one point of view this will add to the quality of debate in your work.

(Higher European and World unit outcomes: 2.2, 2.3)

 Activity 5

Exam style questions

To what extent can the slow pace of civil rights reforms up to 1941 be explained by the activities of the Ku Klux Klan? **(22)**

(Higher European and World unit outcomes: 1.1, 1.2, 1.3, 2.1, 2.2, 2.3)

3 An evaluation of the reasons for the economic crisis of 1929–33

In this section you will learn about:

- Republican government policies in the 1920s.
- Overproduction of goods and underconsumption.
- Weaknesses of the US banking system.
- International economic problems.
- The Wall Street Crash.

Republican government policies in the 1920s

After the First World War, the USA emerged as the richest nation in the world. The Republican government adopted a policy of laissez-faire when it came to economics and because of America's vast natural resources and industrial capability it experienced an economic boom between 1922 and 1929. Businesses were essentially unregulated and businessmen were left to create jobs and decide on wages. The Republican Presidents of the 1920s greatly supported businesses and the stock market and President Calvin Coolidge firmly believed that Federal policies should focus on the principle that businesses should be allowed to operate as far as possible unrestricted by regulation.

Firstly, the Republicans restored free enterprise in 1920 – the government was no longer to control the economy as it had done during the wartime period. Secondly, the Republicans sought to balance the budget and spent as little as possible on public services and tried to not spend more than it made in tax revenue. State Secretary to the Treasury, Andrew Mellon, cut government spending from $6·4 billion to $2·9 billion in seven years. Thirdly, the Fordney-McCumber Act led to strict tariff barriers being imposed on foreign imports. This meant foreign businesses struggled to pay the prices to sell their goods in the USA. This was called 'protectionism' and almost guaranteed that goods made in America would be bought in America. Fourthly, tax reductions were afforded to high earners and businesses, giving more incentive to make their businesses a success. Credit was given out to large businesses to encourage expansion – the credit bill totalled $3·5 billion by 1929. Fifthly, attempts to reduce government spending meant that the law enforcement and regulation of businesses barely existed. Businesses could do what they wanted, not always adhering to an ethical code – for example, child labour was prevalent in the South. During this time there seemed to be a return to very limited government intervention – historian Hugh Brogan calls this era one of

Hint

The two main parties in the USA are the Republicans and the Democrats.

Make the Link

In Business Management you may look at the use of ethical practices in business.

'irresponsibility'. Where government had been perceived to have been too involved in peoples' lives during wartime and in the immediate post-war period, it seemed now that deregulation of banks and businesses was giving people their freedom back. And, for most of the 1920s, it seemed to work.

📖 Historiography

These policies and lack of government regulation created what Peter Clements calls 'a dynamism within the age that encouraged risk and adventure'.

Overproduction of goods and underconsumption

Figure 15: *The Model T Ford has become the iconic image of the American boom years but also a symbol of the overproduction that caused the economic collapse.*

The boom years in the 1920s saw a substantial overproduction of goods. Technical advances meant that electrical goods and cars could be put into mass production. Henry Ford produced the Model T car with the aim that any family earning a reasonable income could have one. As production rose, prices fell and Model Ts went from $850 in 1914 to $295 in 1918. Demand was high and Ford was able to employ thousands of people and pay them well. The motor industry stimulated the other industries like steel, rubber and petrol. The Federal government responded to the high production of cars by employing people to build more roads and by 1929 10 000 miles of highway were being built per year.

New electrical goods were also being sold in their millions. Household items like radios, washing machines and refrigerators were popular with a new industry, advertising, encouraging people to believe they needed the latest model. By 1929, about 160 million electrical goods items were being sold per year.

However, eventually, it became clear that manufacturers were simply making too much. Not everyone could afford to update their car or refrigerator as frequently as the manufacturers wanted them to and, in the motor industry, competition from General Motors and Chrysler meant that there was more choice and availability of cars than there

🔍 **Hint**

Perhaps the explosion of vehicle ownership started here – there are now an estimated 254 million registered vehicles in the USA.

were people to buy them. Once everyone had the latest product, market consumption inevitably slowed down. By encouraging expansion of big business and unregulated credit, government policy did not take into consideration that most businesses cannot grow exponentially without consequence – there comes a point where people cannot afford to borrow more money or buy every new product offered. There was also a lack of acknowledgement by the government that when production of goods had to be halted there was a lack of alternatives in the job market, so people began to lose their jobs. In addition, when the Depression hit properly, the amount of money in circulation fell dramatically which exacerbated the problem. If the government had perhaps decided to tax the rich more and redistribute the wealth then it is possible that businesses and employment could have been given a helping hand. However, to increase taxes would have been anathema to the policies of deregulation at the time.

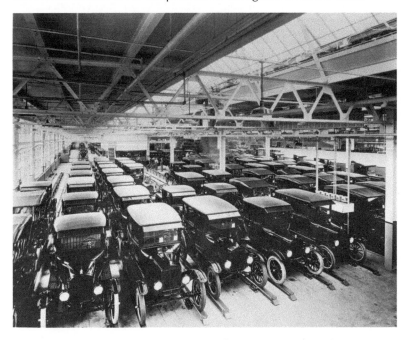

Figure 16: *Mass produced goods eventually flooded the market as there were not enough consumers towards the end of the 1920s.*

Ultimately, by the end of the 1920s there were too many goods and too few buyers. Confidence in the market had led to manufacturers rashly producing goods they expected easily to sell.

There was also a 'land boom' in the early part of the 1920s, Florida being the perfect example. The middle classes began to buy up available land to help secure holiday and retirement homes. Land seemed to hold high value and large profits could be made – people who had bought plots of land for $25 in 1900 were able to sell them for $150 000 25 years later. However, this boom had significantly subsided by 1926 and, after 1926, construction also declined significantly.

'Getting rich quick' greatly characterised the time period before the Great Depression. People invested in the stock market with blind faith that it would return a sure-fire profit. For years it seemed that stocks

Make the Link

In Business Management you learn about supply and demand.

and shares in businesses were only ever on the rise and it was an easy way to make money. People borrowed money to invest thinking that there would never be any issue in repaying the loan.

One area that declined throughout the 1920s was agriculture. America over-produced food and this meant that prices fell. The government would not guarantee prices and farmers therefore would not cut their production for fear of being undercut by other farmers. High levels of cheap food production in the towns and cities meant that farmers struggled to compete. Further, farmers and rural workers experienced higher levels of poverty than those who worked in the towns and could not afford to buy the food made in the cities. In 1930 there were one million fewer farms in the USA than there had been in 1920.

There was a great belief that government should not interfere in people's lives and on the surface it seemed that all was well – Herbert Hoover advocated 'rugged individualism': no government interference. However, it would appear that from 1926 the signs that the boom would end were all present, even if they were to be ignored. Despite this, it is often forgotten that throughout the 1920s about six million families (42% of the population) were below the poverty line.

📖 Historiography

'One-tenth of 1% of the families at the top received as much as 42% of the families at the bottom.'

Howard Zinn

'No one was responsible for the Wall Street crash. No one engineered the speculation that preceded it. Both were the product of the free choice and decisions of thousands of individuals … They were impelled to it by the seminal lunacy which has always seized people who are in turn seized with the notion that they can become very rich.'

John Kenneth Galbraith

In Galbraith's judgement, the 'get rich quick' culture may have been fostered by those on Wall Street, but it was the ordinary American who bought into the idea and could not see that the bubble would have to eventually burst.

Weaknesses of the US banking system

Fundamentally, there was no government regulation of the banking system which essentially meant the banks could do what they wanted. Many of the banks were small and acted in their own interests. Further, there was a progressive abandonment of the Gold Standard in the USA.

Credit became the main way for bankers to make money – people were encouraged to take out loans to buy the new consumer goods and to speculate on the stock market. It is estimated that three quarters

🔅 Make the Link

In Geography you may look at farming in both the developed and the developing world.

🔍 Hint

The Gold Standard was a system whereby the value of a country's currency was fixed by ratio to the amount of the country's gold reserves.

of all cars sold were sold on credit as were half of household appliances. By 1929, $7 billion of goods were sold on credit. Banks gave out loans very easily and almost everyone was in debt. But few questions were asked about the sustainability of this. Bankers in the pre-Depression era did not adequately quantify the risks. Moreover, some historians state that it was the weakness of the European banks that had a knock-on effect on the US banks. The US banks had given out loans to Europe and Europe struggled to pay them back. This decreased the value of US money and contributed to the collapse of the banks in the early 1930s.

> **Hint**
> The lack of regulation of the banking system and unregulated credit also caused the economic crash of 2008.

Historiography

Robert Sobel argues that the Wall Street Crash did not lead to bank failures as they did not fail until 1930–31. He advocates that it was President Hoover's inactivity after the crash that led to the collapse.

International economic problems

At the end of the First World War, America turned into a major creditor. As Europe struggled to get back on its feet, America offered loans to help them do so. Other countries also bought American goods as there was little being produced at home. An immediate post-war boom in production was probably what gave rise to an unalterable faith in the American economy. However, when European nations, such as Germany, struggled to pay back the loans to America in the late 1920s, America simply applied more pressure on them. Some historians think this was at the heart of the economic problem – America could only do so well on its own for so long through policies like protectionism. A prospering world economy would have to be in place for the boom to continue. If other countries were struggling economically, it would only be a matter of time before the USA was struggling too. However, there are also theorists called 'monetarists' who think the Great Depression could have been shortened or even avoided if the Federal Reserve Board (the government body in charge of monetary policy in the USA) had introduced more money into circulation (quantitative easing).

> **Hint**
> The UK government introduced quantitative easing in 2009 to try to stimulate the economy after the 2008 crash. It is debatable if this has been successful.

Historiography

'… war also changed America, rendering the once peripheral New World … central to the planet's concerns.'

Eric Rauchway

In other words, America was the most important economic power in the world and its actions could dictate outcomes for other countries like the European nations.

The Wall Street Crash

Figure 17: *A newspaper details the American Stock Market Crash.*

On Thursday, 24 October 1929 the American stock market crashed. People had been so confident of ever-increasing stock prices that it came as a great shock. Investors began to panic sell and share prices fell dramatically. The stock price of General Electric fell about 15% in one morning. By the end of the day the panic selling had set in again and just shy of 13 million shares had been sold at falling prices. The average number of shares bought/sold each day was about four million. Some bankers had stepped in and bought large numbers of shares but over the weekend the market fell even further and when Wall Street opened again on Monday morning no bankers would step in to rescue the situation. On Tuesday, 29 October, $14 000 million in profit was wiped out in one day. The bubble had well and truly burst.

Stocks had to be sold off at low prices so people could get money to pay their debtors – the banks and creditors were now demanding their loans back immediately. The fall in stock prices meant that people were selling for much less than they had bought and often this would not cover what they owed in debt. People began to lose their homes and possessions as the banks tried to reclaim any money they could. Individuals and businesses lost billions, life savings were wiped out in an instant. Banks collapsed; no new loans were given out. Unemployment spiralled from 3·2% in 1929 to 25·2% by 1932 – a figure of almost 13 million people, although historians think the figure was probably closer to 17 million because so many people, such as illegal immigrants and migrant workers, did not feature in the official count. The heavily industrialised areas were hit hard; by 1932 there were one million out of work in New York City alone. European nations reliant on American money, such as Germany, plunged into depression. It would be fair to say that in this case, 'when America sneezed, the whole world caught a cold'.

Figure 18: *President Herbert Hoover did not know the best way to handle the collapse of the American stock market and its consequences.*

The government did not know what to do. President Hoover, who had taken office earlier that year, stated that: 'We have increased home ownership; we have expanded the investment of the average man … The job of every man and woman has been made more secure. We have in this short period reduced the fear of poverty, the fear of unemployment.' He seemed to cling on to his hope that recovery was just around the corner despite being very aware, probably even as he made his speech about the unfaltering prosperity in the USA, that what was about to hit was the worst economic depression in living memory.

📖 Historiography

Hoover has received a lot of criticism for his apparent inaction at the onset of the Great Depression. However, Peter Clements argues: 'Hoover well understood the seriousness of the Depression … In public, however, he had to be optimistic in spite of all the problems; this has led many to argue that he quite lost touch with reality.'

Conversely, Paul Johnson argues that Hoover should have done less. When the government eventually did intervene and reduced taxes, Johnson argues that this led to a larger government deficit, in turn, prolonging the depression.

The US economy had been so reliant on people buying goods that, because people had no money to invest or buy, it struggled to find a way out of the crisis. The government refused to spend public money on poor relief and people were forced to rely on charitable hand-outs or local government relief. Food could not profitably be harvested, farmers had to let fields of wheat rot and slaughter animals without selling them because the process of transporting and selling was too expensive. Instead, bread queues popped up in every town and city. It is a strange paradox of the Great Depression in the USA that there was probably a substantial amount of food to feed the population but either the unwillingness or the inability of the government to create a suitable intervention policy to access it meant that millions continued to be in a state of desperate need.

Figure 19: *Bread queue in the 1930s.*

Figure 20: *People who lost their homes set up shanty towns called 'Hoovervilles'.*

For the people who had lost their homes, they had to set up temporary accommodation on waste ground that became known as 'Hoovervilles' – blaming their homelessness on President Hoover. Many unemployed men became hoboes – travelling around looking for work and treated appallingly as they went. The Great Depression was surely nothing short of a national emergency.

The government was conflicted about how to solve the problem. Hoover was wary of advocating an interventionist stance, still believing to a great extent in 'rugged individualism'. He thought the government should combine state efforts with private and local initiatives to solve the problem. However, by the end of 1931 most local governments and charities were running out of money. Andrew Mellon – State Secretary to the Treasury – advocated that businessmen fire everyone in their employment and sell everything until the crisis had resolved itself. Hoover promptly sent him to London to be US ambassador to the United Kingdom. It would not be unfair to suggest that the Great Depression paralysed the US government, and seemingly rendered even some of the most able politicians helpless. With hindsight, it is perhaps easy to see that the boom of the 1920s could only be sustained for so long, but either the US government really didn't see the crash coming, or else it did not consider a crisis of such magnitude would ensue following October 1929.

📖 Historiography

Historians regularly debate whether the Wall Street Crash actually caused the Depression or if it coincided with the boom of the 1920s coming to an end. Perhaps it was the first symptom of the economic collapse, rather than the cause of it. Some economists such as Joseph Schumpeter have stated that the crash was just an event in history at the end of the economic cycle of the 1920s. Another economist, Milton Friedman, advocates that the Federal Reserve Bank did not respond quickly enough by introducing more money to the economy after the crash and this is what caused the Depression. Thomas E. Hall and J. David Fergusson wrote that the crash was, to begin with, a recession, but 'Due to a combination of economic ignorance, confusion, and incompetence, U.S. policy makers pursued policies that were highly contractionary. They deepened and transformed the recession into a Great Depression.'

Historian William Manchester argues that it was Hoover himself who coined the phrase the Great Depression – choosing to use the word 'depression' because it was less alarming than 'panic'.

It was going to take an increased level of government intervention on a scale never before seen, or to this point desired, in the USA to sort out the problem.

GO! Activity 6

1. Summarise the key points from each of the headings in this section, making sure you DESCRIBE and EXPLAIN the reasons for the economic crisis of 1929–33.

   (Higher European and World unit outcomes: 1.1, 2.1)

2. With a partner, you now need to analyse how important the reasons you have written down are. Try to show connections between the relevant factors and debate different interpretations of the different factors (use historiography here!).

   (Higher European and World unit outcomes: 2.2, 2.3)

3. With your class, conclude what you think the main reasons for the economic crisis of 1929–33 were. Write your ideas up on the whiteboard and debate your answers – can everyone give a suitable justification for their reason?

4. Using the reasons you have debated, write a short answer to the following question:

   Evaluate the main reasons for the onset of the Great Depression between 1929 and 1933 in the USA.

   (Higher European and World unit outcomes: 1.2, 1.3)

GO! Activity 7

Exam style questions

'The weakness of the US banking system was the main cause of the Great Depression of the 1930s.' How valid is this view? **(22)**

(Higher European and World unit outcomes: 1.1, 1.2, 1.3, 2.1, 2.2, 2.3)

4 An assessment of the effectiveness of the New Deal

Figure 21: *The Hoover Dam was constructed between 1931 and 1936 with government money as part of an attempt to reinvigorate the construction industry during the Depression.*

📖 Make the Link

If you take Economics you will learn about the free market, tariffs, taxes and protectionism.

The role of Roosevelt and 'confidence building'

Herbert Hoover had almost signed his own fate when he stated in 1928 that 'We shall soon be in sight of the day when poverty will be banished from this nation'. Before Franklin Roosevelt was sworn in as President in March 1933, President Hoover did make some attempts to resolve the crisis of the Great Depression. However, the period of the Great Depression seemed to prove that Hoover was out of touch with the population of the USA and lacked an understanding of how to fix the problem, refusing to go back on his principles of low government intervention. Nevertheless, as the situation did not resolve itself quickly he was left with no choice but to introduce some government measures to try to restart the economy and reduce unemployment. A government building programme worth $423 million aimed to get the construction industry going again and was responsible for building the Hoover Dam.

📖 Historiography

William E. Leuchtenburg thinks that Hoover was too modest in his interventions.

The Hawley Smoot Act of 1930 increased tariffs on foreign imports of items such as manufactured goods by almost as much as 50% to try to stop foreign competition. However, it had the adverse effect of encouraging foreign countries to raise the tariffs on American imports so had little positive effect. In 1932 Hoover created the Radical Finance Corporation which was Hoover's most extreme measure to try and get America back on track. State governments were given $1·5 billion for public works and $300 million for relief. Banks were to be given up to $2 billion to rescue them and ailing businesses were given $150 million.

However, despite this government intervention, the attempt to haul America out of the Depression failed. Historians largely attribute this to the fact that the scale of government intervention was not large enough and that more sectors of industry and business were affected than could be helped by the government.

📖 Historiography

'By 1932, Hoover had to admit that voluntary action had failed to stem the Depression. He signed laws creating the Reconstruction Finance Corporation, which loaned money to failing banks, railroads and other businesses … These were dramatic departures from previous federal economic policy. But further than this, Hoover would not go.'

Eric Foner

'The Hawley-Smoot tariff, which limited international trade, made things even worse.'

Peter Clements

Paul Johnson offers an alternative view of Hoover. 'Hoover, in his four years as president, started more public works schemes than had been done by the previous 40 presidents.' He goes on to say that Hoover struggled to make an impact because of the inconsistencies with his tax policies – first he reduced taxes, then increased them when it became clear that public funding was running out very quickly.

Figure 22: *Franklin Delano Roosevelt became the 32nd President of the United States in March 1933.*

In his inauguration speech Franklin Delano Roosevelt said: 'This nation asks for action and action now'. He promised the American people a 'New Deal' that was to try to combat the Depression and stop America from falling too far to the Left (like the Soviet Union) or too far to the Right (like Germany). As well as halt the Depression he wanted to stimulate economic growth and distribute wealth more fairly. Roosevelt also took to addressing the nation on a personal level through his 'fireside chats' on the radio. He appeared to have the common touch and his personality helped rebuild confidence in the early days of the New Deal.

Roosevelt introduced many measures to try to help the US economy and society out of depression. The first wave of measures came to be known as the First New Deal. However, it involved him using his executive powers as President to heavily intervene in people's lives. He needed to have more executive power than any President before him in order to implement his programme. However, rather than give him too much power, there was a worry that Congress would actually deny him the powers he needed to change things. Roosevelt relied on the work of the 'Brain Trust' – enthusiastic young graduates or lawyers employed to improvise ideas for the New Deal and help put them into practice.

🔍 Hint

Roosevelt knew the importance of his image in giving the public confidence. He was actually wheelchair-bound because of polio but always managed without using his wheelchair in public.

Make the Link

You may learn more about the executive powers of the President in Modern Studies.

📖 **Historiography**

'Never in American history had a president exercised such power or so rapidly expanded the role of the federal government in people's lives.'

Eric Foner

Banking

Make the Link

If you studied Britain, 1851–1951 you will know that the effects of depression in the 1930s prompted large scale reform in Britain 1945–51.

The First New Deal (1933–34)

Emergency Banking Act, March 1933 – This sought to restore public confidence in the banking system by having government officials inspect banks over the period of a four day closure and only allowing the solvent ones to reopen. Roosevelt himself encouraged people to put their money back into the banks, stating that 'I can assure you that it is much safer to keep your money in a reopened bank than under your mattress.' People listened and put their money back in the banks. By bringing all the banks under Federal Control and only allowing those under licence to reopen, Roosevelt seemingly very quickly resolved the banking crisis. He aimed to increase the confidence of Americans so they would reinvest in the banking system and the economy.

Agriculture

During the 1920s, farmers in America had struggled to prosper. They were not as successful as other areas of the economy had been in the 1920s. This was largely because farmers had produced too much to sell in the USA and there was limited trade taking place overseas because of a tariff war. By the 1930s, and the onset of the Great Depression, farmers found themselves in crisis with many going bankrupt.

In May 1933, the **Agricultural Adjustment Act** (AAA) was passed. This act focussed on reducing surplus food. Commodities like wheat, sugar and pigs were a key target for reduction of surplus as they were overproduced but also required a lot of processing for consumption. The intended consequence would be to have less produce on the market and have prices raised for the farmers. In 1933, $100 million was paid out to cotton farmers to plough their crops back into the ground. Six million piglets were slaughtered after the government had bought them from the farmers.

There were some significant consequences of this Act. Enaction of the policy included burning corn and destroying large fruit crops from being consumed. However, at the same time many people found themselves starving. The farming families of the mid-West found themselves the victims of severe drought and dust storms and the area became known as the 'Dust Bowl'. Many had to abandon their farms as they were unable to pay mortgages or grow crops. Around 350 000 people migrated to California but found that the economic conditions were not much different there.

The AAA also had an impact on Tenant Farmers or Sharecroppers. In an attempt to stop over-production, the government agreed to pay money to sharecroppers to have them stop growing crops like cotton and tobacco on portions of their land. However, after complaints, the payments went to the landlords instead of the tenants. The landlords had protested that they had been left out of pocket and the sharecroppers were unable to pay them their dues as they had no crops to sell. This left many sharecroppers in desperate poverty. It affected African American sharecroppers in particular, many of whom left and migrated to the larger cities. On the other hand, some sharecroppers benefitted. With the extra land available they were able to grow crops for personal use which helped to raise their standards of living.

By 1936, benefit payments to farmers had risen by $1.5 billion. However, the same year the Supreme Court declared the AAA unconstitutional as it allowed the central government to interfere in State affairs.

In 1938, the AAA was renewed but with a different focus. It was designed to continue to subsidise farmers where necessary but also soil conservation – the Dust Bowl era had raised the idea of preserving land appropriately so that the adverse effects of climate and drought could be managed better. Any subsidies were also to come directly from the Federal government rather than the produce processors taxes. The monetary provisions were designed to maintain a price support for crops like cotton, wheat and corn to ensure efficient supply in low production periods. It also created marketing quotas to keep supply in line with demand.

> ### 📖 Historiography
>
> 'In 1933, the government ordered more than 6 million pigs slaughtered as part of the policy, a step critics found strange at a time of widespread hunger.'
>
> Eric Foner

> ### 🔗 Make the Link
>
> John Steinbeck's *The Grapes of Wrath* written in 1939 follows a family and their journey from Oklahoma to California during the agricultural crisis.

Industry

The First New Deal (1933–34)

Tennessee Valley Authority (TVA), May 1933 – This was a plan to build 16 dams on the Tennessee river covering 16 states where about 45 million people had been affected badly by the Depression. Construction work would provide employment for thousands and other jobs would be created as well as generating hydro-electricity for use in industry. This is regarded as one of the real success stories of the New Deal.

National Recovery Act (NRA), June 1933 – The government tried to encourage businesses and employers to introduce a minimum wage and increase the number of people employed. However, many employers refused to follow the Act. The Act also tried to stop overproduction and some industries were given money to halt

Figure 23: *Workers in construction employment as part of the TVA programme in 1933.*

Figure 24: *Detroit motor workers on strike in winter 1936.*

overproduction. The government thought that this would stop high inflation but it had the opposite effect. The Supreme Court decided the NRA was a failure in 1936 and revoked the Act.

The Second New Deal (1935–36)

Works Progress Administration, 1935 – This aided unskilled workers and employed 20% of America's workforce. Public buildings and roads were its main focus. Many unskilled workers experienced employment and a rise in their feeling of self-worth.

National Labor Relations Act, July 1935 – This gave workers the right to form and join trade unions. By 1938, union membership had risen to nine million. Although this Act included the right to strike, employers often fought back with lockouts and strike-breakers, as well as getting help from private armies or 'goon squads'.

Strikes sometimes worked to the benefit of employees, with government support, but often added to Roosevelt's unpopularity.

Society

The First New Deal (1933–34)

Economy Act, March 1933 – This cut government spending by $1 billion but did so at the expense of government employees and soldiers' pensions.

Federal Emergency Relief Administration, May 1933 – $500 million granted to give food and necessities to the unemployed. This represented a huge increase in the level of Federal responsibility for the poor and unemployed.

Historiography

'But the FERA programme left much to be desired. People of direct relief felt humiliated. Applying for assistance was like making a formal admission of inadequacy.'

W.E. Leuchtenburg

Public Works Administration (PWA), June 1933 – The PWA aimed to help give people back purchasing power to get the economy going again. It spent $3·3 billion and built schools and hospitals, and helped militarise the army.

The Second New Deal (1935–36)

Wealth Tax Act, 1935 – Known as the 'Soak the Successful' tax, Roosevelt introduced higher taxes for higher earners to help pay for the New Deal initiatives. It met with great unpopularity and many of the richer people found loopholes to get out of paying. It won Roosevelt no support from big business – the very sector he felt he needed to support him to boost the economy.

Social Security Act, 1935 – This set up a national pensions system, child benefit and unemployment insurance. However, the Federal and State governments were both responsible for administering benefits and those in better off states inevitably got more. Another difficulty of the system was that it was simply not comprehensive enough. Also, some Americans thought unemployment benefit encouraged people to be lazy and went against the ideology of 'rugged individualism'. Many did not like the Federal government interfering on such a large scale.

 Historiography

'Roosevelt's goal was … to protect social stability.'

Michael Hiltzik

Roosevelt was proudest of the Social Security Act although now its scope seems limited.

The Federal government became interventionist on a previously unseen scale. Gone was the 'rugged individualism' of Hoover's days. With the move away from laissez-faire policies, and the introduction of legislation like the Social Security Act, the role of Federal government shifted away from not intervening in people's lives to instigating the beginnings of a welfare state.

 Historiography

Peter Clements writes of the Social Security Act: 'The amounts spent were inadequate for the needs of a population suffering from a prolonged depression. Nevertheless, important precedents were set by this legislation.'

Figure 25: *Roosevelt signs the Social Security Act, 14 August 1935.*

🔍 **Hint**

Every American citizen now has a social security number. You cannot legally find work in the USA without one.

The First New Deal (1933–34) made a significant impact. It saw the largest scale of government intervention ever known in the USA. People had jobs, food was available to buy and the economy seemed to make a recovery. However, any success was only temporary and by 1935 the New Deal was facing significant difficulties. For many, the provisions made by government through the New Deal did not go far enough, and trade unions began to organise strikes. Big business showed Roosevelt little support, and flouted the rules he set. Further, the Supreme Court began to rule that many of the Acts passed were unconstitutional and began to overrule much of the legislation. They felt that increased government intervention, especially limiting the free market, was against the founding principles of the USA. Thus, more significant steps had to be taken with the Acts of the Second New Deal.

🔍 **Hint**

The Supreme Court exists to check that any laws introduced by Federal or state governments adhere to the rules set out in the Constitution. If they are found not to adhere to these rules they can be taken out of law.

The first problem Roosevelt had to overcome was the problem of the Supreme Court. If it deemed every action by the Federal government unconstitutional then further progress would be thwarted. Roosevelt threatened to change the way the Supreme Court worked by introducing the Judicial Reform Act. It proposed that Roosevelt be able to appoint six new judges. The judges in the Supreme Court disliked this – they did not want their jurisdiction to be undermined by new judges so immediately backed down and stopped opposing the Acts Roosevelt wanted to introduce.

The period that followed from 1935 to 1936 is known as the Second New Deal. Roosevelt needed to introduce more Acts to resolve the shortfalls in the Acts of the First New Deal.

However, historians continue to dispute how interventionist the government actually became and how extensive the legacy of the New Deal actually is. The behaviour of the Supreme Court in trying to limit what the New Deal could achieve by nullifying particular Acts like the NRA and declaring them unconstitutional points towards the idea that the government could never fully depart from the idea of being laissez-faire. Further, Roosevelt himself can be criticised for not intervening enough, as he was very aware that Congress would only go so far in supporting interventionist policies and, ultimately, he was in favour of any policies being temporary in nature in order to merely 'prime the pump' of economic recovery.

The long-term goal of the Federal government was to return America to the prosperity of the 1920s and it did not seem to acknowledge that perhaps more permanent regulation of the economy and banking system was required to avoid a crisis from happening again. It seemed that America could never deviate from the laissez-faire path it had set out on, even for its collective benefit.

The effects of the First New Deal were impressive. Between 1933 and 1934, national income rose by 23%. Unemployment dropped by two million, which sounds a lot but in January of 1934 unemployment was still running at 21·2%. The banking crisis appeared to be resolved in a matter of days. The economy grew by 8% per year between 1933 and 1937. Yet the USA seemed unable to return to the halcyon days of the 1920s. The New Deal only ever was an American answer to a global problem – the economy would have to improve on a global scale before the impact was felt in the USA. By 1937 America was facing problems again and in 1937–38 dipped back into recession. By 1938–39 the New Deal was all but over. In any case, there was a European war on the horizon and, if anything, it was the Second World War that resolved the unemployment and economic crises.

📖 Historiography

'The New Deal did not end the Great Depression. As one American who lived through the 1930s [said]: "it was the industries needed to make guns for World War II made that happen".'
Eric Rauchway

Historiography – asssessments of the New Deal

Most historians would agree that the New Deal, whether successful or not, changed attitudes towards the Federal government in the USA forever. There was a more flexible approach to the Constitution and both state and local government expenditure increased – from $1 billion per year in 1902 to $10 billion in 1938. Arthur Schlesinger, Junior argues that this level of progress would have happened without the Great Depression and that, as most progress happens in times of prosperity, there would have been more without the crisis.

William Leuchtenburg states that the New Deal was a compassionate response to a major crisis: 'it is hard to think of another period in the whole history of the republic that was so fruitful or a crisis that was met with such imagination'.

Howard Zinn and Paul Conkin think that the New Deal was an opportunity for more radical change to take place that was wasted, that the people were not consulted on their needs and that ultimately capitalism was allowed to prevail.

More recent historians, like David Kennedy, assess that opportunities to better exploit the benefits of a capitalist system were missed, i.e. that the wealth could have been better distributed but the New Deal needed to be careful to avoid too radical a change to government.

GO! Activity 8

1. Describe the background to the New Deal. You can include details you have studied in the previous section about the causes and the extent of the Great Depression.
    (Higher European and World unit outcomes: 2.1)

2. With a partner, work through the section to explain two reasons you think the New Deal was a success and two reasons you think it was a failure. You must put the factors into their historical context.

    Now share your ideas with the rest of the class. Have you come up with similar or very different arguments?
    (Higher European and World unit outcomes: 1.1)

3. With your partner, take two of the following factors each:

    - Banking
    - Agriculture
    - Industry
    - Society.

    For each factor, write a short paragraph analysing the effectiveness of the policies applied to each area. You should show the connections between relevant factors, giving detail, examples and evidence. You could use historiography from the section to help prove the points you have made.
    (Higher European and World unit outcomes: 2.2, 2.3)

4. Below is an extract from Eric Foner's *Give Me Liberty! An American History,* in which he details Roosevelt's inauguration.

Source A

'This nation asks for action and action now,' Roosevelt announced on taking office on March 4, 1933. The country, wrote the journalist and political commentator Walter Lipmann, 'was in such a state of confused desperation that it would have followed almost any leader anywhere he chose to go.' FDR spent much of 1933 trying to reassure the public. In his inaugural address, he declared that 'the only thing we have to fear is fear itself'.

Use at least four pieces of information from Source A and at least two points from your own knowledge to explain how Roosevelt tried to restore public confidence in the USA.

(Higher European and World unit outcomes: 1.1, 1.2, 2.2)

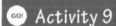 Activity 9

Exam style questions

How effective was the New Deal in solving America's problems in the 1930s? **(22)**

(Higher European and World unit outcomes: 1.1, 1.2, 1.3, 2.1, 2.2, 2.3)

5 An evaluation of the reasons for the development of the civil rights campaign after 1945

In this section you will learn about:

- Prejudice and discrimination.
- The experience of black servicemen in the Second World War.
- The role of black civil rights organisations.
- The emergence of effective black leaders.
- The role of Martin Luther King.

Prejudice and discrimination

By 1945, black people continued to suffer prejudice and discrimination as they had during the first half of the twentieth century. Jim Crow was prevalent and lynchings still common. However, the case of Emmett Till highlighted the extreme levels of continued prejudice and brought it to national attention.

Emmett Till was a black fourteen year old who was kidnapped and murdered in 1955. He was visiting family in Money, Mississippi, from his home in Chicago. He had experienced his fair share of discrimination in the North but nothing like the treatment that was about to befall him. Emmett's confidence got the better of him and, when dared by his friends to speak to a white girl in a store, he did so. When he left, he said 'Bye baby' to the white store owner, Carol Bryant.

Days later, two men, Rob Bryant, Carol's husband and J.W. Milam, drove to Emmett's relatives' house. They took Emmett away in the car. A few days later Emmett was found brutally murdered in the Tallahatchie River with his skull crushed in, seemingly having been shot in the head after having his eye gouged out.

Both black and white people were horrified by the murder and Rob Bryant was arrested. Emmett's mother, Mamie Till, had his body brought back to Chicago and had it lie in an open coffin so the extent of his injuries could be seen. The case attracted national attention and all eyes fell on the Southern justice system to see what would become of Rob Bryant.

No lawyers were at first prepared to defend Bryant and Milam but eventually five Southern lawyers, seeing that there was a real risk of the Southern justice system being challenged, offered their services free of charge.

Figure 26: *The case of Emmett Till highlighted the continuation of extreme prejudice against black people.*

Figure 27: *The Emmett Till case hit the headlines and an enquiry was called for into the murder.*

The trial took place in September 1955 in a segregated courthouse with an all-white jury. Emmett Till's uncle was asked to identify the murderers and he pointed out Bryant and Milam but still a 'not guilty' verdict was returned.

The case of Emmett Till attracted widespread publicity and had a huge impact on the awareness of the civil rights issue, especially in the North. Before this, neither black nor white people in the North had truly understood the extent of the cruelty of segregation in the South. As Emmett Till's mother, Mamie Till, stated: 'When something happened to the Negroes in the South I said, "That's their business, not mine."' Now, with such a high profile case, the plight of black people in the South could not be ignored. It also brought the disparity in civil rights in the North to the fore and highlighted the existence of racism there also.

📖 Historiography

Clenora Hudson-Weems calls Emmett Till 'The Sacrificial Lamb of the Civil Rights Movement' because it took the sacrifice of his life to push civil rights to the top of the political agenda.

The experience of black servicemen in the Second World War

📖 Historiography

'… the wartime message of freedom portended a major transformation in the status of Blacks … The war years witnessed the birth of the modern civil rights movement.'

Eric Foner

Figure 28: *After 1945 the contribution of black servicemen in the Second World War prompted the 'double V' campaign – Victory in Europe and Victory at home for civil rights.*

The focus of America's wartime campaign was the 'Four Freedoms' – freedom of speech, freedom of worship, freedom from want, freedom from fear. Yet black Americans were denied these freedoms and other civil liberties. The need for workers in the heavy industries in the 1940s prompted about 700 000 black people to move north in search of work. They experienced violence and hostility from white Americans worried about the social, political and economic effects of black migration. In many of the war industries like aircraft production, black people found themselves almost entirely excluded. A. Philip Randolph called for a march on Washington to demand an end to segregation, access to employment in the defence industry and an anti-lynching law.

The threat of a march on Washington worked – Roosevelt issued Executive Order 8802 which banned discrimination in defence jobs and set up an agency to monitor that the law was being followed. Industries began to employ black people and by 1944 there were one million black people employed in manufacturing. 'Hitler got us out of the white folks' kitchen' remarked one black woman. The irony of America fighting for freedom in Europe when so many black people were denied so many civil liberties at home had been recognised.

It was this idea that encouraged the 'double V' campaign – Victory in Europe and Victory at home. As black servicemen fought for freedom in Europe the campaign for civil rights at home stepped up. Membership of the NAACP increased from 50 000 to 500 000.

However, change was slow, and after the war it was clear that not a great deal of headway had been made towards civil rights. Roosevelt himself acknowledged that if there was to be change it would have to happen at a relatively slow pace. Nevertheless, the wartime struggle and small steps made towards equality had set the agenda for change that was to gather pace in the 1950s and 1960s.

📖 Historiography

'If there was a Negro revolution in the 1950s and 60s it was a revolution born out of frustrated expectations … The events of 1955–56 suggest strong elements of continuity with preceding decades.'

Neil Wynn

The role of black civil rights organisations

The National Association for the Advancement of Colored People (NAACP) was formed in 1909 and, between then and the Second World War, had been a formidable challenge to Jim Crow in the South. By the post-war era NAACP membership had increased significantly and in the 1950s they supported individuals when they openly began to challenge segregation in courts of law. The NAACP highlighted inequalities and pointed out the absurdity and hypocrisy of having black soldiers fight for freedom, democracy and equality in Europe when black people experienced such startling inequalities at home. However, in 1956 it lost its leadership in the civil rights movement because of a legal challenge to its actions that prevented it from operating in Alabama. The NAACP was apparently in violation of not registering properly to conduct business in the state. They were registered in New York which meant the NAACP was viewed as a 'foreign business' and Alabama state law prohibited their activities.

The Congress of Racial Equality (CORE) was founded by an interracial group of pacifists in 1942. They aimed to exert political pressure and planted the seeds for later change. The publication of *An American*

Figure 29: *A. Philip Randolph was the first to call a march on Washington demanding civil rights in 1941.*

Figure 30: *Ralph Abernathy was one of the key civil rights leaders.*

Make the Link

You may learn about effective leadership in Business Management and PE.

Dilemma by social scientist Gunnar Myrdal pointed out the irony of an America that believed in equality, justice, equal opportunities and freedom yet denied this to black people.

The Southern Christian Leadership Conference (SCLC) was founded by Martin Luther King and Ralph Abernathy in 1957 after the famous Montgomery bus boycott. They joined in the civil rights campaign spearheaded by the NAACP and ended up emerging as the leading group with Martin Luther King at the helm, advocating non-violent tactics to achieve their aims.

📖 Historiography

Historians debate the importance of the different civil rights groups. Mark Newman states that the SCLC 'developed much of the civil rights movement's infrastructure' but the SCLC 'assisted, rather than initiated' many of the famous protests in the 1950s and 1960s. Credit, he says, should rather go to the great number of participants of the movement as a whole rather than attribute the responsibility to any one organisation.

Hugh Brogan states that 'The NAACP addressed itself to the consciousness of judges' – he is saying that the NAACP fundamentally tried to challenge the legality of segregation and racism.

The emergence of effective black leaders

There were many effective black leaders in the struggle for civil rights, for example Roy Wilkins, who led the NAACP from 1955 until 1977. Within the NAACP there were many others who took a leadership role including Rosa Parks, whose actions started the Montgomery bus boycott. A. Philip Randolph and Ralph Abernathy also played significant roles in the civil rights movement. These black leaders openly challenged the segregation laws and gave black people a public voice in both the South and North, motivating both black and white people to campaign for civil rights. However, none has been so revered by history as Martin Luther King, Junior.

The role of Martin Luther King

Martin Luther King was a Baptist minister from Atlanta, Georgia. He had experienced segregation in his youth and was dedicated to defending the poor and challenging segregation. In 1955 he was working in Montgomery, Alabama, when Rosa Parks refused to give up her seat to a white man on the bus. Along with Parks and Abernathy, King helped to organise the bus boycott and from there he became the public voice of civil rights, speaking up and down the country. He wrote *Stride Toward Freedom* in 1958 in which he detailed the plight of black people living in the South, his thoughts about the boycott and his plans thereafter. He became leader of the SCLC in

1960 and particularly advocated non-violent tactics to achieve the goal of civil rights. In 1955, King spoke of his non-violent tactics and said quite clearly that he did not want the protestors of the Civil Rights Movement to use the same levels of violence as many black people had experienced from white people. He believed this would hinder their cause. King's leadership in conjunction with the activities of others like Rosa Parks and the activists of the civil rights campaign culminated in the Civil Rights Acts of 1964 and 1965. He won the Nobel Peace Prize in 1964. However, he had many enemies and in 1968 he was assassinated at the age of 35. The death of Martin Luther King sparked riots and in-fighting among those who had so unquestioningly supported his non-violent methods and inspirational leadership. It seemed without King as the figurehead, the civil rights movement would lose its way.

📖 Historiography

Historian Clayborne Carson details his stance on the role of Martin Luther King and the civil rights movement: 'I believe that people like Rosa Parks made it possible for King to display his singular leadership qualities. The movement would have happened even without King.'

Figure 31: *Martin Luther King, Junior.*

Activity 10

1. Get into groups of four. Come up with five different questions asking another group to describe the development of the civil rights movement. Swap papers and answer the other group's questions as best you can. Now swap back your papers and mark each other's work.

   Has each group managed to describe the development of the civil rights movement, especially after 1945, effectively?

   (Higher European and World unit outcomes: 2.1)

2. Read Source B, from *Eyes on the Prize: America's Civil Rights Years* by Juan Williams and Julian Bond (2013) and Source C, in which a black writer, Dempsey Travis writes about his experience in the Second World War.

Source B

> The Emmett Till case shook the foundations of Mississippi, both black and white – with the white community because it had become nationally publicised … because it said that not even a child was safe from racism and bigotry and death.

Source C

> The army was an experience unlike anything I've had in my life. I think of two armies, one black, one white. I saw German prisoners free to move around the camp, unlike black soldiers, who were restricted. The Germans walked right into the doggone places like any white American. We were wearin' the same uniform, but we were excluded.

(continued)

Use at least four pieces of information from Sources B and C and at least two points from your own knowledge to explain how the civil rights campaign developed.

(Higher European and World unit outcomes: 1.1, 1.2, 2.2)

3. Now analyse how important the reasons you have written down are. Try to show connections between the relevant factors and debate different interpretations of the different factors (use historiography here!).

(Higher European and World unit outcomes: 2.2, 2.3)

4. Now conclude why you think the civil rights campaign developed. Give a justified reason!

5. Using the reasons you have written, write a short answer to the following question:

Do you agree that it was the treatment of black soldiers in the Second World War that prompted the rise of the civil rights movement?

(Higher European and World unit outcomes: 1.2, 1.3)

GO! Activity 11

Exam style questions

How important was the role of black civil rights organisations in the development of the civil rights campaigns after 1945? **(22)**

(Higher European and World unit outcomes: 1.1, 1.2, 1.3, 2.1, 2.2, 2.3)

6 An assessment of the effectiveness of the civil rights movement in meeting the needs of black Americans, up to 1968

In this section you will learn about:

- The roles of the NAACP, CORE and the SCLC.
- The role of Martin Luther King.
- Changes in Federal policy.
- Social, economic and political changes.
- The resultant rise of black radical movements.

The roles of the NAACP, CORE and the SCLC

The main aims of the civil rights movement were to end racial discrimination and segregation against black Americans and gain equal constitutional voting rights with white people. In addition, the movement wanted better social and economic conditions for black people and fairer employment opportunities. Several groups played a significant role in furthering civil rights; these were the NAACP (National Association for the Advancement of Colored People), CORE (Congress of Racial Equality) and the SCLC (Southern Christian Leadership Conference). Each of the groups had a role either separately or collectively in the civil rights movement.

Figure 32: *The civil rights movement had several aims, but above all equality was the main goal.*

Below are some examples of the key methods of protest spearheaded by the NAACP, CORE and the SCLC.

The two key events that kick-started the nationwide civil rights campaigns were *Brown v. Board of Education* in 1954 and the Montgomery bus boycott of 1955.

In Topeka, Kansas, Linda Brown's father Oliver Brown decided she should not have to travel to a separate school for black children when there was a 'whites only' school closer to home. The NAACP helped Oliver Brown to take the case to the Supreme Court. The decision by the Supreme Court to overturn the 'separate but equal' decision it had made 60 years earlier marked a watershed for civil rights. However, it did not stop segregation, and white mobs and the Ku Klux Klan continued to attack both black and white Americans who supported desegregation.

📖 Historiography

'Brown v. Board of Education turned out to be only the first blow in a new battle in the long, long war.'

Hugh Brogan

'But of course, the process of dismantling segregation could not be plain sailing. For one thing, to attack it in the schools was to attack it everywhere. The structure of White Supremacy tottered.'

Hugh Brogan

Figure 33: *Rosa Parks after her arrest. Parks is often hailed as one of the first people to really kick-start the civil rights campaign with her refusal to give up her seat on a bus in Montgomery in 1955.*

Rosa Parks was from Montgomery, Alabama. In December 1955 she made history when she refused to give up her seat to a white man on a segregated bus. Parks was arrested and charged with violating the segregation laws of Alabama. It had been a preconceived plan by the NAACP of which Parks was, and continued to be, an active member. The bus boycott of Baton Rouge in 1953 had highlighted the power of civil disobedience. The NAACP had already pointed out to the Mayor of Montgomery that 75% of bus users were black and that an active boycott could damage bus companies' profits. The arrest of Parks was the publicity the NAACP needed to launch the Montgomery bus boycott, one of the first major coordinated acts of civil disobedience in the civil rights movement. The boycott was extremely effective and, as planned, forced the buses to desegregate or go out of business. The boycott lasted just over a year and its success proved the economic power of the black population.

📖 Historiography

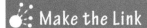

If you studied Britain, 1851–1951 you will have learned about the different tactics, both violent and non-violent, used by protestors in Britain earlier in the twentieth century.

'Rosa Parks … was a civil rights activist who so frequently defied jim crow [sic] laws that some Montgomery bus drivers drove right past her rather than allow her to board their buses.'

Charles Payne

'The Montgomery Bus Boycott marked a turning point in post-war American history. It launched the movement for racial justice as a nonviolent crusade based in the black churches of the South. It gained the support of northern liberals and focused unprecedented and unwelcome international attention on the country's racial policies. And it marked the emergence of twenty-six year-old Martin Luther King Jr … as the movement's national symbol.'

Eric Foner

Little Rock, Arkansas – Following the overturning of the 'separate but equal' law by the Supreme Court in *Brown v. Board of Education*, Southern states tried to ignore the fact that schools were to be desegregated. In 1957, the Central High School in Little Rock decided to admit nine black students. Orval Faubus, the governor of Arkansas was vehemently against desegregation and sent the army to stop the black students from going to school. White protestors and the KKK also tried to intimidate the black students from entering. The first student to try to go to Central High School was Elizabeth Eckford who was met with racist vitriol and attacked by white, middle-class people, many of them young women like herself.

Figure 34: *Elizabeth Eckford tries to go to school in Little Rock, 1957.*

The Federal government reacted quickly to the state forces surrounding the school. President Eisenhower could not have individual states ignoring Federal law so he sent the US army to enforce desegregation. The army stayed in Little Rock throughout the following year. This high-profile case attracted media attention from around the country.

Sit-ins – In February 1960 in Greensboro, North Carolina, four black students were refused service at a whites-only restaurant. They were asked to leave but refused and the next day returned with more protesters, both black and white – about 80 in total. The idea of sit-ins as a form of non-violent protest quickly spread and by the end of 1960 about 70 000 people had taken part in sit-ins. Many white people verbally and physically attacked the protestors. However, rather than having the desired effect of stopping the protests, it served to publicise the campaign even more because it was picked up by newspapers and the new medium of the day, television.

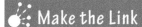
Make the Link

You may learn about the interaction between the media and current events in Modern Studies or Media Studies.

Figure 35: *Sit-ins became a very effective method of non-violent protest but evoked strong public reaction from white people.*

Freedom rides – In 1961 Members of CORE wanted to highlight the fact that segregation still existed in the Southern states so began to make 'freedom rides' from Washington to New Orleans using 'whites only' facilities along the way to prove their point. They were met with racism and violence from white southerners and in some cases the KKK attacked the protestors on the buses. In Birmingham, Alabama, a bus was burned and the passengers violently beaten. By this time Eisenhower had been replaced by President John F. Kennedy and he put through the change that was required – the interstate bus services were required to desegregate bus stations in the South and, following this, desegregation followed in 1961 for all airports, rail and bus stations. The Freedom Riders did not succeed in making great changes to the Constitution. However, they certainly increased the momentum for change.

📖 Historiography

'Deliberately provoking a crisis of authority, the Riders challenged Federal officials to enforce the law and uphold the constitutional right to travel without being subjected to degrading and humiliating racial restrictions … Invoking the philosophy of nonviolent direct action they willingly put their bodies on the line for the cause of racial justice.'

Raymond Arsenault

The role of Martin Luther King

Martin Luther King and the SCLC certainly emerged as the 'leaders' of the civil rights movement but the years of groundwork laid by the NAACP and CORE cannot be ignored. Martin Luther King certainly did not 'come from nowhere' and it is arguably the case that the enormous public support for the civil rights movement propelled King into the spotlight rather than the reverse.

Birmingham, Alabama, 1963 – In 1963 Martin Luther King made the decision to protest against segregation in Birmingham, Alabama, one of the most violent anti-desegregation cities in the South. If they could overcome segregation there it would encourage the rest of the South to also desegregate. King also wanted to show the world the level of police brutality in Birmingham. King and his colleague, Reverend Fred Shuttlesworth, were imprisoned as soon as they came to Birmingham. From his jail cell, King answered the calls of those who asked him to stop the protests and let desegregation happen at a slower pace. King replied that it would be easy for those who had not experienced the segregation of the South and the lawless behaviour towards black people to want to halt the protests and wait longer for change. His argument, however, was that it was because of the abhorrent treatment of black people that the continuation of the protests, even though they had become very dangerous, was absolutely necessary. On 20 April King and Shuttlesworth were released from prison and the march began on 2 May with school children leading. As expected, the chief of police 'Bull' Connor reacted violently, attacking the protestors with water cannon and dogs. The protestors did not retaliate and the nation was outraged as children and adults were bitten and beaten live on television.

Make the Link

You learn about a citizen's right to peaceful protest in Modern Studies.

Figure 36: *Protestors were met with extreme violence in Birmingham in 1963, including being bitten by dogs and hit by water cannon.*

By the second day, the police and authorities were doubting the strategy of taking violent action against the protestors. Businessmen were extremely concerned that the bad publicity was damaging the local economy. They offered to desegregate public facilities and restaurants within 90 days.

March on Washington – After events in Alabama, President Kennedy had called on Congress to legally desegregate public facilities and public schools, and offered greater support for the right to vote. On 28 August 1963 about 250 000 black and white protestors gathered at the Lincoln Memorial to protest in favour of the Civil Rights Act. It achieved huge publicity as the protest was broadcast live on television. The famous 'I Have a Dream' speech was delivered by King and became one of the most famous and important speeches of the twentieth century.

Figure 37: *Martin Luther King at the Lincoln Memorial, 28 August 1963.*

The march raised publicity to a new level and, despite some acts of violence against the protest and the assassination of President Kennedy in November 1963, the Civil Rights Act was passed in 1964. The new President, Lyndon B. Johnson, ensured that the Act became law.

📖 Historiography

'The March on Washington had a huge impact on Americans. People across the nation were awakened to the racism that still existed in parts of the United States … Americans were equally impressed by the marchers, who were peaceful yet determined to bring about change. The March on Washington proved that the civil rights movement could not be ignored.'

Robin S. Doak

'Martin Luther King, Jr. remains arguably the most recognisable African American figure in world history. First thrust into the international spotlight courtesy of his leadership of a boycott of the public bus system in Montgomery, Alabama, where he was a pastor of a local church, King became the lightning rod for the civil rights movement that emerged in the wake of the successful boycott. During the 1960s he gave innumerable speeches

characterised by oratorical genius, led a succession of mass marches in the heart of segregated America and helped to reconstruct American race relations before his assassination in 1968.'

Dr Joe Street

Changes in Federal policy

In 1957 a Civil Rights Act had been passed by President Eisenhower. It stated that a Civil Rights Commission would be started and vowed to support black Americans if they went to court because they could not vote freely. On the one hand, this was a step in the right direction, an acknowledgement that Southern states could not just ignore Federal law as they pleased. On the other hand, it did not award true civil and voting rights to all black Americans. Eisenhower himself was wary of passing any Civil Rights Act, fearful of alienating voters in the South and unsure himself about how he felt about civil rights.

The 1964 Civil Rights Act legislated that discrimination on the basis of race in public places in the USA was banned, that employers could no longer discriminate on the basis of race, national origin, religion or sex if they employed more than 25 people and the Justice department was allowed to take a state to court if it continued to discriminate against black people.

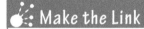

Make the Link

In Modern Studies you learn about the passage of an Act through Parliament in Scotland, and about equality laws in place in the UK today.

In August 1965, following further protests, the Voting Rights Act was passed. The protests had taken place in Selma, Alabama and again the televised events of protestors being beaten, trampled on by horses and the arrest of Martin Luther King (now a Nobel Peace Prize winner) brought the voting rights question to Federal attention. The Voting Rights Act abolished literacy tests and checks on poll tax payments of black people, which in the past had been used as restrictions to stop them from voting. The number of black voters in the South increased substantially. For example, in Alabama in 1960 there were 66 000 black voters but by 1966 there were 250 000 black voters. Despite this progress, it would be ten more years before an African American won a state-wide election in the South. Further, as black people moved north to the cities, the white populations moved out to the suburbs. 'White flight' proved the continuation of discrimination and black incomers experienced poorer housing and education, and relied more on welfare as the employment opportunities were fewer.

Hint

Poorer areas in US cities populated largely by black people are called ghettos.

Social, economic and political changes

Make the Link

You may study inequalities in wealth and race in Modern Studies.

Following on from the key Civil Rights Acts, there were further changes in marriage laws, allowing interracial marriages to take place. There could be no discrimination when it came to buying or renting houses. The political status of black Americans had dramatically improved: black senator Edward William Brooke took office in 1967 and African American Supreme Court judge Thurgood Marshall was appointed in

1967. In court, black people had a much fairer chance of representation. The armed forces were successfully desegregated and many black people held prominent positions. However, educational success was limited. 58% of black southerners were still segregated in schools in 1968 and it would take a number of Supreme Court decisions to reduce this to 10% by 1972. There was continuing inequality in unemployment with the figure for blacks remaining 7 to 12% higher than whites. But the economic situation did improve overall. Incomes of black people doubled in the 1960s and a black middle class grew rapidly. However, black wages were still to remain typically about 60% of the average white wage. Further, segregation still existed in transport and was enforced in parts of the South, like Alabama. Discrimination and racism on a large scale still continued.

There was a large number of black people who did not support Martin Luther King, his methods or his aims. The civil rights movement split in the mid-1960s and there were several race riots in the North and South. There were strikes in Harlem in 1963 and race riots in 1965 in the Watt Ghetto in Los Angeles. In the North, alternative leaders began to emerge.

> ### 🔍 Hint
>
> The end of the civil rights movement did not mark the end of inequalities for black people and they have experienced difficulties up to the present day. Race riots were common in the 1990s.

📖 Historiography

'The remedies applied to the South proved to be of little use elsewhere.'

Hugh Brogan

The resultant rise of black radical movements

Many of those who did not participate in the peaceful protests to gain civil rights felt that progress was too slow and that black and white would never be considered equal. They therefore began to support the idea of black separatism.

Figure 38: *Malcolm X was one of the main leaders who advocated black separatism.*

Malcolm X was born Malcolm Little. His father was murdered when he was young, possibly by the KKK. His father had followed Marcus Garvey and his teachings of separatism. Malcolm X spent time in prison where he heard about the Nation of Islam headed by Elijah Muhammad which rejected ideas of integration and advocated that the white man is the devil. He gave himself the last name 'X' as a rejection of his slave name, 'Little'. He was critical of Martin Luther King and his methods and was of great concern to the authorities. The FBI kept him under constant surveillance. After 1963, he split from the Nation of Islam after arguments with Elijah Muhammad and went to the Middle East. There, he discovered that Muslims came from all racial backgrounds and changed his views on racism significantly. In 1965 he was murdered.

📖 Historiography

'Malcolm X offered a unique combination that attracted many young activist artists: a core of black nationalism together with an insistence that the African American freedom struggle must be understood within a global context.'

James Smethurst

⁂ Make the Link

If you study RMPS you will learn more about Islam.

Another black radical who disagreed with the main civil rights movement was Stokely Carmichael. Carmichael was president of the Student Non-Violent Coordinating Committee (SNCC) but had become frustrated with the slow progress of the civil rights movement and coined the phrase 'Black Power'. He began to advocate the use of violence and said they should not wait on whites giving black people civil rights but should start their own schools, hospitals and, in effect, a separate society. The SNCC changed its name to the Student National Coordinating Committee. However, by 1968 Carmichael had left to head the 'Black Panthers' and was replaced by H. Rapp Brown.

Figure 39: *Stokely Carmichael.*

The Black Panthers, started by Huey Newton and Bobby Seale, had a branch established in most US cities by 1968. They supported violent protest and the use of guns for self-defence – Huey Newton said himself, 'what good is non-violence when the police are determined to rule by force?' Their slogans included 'Black Power'. However, another aim of the Black Panthers was to help black communities out of poverty. In ghettos they organised breakfast clubs for children, free clothing and free healthcare as well as trying to improve crime rates and drug abuse. Violence broke out between the Panthers and law enforcement regularly in the 1960s and the FBI had them under constant surveillance. The FBI even antagonised the Panthers deliberately in an attempt to cause infighting. The FBI also destroyed the Black Panthers' programmes to help the poor in the ghettos. By the 1970s the Panthers no longer existed. Their attempts to promote 'Black Power' and their violent methods had never been fully supported by a majority of black people. Nevertheless, the existence of groups like the Nation of Islam and the Black Panthers proved that not all black Americans supported non-violent methods, and the seemingly slow progress of civil rights and continuing racism fuelled feelings of discontent among black and white Americans throughout the 1960s and beyond.

📖 Historiography

'... the Black Panthers ... [were] involved in numerous violent confrontations with the police. This tended to distract attention from some of their more philanthropic activities, such as the provision of food for black ghetto children and legal aid for the ghetto blacks.'

Ron Field

Figure 40: *Huey Newton and Bobby Seale standing armed in the street.*

GO! Activity 12

You are going to present a group presentation on an assessment of the Civil Rights Movement up until 1968 in the USA.

To what extent did the civil rights campaigns of the 1950s and 1960s result in significant improvements in the lives of black Americans?

Your presentation must contain the following:

Introduction

A detailed description of the background to and events of the civil rights movement.

(Higher European and World unit outcomes: 2.1)

An explanation of two reasons why you think the civil rights movement resulted in improvements in the lives of black Americans.

(Higher European and World unit outcomes: 1.1)

Main presentation – can be done on PowerPoint, poster – you choose!

An analysis of the extent to which the civil rights campaigns improved the lives of black Americans. You should show the connections between relevant factors, giving detail, examples and evidence. You could use historiography from the section to help prove the points you have made.

Include information from the following headings:

- Aims of the civil rights movement
- The roles of the NAACP, CORE and the SCLC
- The role of Martin Luther King
- Changes in Federal policy
- Social, economic and political changes
- The resultant rise of black radical movements.

(Higher European and World unit outcomes: 1.1, 2.2, 2.3)

Conclusion

Summarise the key factors to the audience and make a judgement on the issue. Provide two developed points to support your overall judgement.

(Higher European and World unit outcomes: 1.2, 1.3)

GO! Activity 13

Exam style questions

To what extent did the civil rights campaigns of the 1950s and 1960s result in significant improvements in the lives of black Americans? **(22)**

(Higher European and World unit outcomes: 1.1, 1.2, 1.3, 2.1, 2.2, 2.3)

Summary

In this topic you have learned:

- The reasons for changing attitudes towards immigration in the 1920s
- The obstacles to the achievement of civil rights for black people up to 1941
- The reasons for the economic crisis of 1929–33
- How effective the New Deal was
- The reasons for the development of the civil rights campaign after 1945
- How effective the civil rights movement was in meeting the needs of black Americans, up to 1968.

You should have developed your skills and be able to:

- construct an essay that describes and explains an issue in detail
- analyse an historical issue in a structured essay
- interpret and make use of historiography.

Learning checklist

Now that you have finished **USA, 1918–68**, complete a self-evaluation of your knowledge and skills to assess what you have understood. Use traffic lights to help you make up a revision plan to help you improve in the areas you identified as red or amber.

- Describe and explain what is meant by isolationism and its effect on USA immigration policy.

- Explain why there was a fear of revolution in the 1920s in the USA.

- Explain why new immigrants experienced prejudice and discrimination.

- Explain the social fears with regard to new immigrants.

- Analyse the importance of economic fears on immigration.

- Describe the legal impediments experienced by black people up until 1941.

- Explain the 'Separate but Equal' decision of the Supreme Court.

- Describe the activities of the Ku Klux Klan.

- Explain the popular prejudice experienced by black people.

- Analyse the political influence, or lack of political influence, of black people up until 1941.

- Explain and analyse the divisions in the black community.

- Describe Republican government policies in the 1920s.

- Describe the overproduction of goods and explain the problems caused by this.

- Describe and explain the problem of under-consumption and the saturation of the US market.

- Describe the weaknesses of the US banking system in the 1920s.

- Analyse the international economic problems in the 1920s.

- Describe, explain and analyse the effects of the Wall Street Crash.

- Describe the role of Roosevelt and 'confidence building'.

- Describe the role of the Federal government during the Depression Analyse the effects of the New Deal on banking.

- Analyse the effects of the New Deal on industry.

- Analyse the effects of the New Deal on society.

- Analyse the effects of the New Deal on agriculture.

- Describe the continuation of prejudice and discrimination experienced by black people after 1945.

- Describe the experience of black servicemen in the Second World War.

- Describe the formation of civil rights organisations.

- Describe the emergence of effective black leaders.

- Analyse the importance of Martin Luther King.

- Describe the roles of the NAACP, CORE and the SCLC.

- Describe the role of Martin Luther King.

- Describe the changes in Federal policy.

- Explain the social, economic and political changes.

- Analyse the resultant rise of black radical movements.

Bibliography

Scotland, 1249–1328

Barrell, A.D.M., Medieval Scotland, Cambridge University Press (2000)

Barrow, Geoffrey W.S., Robert Bruce and the Community of the Realm of Scotland, Edinburgh University Press (2005)

Bingham, Caroline, Robert The Bruce, Constable (1999)

McNamee, Colm, Robert Bruce: Our Most Valiant Prince, King and Lord, Birlinn (2006)

Nicholson, Ranald, Scotland: The Later Middle Ages, Barnes & Noble (1974)

Penman, Michael, The Scottish Civil War: The Bruces and Balliols and the War for Control of Scotland, The History Press (2002)

Scotland, 1830–1939

McMahon, Professor Richard, Images, the Irish and the history of violence in Scotland, https://headlong.co.uk/ideas/images-irish-and-history-violence-scotland, online article (31 May 2016)

Mitchell, Martin J., New Perspectives on the Irish in Scotland, Birlinn (2008)

Britain, 1851–1951

Addison, Paul, Now the War is Over: A Social History of Britain, 1945–1951, Jonathan Cape (1985)

Barnett, Correlli, The Lost Victory. British Dreams, British Realities 1945–50, Macmillan (1995)

Bartley, Paula, Access to History, Votes for Women, Hodder Education (2007)

Birch, R.C., The Shaping of the Welfare State, Prentice Hall (1974)

Brooke, Stephen (ed.), Reform and Reconstruction: Britain After the War, 1945–51, Manchester University Press (1995)

Clarke, Peter, Liberals and Social Democrats, Cambridge University Press (1978)

Cowling, Maurice, 1867: Disraeli, Gladstone and Revolution, Cambridge University Press (1967)

Evans, Eric, The Shaping of Modern Britain: Identity, Industry and Empire, 1780–1914, Longman Pearson (2011)

Fraser, Derek, The Evolution of the British Welfare State, Palgrave Macmillan (2002)

Goodlad, Graham and Staton, Richard, Flagship History: Britain 1895–1951, Collins Educational (2008)

Harrison, Royden, Before the Socialists: Studies in Labour and Politics 1861–1881, Routledge (1994)

Himmelfarb, Gertrude, 'The Politics of Democracy: the English Reform Act of 1867', Journal of British Studies, Cambridge University Press (1966)

Holton, Sandra Stanley, Feminism and Democracy, Women's Suffrage and Reform Politics in Britain, 1900–1918, Cambridge University Press (1986)

Kerr, John and McGonigle, James, New Higher History: Britain & Scotland and Germany, Hodder Gibson (2010)

Kinser, Brent E., The American Civil War in the Shaping of British Democracy, Ashgate (2011)

Mackenzie, Midge, Shoulder to Shoulder, Vintage (1988)

Morgan, Kenneth, Labour in Power, 1945–1951, Clarendon Press (1984)

Morrison, Donald, Morrison, Elliot and Monaghan, Tom, Changing Britain 1850–1979, Pulse (2000)

Murray, Peter, Poverty and Welfare, 1830–1914, Hodder Education (1999)

Pearce, Malcolm and Stewart, Geoffrey, British Political History 1867–2001 Democracy and Decline, Routledge (2002)

Pearce, Robert and Stearn, Roger, Access to History: Government and Reform – Britain 1815–1918, Hodder and Stoughton (2000)

Pollard, Sidney, The Wasting of the British Economy, Routledge (2012)

Pugh, Martin, Britain since 1789 A Concise History, St Martin's Press (1999)

Rover, Constance, Women's Suffrage and Party Politics in Britain 1866–1914, Routledge (1967)

Sked, Alan and Cook, Chris, Post-war Britain: A Political History, 1945–92, Penguin (1993)

Smith, F.B., The Making of the Second Reform Bill, Cambridge University Press (1966)

Sykes, Alan, The Rise and Fall of British Liberalism 1776–1988, Longman (1998)

Taylor, A.J.P., English History, 1914–1945, Oxford University Press (1965)

Thane, Pat, The Foundations of the Welfare State: Social Policy in Modern Britain, Longman (1982)

Webster, Charles, The National Health Service: A Political History, Oxford University Press (2002)

Wright, D.G., Democracy and Reform, Longman (1970)

Germany, 1815–1939

Adam, P., The Arts of the Third Reich, N. Harry Abrahams (1992)

Bullock, Alan, Hitler and Stalin, Fontana (2nd ed. 1998)

Burleigh, Michael, The Third Reich, MacMillan (2000)

Cameron, Ronald, Henderson, Christine and Robertson, Charles, The Growth of Nationalism in Germany and Italy, Pulse (2005)

Carr, William, A History of Germany 1815–1990, Bloomsbury Academic (1991)

Comay, Rebecca, Mourning Sickness: Hegel and the French Revolution (Cultural Memory in the Present), Stanford University Press (2010)

Craig, Gordon, Germany 1866–1945, Oxford Paperbacks (1980 edition)

Evans, Richard, The Coming of the Third Reich, Penguin Press (2003)

Eyck, Erich, Bismarck and the German Empire, Norton (1964)

Feuchtwanger, Edgar, Bismarck, Routledge (2002)

Feuchtwanger, Edgar, Imperial Germany 1850–1918, Routledge (2001)

Fulbrook, Mary, A Concise History of Germany, Cambridge University Press (2nd ed. 2004)

Gorman, Michael, The Unification of Germany, Cambridge University Press (1990)

Grenville, J.A.S., Europe Reshaped 1848–78, Wiley-Blackwell (1999)

Hamerow, Theodore, Otto von Bismarck and Imperial Germany, D C Heath (3rd ed. 1993)

Hiden, John, Republican and Fascist Germany. Themes and Variations in the History of Weimar and the Third Reich, 1918–1945, Routledge (1996)

Hiden, John, The Weimar Republic, Routledge (2nd ed. 1996)

Holborn, Hajo, A History of Modern Germany, Volume 3: 1840–1945, Princeton University Press (1982 edition)

James, Leighton, 'For the Fatherland? The Motivations of Austrian and Prussian Volunteers during the Revolutionary and Napoleonic Wars'. In Krüger, C. and Levsen, S. (eds), War Volunteering in Modern Times: From the French Revolution to the Second World War, Palgrave (2011)

Kerr, John and McGonigle, James, New Higher History: Britain & Scotland and Germany, Hodder Gibson (2010)

Kershaw, Ian, Hitler, Penguin (2013)

McKichan, Finlay, Germany 1815–39: The Rise of Nationalism, Oliver and Boyd (1992)

Mann, Golo, The History of Germany since 1789, Pimlico (1996)

Mitchell, Ian, Bismarck and the Development of Germany, Holmes McDougall (1980)

Murphy, Derrick, Morris, Terry and Fulbrook, Mary, Germany 1848–1991, Collins Educational (2008)

Noakes, Jeremy and Pridham, Geoffrey, Nazism 1919–1945 Volume 2: State, Economy and Society 1933–39, Liverpool University Press (5th ed. 2000)

Ritschl, A., 'Reparations, deficits and debt default: The Great Depression in Germany' in London School of Economics Discussion Paper, no. 1149, (June 2012)

Rothfels, Hans, The German Opposition to Hitler, an Appraisal, Literary Licensing (2011)

Schulze, Hagen, The Course of German Nationalism 1763–1867, Cambridge University Press (1991)

Simpson, William, Hitler and Germany, Cambridge University Press (1991)

Steinberg, Jonathan, Bismarck: A Life, Oxford University Press (2012)

Stiles, Andrina, Access to History: The Unification of Germany 1815–1919, Hodder Education (3rd ed. 2007)

Taylor, A.J.P., The Course of German History, Routledge (2001 edition)

Taylor, A.J.P., The Origins of the Second World War, Penguin (1991 edition)

Thomson, David, Europe since Napoleon, Penguin (1990 edition)

Tipton, Frank B., A History of Modern Germany since 1815, Bloomsbury (2003)

Williamson, D.G., Bismarck and Germany 1862–1890, Routledge (3rd ed. 2010)

Russia, 1881–1921

Acton, Edward, Rethinking the Russian Revolution, Bloomsbury Academic (1990)

Darby, Graham, The Russian Revolution: Tsarism to Bolshevism, 1861–1924, Longman (1998)

Figes, Orlando, A People's Tragedy: The Russian Revolution, 1891–1924, Pimlico (1997)

Hill, Christopher, Lenin and the Russian Revolution, Hodder and Stoughton (1947)

Lynch, Michael, Reaction and Revolutions: Russia, 1881–1924, Hodder Arnold (1992)

McColgan, Martin, Russia, 1881–1921: From Tsarism to Communism, Oliver and Boyd (1994)

Mawdsley, Evan, The Russian Civil War, Birlinn (2008)

Nettl, J.P., Rosa Luxemburg, Schocken (1989)

Pipes, Richard, The Russian Revolution 1899–1919, Fontana (1992)

Service, Robert, A History of Twentieth-Century Russia, Harvard University Press (1999)

Smith, S.A., The Russian Revolution: A Very Short Introduction, Oxford Paperbacks (2002)

Suny, Ronald, 'Toward a Social History of the October Revolution' in The American Historical Review, Vol. 88, No. 1, pp. 31–52, American Historical Association (1983)

Welch, David, Modern European History, 1871–2000: A Documentary Reader, Routledge (1999)

Wood, Alan, The Origins of the Russian Revolution, 1861–1917, Routledge (2003)

USA, 1918–68

Allen, F.L., cited in Patrick O'Donnell, Ku Klux Klan: America's First Terrorists Exposed, Idea Men Productions (2006)

Arsenault, Raymond, Freedom Riders: 1961 and the Struggle for Racial Justice, Oxford University Press (2007)

Brogan, Hugh, Penguin History of the USA, Penguin (2001 edition)

Carson, Clayborne, http://news.stanford.edu/news/2013/january/carson-king-legacy-01173.html online article on Martin Luther King's legacy

Chalmers, David M., Hooded Americanism, Duke University Press (1987 edition)

Clements, Peter, Access to History: Prosperity, Depression and the New Deal: The USA 1890 to 1954, Hodder Education (2008)

Conkin, Paul, cited in: Peter Clements, Access to History: Prosperity, Depression and the New Deal: The USA 1890 to 1954, Hodder Education (2008)

Cooke, Alistair, America, Penguin (2008)

Doak, Robin S., The March on Washington: Uniting against Racism, Compass Point (2007)

Field, Ron, Civil Rights in America, 1865–1980, Cambridge University Press (2002)

Foner, Eric, Give me Liberty! An American History, Norton (2011 edition)

Galbraith, John Kenneth, The Great Crash, 1929, Penguin (2009 edition)

Grant, Susan-Mary, A Concise History of the United States, Cambridge University Press (2010)

Hall, Thomas E. and Fergusson, J. David, The Great Depression, an International Disaster of Perverse Economic Policies, University of Michigan Press (1998)

Hiltzik, Michael, The New Deal, Free Press (2012)

Hofstadter, Richard, The American Political Tradition, cited in Stephen M. Kohn: American Political Prisoners: Prosecutions under the Espionage and Sedition Acts, Praeger (1994)

Hudson-Weems, Clenora, Emmett Till: The Sacrificial Lamb of the Civil Rights Movement, Bedford (1994)

Johnson, Paul, Modern Times, Harper Perennial (2001 edition)

Jones, M.A., American Immigration, University of Chicago Press (1992)

Kennedy, David, Freedom from Fear: The American People in Depression and War 1929–1945 (Oxford History of the United States), Oxford University Press (2001)

Leuchtenburg, William E., Franklin D. Roosevelt and the New Deal, Harper Perennial (2009)

Manchester, William, The Glory and the Dream: A Narrative History of America, 1932–1972, Bantam Dell (1990 edition)

Newman, Mark, The Civil Rights Movement, Edinburgh University Press (2004)

Payne, Charles, Light of Freedom, University of California Press (2007 edition)

Rauchway, Eric, The Great Depression and the New Deal, A Very Short Introduction, Oxford University Press (2008)

Saunders, Vivien, Access to History: Race Relations in the USA, Hodder Education (3rd ed. 2006)

Schlesinger Junior, Arthur, cited in: Peter Clements, Access to History: Prosperity, Depression and the New Deal: The USA 1890 to 1954, Hodder Education (2008)

Smethurst, James in Robert Terrill (ed.) The Cambridge Companion to Malcom X, Cambridge University Press (2010)

Sobel, Robert, The Great Bull Market, Norton (1968)

Verney, Kervern, Black Civil Rights in America, Routledge (2000)

Williams, Juan and Bond, Julian, Eyes on the Prize, America's Civil Rights Years, Penguin (2013)

Willoughby, Susan, Heinemann Advanced History: Civil Rights in the USA 1863–1980, Heinemann (2001)

Wynn, Neil, The Afro-American Experience in World War II, Rowman and Littlefield (2011)

Zinn, Howard, A People's History of the United States, Harper Perennial (1995 edition)

Text permissions

Quotation from: Post-war Britain: A Political History, 1945–92 by Alan Sked & Chris Cook © 1993. Reproduced by permission of Penguin Books Ltd.

Quotation from: Reform and Reconstruction: Britain After the War, 1945–51 by Stephen Brooke ed. © 1995. Reproduced courtesy of Manchester University Press.

Quotation from: Now the War is Over: A Social History of Britain, 1945–1951 by Paul Addison © 2013. Published by Jonathan Cape reproduced by permission of The Random House Group Ltd.

Quotations from: British Political History, 1867–2001: Democracy and Decline by Malcolm Pierce & Geoffrey Stewart © 2002. Reproduced courtesy of Routledge.

Page 126, Activity 12, Question 1; Page 133, Activity 15, Question 1 and Page 142, Activity 19, Question 1 adapted from SQA questions © Scottish Qualifications Authority. All worked examples have been written by the authors and do not emanate from the SQA.

Historical Study: European and World: Germany, 1815–1939

Quotations from: The Course of German History by AJP Taylor © 2001, published by Routledge. Reproduced courtesy of David Higham Associates Limited.

Quotations from: Mourning Sickness: Hegel and the French Revolution (Cultural Memory in the present) by Rebecca Comay © 2010. Published by Stanford University Press.

Quotations from: The Growth of Nationalism in Germany and Italy by Cameron, Henderson and Robertson © 2005. Published by Pulse.

Quotations from: The Origins of the Second World War by AJP Taylor © 1991. Reproduced by permission of Penguin Books Ltd.

Quotations from: Bismark and the German Empire by Erich Eyck © 1964. Published by Norton.

Quotations from: The Course of German Nationalism 1763–1867 by Hagen Schulze © 1991. Reproduced courtesy of Cambridge University Press.

Quotations from: A History of Germany 1815–1990 reproduced courtesy of Bloomsbury Publishing Plc. © William Carr, 1987, A History of Germany 1815–1990, Bloomsbury Academic, an imprint of Bloomsbury Publishing Plc.

Quotation from: Access to History: The Unification of Germany 1815–1919 by Andrina Stiles © 2007. Reproduced by permission of Hodder Education.

Quotation from: The Unification of Germany by Michael Gorman © 1990. Reproduced courtesy of Cambridge University Press.

Quotation from: Bismark and the Development of Germany by Ian Mitchell © 1980. Published by Holmes McDougal.

Quotations from: New Higher History: Britain & Scotland and Germany by John Kerr & Jim McGonigle © 2010. Reproduced by permission of Hodder Education.

Quotations from: Germany 1815–39, The Rise of Nationalism by Finlay McKichan © 1992. Reproduced courtesy of Pearson Education Limited.

Quotation from: Bismarck and Germany 1862–1890, D.G. Williamson, © 2010 Routledge, reproduced by permission of Taylor & Francis Books UK.

Quotation from: Otto Von Bismark and Imperial Germany by Theodore Hamerow © 1993. Published by DC Heath.

Quotation from: Europe since Napoleon by David Thomson © 1990. Reproduced courtesy of Penguin Random House.

Quotation from: Europe Reshaped 1848–78 by J.A.S. Grenville, © 1999. Reproduced courtesy of Wiley-Blackwell.

Quotation from: Bismarck by Edgar Feuchtwanger © 2002. Reproduced courtesy of Routledge.

Quotation from: Bismarck: A Life, by Jonathan Steinberg © 2012. Reproduced by permission © Jonathan Steinberg, 2011.

Quotation from: The Weimar Republic, John Hiden © 1996 published by Routledge, reproduced by permission of Taylor & Francis Books UK.

Quotation from: Republican and Fascist Germany. Themes and Variations in the History of Weimar and the Third Reich, 1918–1945, John Hiden, copyright 1996 Routledge, reproduced by permission of Taylor & Francis Books UK.

Quotations from: Germany 1866–1945 by Gordon Craig © 1990. Reproduced by permission of Oxford University Press.

Quotations from: The History of Germany since 1789 by Golo Mann ©1996. Published by Pimlico reproduced by permission of The Random House Group Ltd.

Quotation from: A Concise History of Germany by Mary Fulbrook © 2004. Reproduced courtesy of Cambridge University Press.

Quotation from: Hitler and Germany (Cambridge Topics in History) by William Simpson © 2010. Published by Cambridge University Press.

Quotations from: Nazism 1919–1945 Volume 2: State, Economy and Society 1933–39 by Noakes & Pridham © 2000. Reproduced courtesy of Liverpool University Press.

Quotations from: The German Opposition to Hitler, an Appraisal by Hans Rothfels © 1962. Published by Henry Regnery Company.

Historical Study: European and World: Russia 1881–1921

Quotations from: A History of Twentieth-Century Russia by Robert Service © 1999. Reproduced by permission of Penguin Books Ltd.

Quotations from: A People's Tragedy: The Russian Revolution, 1891–1924 by Orlando Figes © 1997. Published by Pimlico reproduced by permission of The Random House Group Ltd.

Quotations from: Reaction and Revolutions: Russia, 1881–1924 by Michael Lynch © 1992. Reproduced by permission of Hodder Education.

Historical Study: European and World: USA, 1918–68